Southern Living.

# The SOUTHERN HERITAGE COOKBOOK LIBRARY

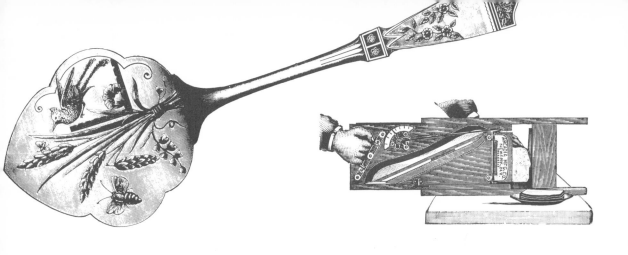

# The SOUTHERN HERITAGE
## COOKBOOK LIBRARY
# INDEX

OXMOOR HOUSE
Birmingham, Alabama

**Southern Living** .

**The Southern Heritage Cookbook Library**

**The Southern Heritage Cookbook Index**

*Executive Editor:* Ann H. Harvey
*Southern Living*® *Foods Editor:* Jean W. Liles
*Senior Editor:* Joan E. Denman
*Senior Foods Editor:* Katherine M. Eakin
*Assistant Editor:* Ellen de Lathouder
*Copy Editor:* Melinda E. West
*Assistant Foods Editor:* Helen R. Turk
*Director, Test Kitchen:* Laura N. Massey
*Test Kitchen Home Economists:* Kay E. Clarke, Rebecca J. Riddle,
    Elizabeth J. Taliaferro, Elise Wright Walker
*Production Manager:* Jerry R. Higdon
*Editorial Assistants:* Mary Ann Laurens, Donna A. Rumbarger,
    Karen P. Traccarella
*Food Photographer:* Jim Bathie
*Food Stylist:* Sara Jane Ball
*Layout Designer:* Christian von Rosenvinge
*Mechanical Artist:* Faith Nance
*Research Editor:* Alicia Hathaway

**Special Consultants**

*Art Director:* Irwin Glusker
*Heritage Consultant:* Meryle Evans
*Foods Writer:* Lillian B. Marshall
*Food and Recipe Consultants:* Marilyn Wyrick Ingram,
    Audrey P. Stehle

*Cover:* The library of *Southern Heritage* cookbooks links the people,
places, and events of Southern history with the recipes that have made
Southern cooking a favorite in America.

Brown Brothers

# CONTENTS

Southern Heritage Recipes     7

Index to Recipes     8

Southern Heritage Subjects     93

Index to Subjects     96

Favorite Recipes     109

# SOUTHERN HERITAGE RECIPES

**W**ith this volume, you hold the key to locating some 4,000 recipes that comprise *The Southern Heritage Cookbook Library*. The abbreviations repeated throughout will make it possible for you to pull just which book you need and go straight to the recipe of your choice.

In this series, as you know, we have alternated between menu books and books on single subjects. You will find breads and cakes, for example, not only in the *Breads* and *Cakes* volumes, but also in the menu cookbooks: *Family Gatherings, Celebrations, Breakfast and Brunch, Company's Coming, Sporting Scene*, and *Socials and Soirees*.

You will find the cross-references invaluable; Salmon Mousse is listed not only under "Salmon," but also under "Appetizers" and "Mousses." Mainly, though, this index places all breads under "Breads" and pies under "Pies," and so on, identifying each recipe by its title; thus, the reader is speedily referred to the right volume and page number. If it's biscuits you need, the "Breads" category will tell you to *see also* specific types, which will send you to "Biscuits." Bread puddings are conveniently listed under the general category "Breads" and the subcategory "Puddings" or the general category "Desserts." You simply can't NOT find it!

Use this index to good advantage by finding a recipe to suit the ingredients you have at hand. A pâté for a party, for example: under "Appetizers," you will find a pâté of black-eyed peas in *Socials and Soirees*, chicken liver pâté in *Plain and Fancy Poultry*, and a pâté made of pork liver in the *All Pork* volume. You may have the makings of one or another without taking an extra trip to the market.

Or you may want to make a tasty party dish of pecans. Look under "Pecans" and decide which way you wish to go; you may have them salted, butter-toasted, hot-peppered, sherried, or sugared, as you wish. And, as you'd suspect, they are all listed under "Appetizers" as well.

This comprehensive index is the key to your treasury of authentic Southern heritage cookery; use it to unlock a lifetime of good eating for your family and friends.

## LIBRARY VOLUMES

ALL PORK

BEEF, VEAL AND LAMB

BREADS

BREAKFAST AND BRUNCH

CAKES

CELEBRATIONS

COMPANY'S COMING

COOKIE JAR

FAMILY GATHERINGS

GIFT RECEIPTS

JUST DESSERTS

PIES AND PASTRY

PLAIN AND FANCY POULTRY

SEA AND STREAM

SOCIALS AND SOIREES

SOUPS AND STEWS

SPORTING SCENE

VEGETABLES

*This 1880 illustration by Albert R. Waud shows the lady of the household cooking on the iron stove.*

To use index: Each entry is followed by the page number
and, in parenthesis, the code
for the book where the entry
can be found. The book codes
are identified in the key below.

**Almonds**
Acorns, Almond, 91 (GR)
Asparagus with Almonds,
    Scalloped, 14 (VE)
Blancmange, 123 (CC); 59 (DE)
Butter, Almond, 132 (VE)
Cake, Almond Sponge, 122 (CA)
Cake, Tarboro Tipsy, 60 (DE)
Candied Almonds, 91 (GR)
Charlotte,
    Pumpkin-Almond, 63 (CC)
Coffee Cake, Almond
    Puff, 77 (BB)
Coleslaw, Almond, 74 (SP)
Cookies, Almond
    Christmas, 112 (CJ)
Cookies, Almond Icebox, 66 (CJ)
Cookies, Almond
    Meringue, 23 (SS)
Cookies, Christmas
    Butter, 115 (CJ)
Cookies, Greek Almond, 53 (CJ)
Cookies, Linzer, 63 (CJ)
Filling, Almond-
    Coconut, 117 (FG)
Florentines, 54 (CJ)
Frosting, Almond, 126 (DE)
Gâteau aux Amandes, 136 (SS)
Green Beans Amandine, 55 (SP)
Green Beans with
    Almonds, 124 (CC)
Grilled Almonds, 68 (SS)
Holiday Nuts, 96 (GR)
Lebkuchen,
    Nürnberger, 128 (CJ)
Macaroons, 123 (CC); 66 (SS)
Macaroons, Mary
    Randolph's, 13 (CJ)
Macaroons, Monticello, 13 (CJ)
Macaroons, New Bern
    Almond, 14 (CJ)
Macaroons, Passover, 14 (CJ)
Marzipan, 20 (CE); 92 (GR)
Mullet Amandine, 75 (SE)
Nougat, Honey-
    Pistachio, 102 (GR)
Parfait, Burnt Almond, 111 (DE)
Pie, Coffee-Almond
    Cream, 93 (PP)
Pompano Amandine, 80 (SE)
Rolls, Anna Maude's Honey
    Almond, 69 (BR)

Salad, Amandine
    Chicken, 113 (PO)
Salted Almonds, 91 (GR)
Salted Nuts, 21 (CE)
Sandwiches, Amandine
    Chicken, 87 (CC); 11 (SS)
Sandwiches,
    Chicken-Almond, 51 (SS)
Sauce, Almond-
    Mushroom, 134 (BB)
Sauce, Trout with
    Almond-Lemon, 121 (SE)
Shortbread, Almond, 17 (CJ)
Spiced Almonds, 136 (CE)
Sugar Almonds, 63 (CC)
Sugar and Spice Nuts, 97 (GR)
Torte, Almond Brittle, 126 (DE)
Trout Amandine, 120 (SE)
Tuilles with Almonds, 83 (CJ)
Wafers, Almond Lace, 84 (SP)
Zimtsterne, 130 (CJ)
**Ambrosia**
Ambrosia, 30 (DE); 57 (FG)
Cake, Ambrosia, 22 (CA);
    20 (CE)
Cake, Pineapple-Ambrosia
    Upside-Down, 71 (CA)
Cookies, Ambrosia, 112 (CJ)
Holiday Ambrosia, 30 (DE)

Orange-Pineapple
    Ambrosia, 136 (SS)
Oranges, Ambrosial, 31 (DE)
**Anchovies**
Eggs with Anchovies,
    Deviled, 52 (SS)
Lamb with Anchovies,
    Roast, 88 (BE)
Toast, Buttered
    Anchovy, 65 (SS)
**Appetizers**
Almonds, Grilled, 68 (SS)
Almonds, Spiced, 136 (CE)
Anchovy Toast,
    Buttered, 65 (SS)
Angels on Horseback, 24 (FG);
    37 (SE)
Artichokes, Pickled
    Jerusalem, 78 (CE)
Asparagus, Fried Fresh, 14 (VE)
Beef Barbecue, Chafing
    Dish, 36 (CE)

Beef Empanadas, 47 (BE)
Beef Mold, Cold, 36 (CE)
Carrot Fritters, 36 (VE)
Caviar Canapés, 79 (CE);
    37 (SS)
Caviar Ring, 11 (SP)
Caviar, Texas, 129 (SP)
Celery Roll, Stuffed, 131 (CE)
Cheese
    Ball, Pecan Cheese, 92 (SP)
    Bells, Cheese, 115 (FG)
    Biscuits, Tiny
        Cheddar, 107 (CE)
    Brambles, Cheese, 103 (SS)
    Butter, English Muffins
        Toasted with
        Cheese, 123 (SP)
    Celery, Pimiento Cheese
        Stuffed, 69 (CE)
    Celery, Stuffed, 121 (FG);
        75 (SP)
    Crescents, Cheese, 68 (SS)
    Dates, Cheese, 12 (CE)
    Dip, Cream Cheese, 16 (SS)
    Dip, Sausage-
        Cheese, 107 (PK)
    Dreams, Cheese, 23 (SP)
    Eggs au Gratin, 46 (SS)
    Flambé, Fried Cheese, 62 (FG)
    Ham and Cheese
        Appetizers, 124 (SS)
    Heart, Herbed Cheese, 80 (SP)
    Log, Cheddar Cheese, 57 (SS)
    Mold, Horseshoe
        Cheese, 10 (SP)
    Mound, Caraway
        Cheese, 83 (CC)
    Mounds, Cheddar
        Cheese, 129 (SP)
    Mousse, Blue Cheese,
        97 (SS)
    Puffs, Cheese, 118 (SP)
    Puffs, Cheese-Bacon, 11 (SS)
    Puffs, Chicken Salad in
        Cheese, 74 (SS)
    Roll, Roquefort, 103 (SS)
    Sandwiches,
        Cucumber-Cheese, 87 (CC)
    Sandwiches, Cucumber-Cream
        Cheese, 28 (SS)
    Sandwiches, Heart and
        Diamond, 72 (CC)
    Sandwich Loaf,
        Ribbon, 71 (CC)
    Sticks, Cheese, 49 (SS)
    Strata, Cheese, 36 (SS)
    Straws, Cheese, 12 (SP);
        61 (SS)
    Straws, Old-Fashioned
        Cheese, 125 (FG)
    Toast Rounds, Ham and
        Cheese, 115 (SS)
    Triangles, Ginger
        Cream, 69 (CE)
    Triangles, Herbed
        Party, 68 (SS)

**BB** Breakfast & Brunch   **BE** Beef, Veal & Lamb   **BR** Breads   **CA** Cakes   **CC** Company's Coming   **CE** Celebrations
**CJ** Cookie Jar   **DE** Just Desserts   **FG** Family Gatherings   **GR** Gift Receipts   **PK** All Pork   **PO** Plain & Fancy Poultry
**PP** Pies & Pastry   **SE** Sea & Stream   **SO** Soups & Stews   **SP** Sporting Scene   **SS** Socials & Soirees   **VE** Vegetables

Appetizers, Cheese, *continued*
    Triangles, Shrimp and Cream
      Cheese, 81 (SS)
    Vegetables with Blue Cheese
      Whip, 88 (SS)
Chicken Canapés, Hot,
  123 (SP)
Chicken Liver
  Appetizers, 126 (PO)
Chicken Salad in Tart
  Shells, 80 (SS)
Chicken Sandwiches, 71 (CC);
  27 (FG)
Chicken Sandwiches,
  Amandine, 87 (CC)
Chicken Wings, Sesame,
  87 (SS)
Clam Fritters, 11 (SE)
Clams Casino, 10 (SE)
Clams, Fried Chesapeake Bay
  Soft-Shell, 11 (SE)
Clams, Steamed, 10 (SE)
Clams, Stuffed, 80 (CE)
Crab Croquettes, 115 (SS)
Crabmeat Imperial, 37 (CE)
Crabmeat Mold, 11 (CE)
Creole Canapés, 29 (CC)
Cucumber Ring
  Canapés, 11 (CE)
Deviled Wafers, 57 (SS)
Dips
  Artichoke Dip, Hot, 88 (FG)
  Bacon-Horseradish
    Dip, 125 (SP)
  Blue Cheese Whip, 88 (SS)
  Caviar Dip, 94 (SE)
  Crab Dip, Chafing
    Dish, 96 (SS)
  Cream Cheese Dip, 16 (SS)
  Garlic-Mayonnaise
    Dip, 95 (FG)
  Guacamole Dip, 34 (CC)
  Herb Dip with
    Vegetables, 22 (SP)
  Sausage-Cheese Dip, 107 (PK)
  Sour Cream Spinach
    Dip, 115 (FG)
Dove, Plantation, 50 (SP)
Egg Salad Finger
  Sandwiches, 84 (FG)
Escargots, 81 (CE)
Fish Balls, Fried, 122 (SE)
Forfar Bridies, 13 (CE)
Fruit, Stuffed Dried, 23 (SS)
Gazpacho Tarts, 106 (SS)
Ginger Cream
  Triangles, 69 (CE)
Gorp, 78 (SP)
Guacamole with Pomegranate
  Seeds, 126 (CE)
Ham Balls in Sauce,
  89 (PK)
Ham Biscuits,
  Smithfield, 91 (PK)
Ham, Deviled, 89 (PK)
Ham Mousse, 86 (PK)
Ham Puffs, Deviled, 18 (SS)
Ham Rolls, 91 (PK)
Ham Turnovers, 91 (PK)
Head Cheese, 129 (PK)

Kraut Balls, 103 (SS)
Lemon Triangles, 11 (SS)
Liver Nips, 114 (BE)
Lobster Cocktail, 33 (SE)
Marlin, Barbecued, 106 (SP)
Meatballs, Danish, 11 (CE)
Meatballs in Wine
  Gravy, 91 (FG)
Meatballs,
  Scandinavian, 18 (FG)
Meat Roll, Norwegian, 19 (FG)
Meat Tray, Cold, 104 (SS)
Mushrooms, Baked
  Stuffed, 63 (VE)
Mushrooms, Herbed, 11 (SP)
Mushrooms, Marinated, 11 (CE)
Mushrooms, Stuffed, 103 (SS)
Nuts, Minted, 31 (CE)
Nuts, Peppery Spiced, 83 (CC)
Nuts, Salted, 21 (CE)
Nuts, Sugared, 25 (CE)
Olive-Mustard
  Sandwiches, 28 (FG)
Oysters, Broiled, 110 (SP)
Oysters, Deviled, 25 (FG);
  133 (SS)
Oysters, Fried, 25 (FG)
Oysters, Smokehouse, 37 (SE)
Pancakes, Scotch, 112 (SS)
Parsnip Fritters, 74 (VE)
Pâtés
  Black-Eyed Pea Pâté, 106 (SS)
  Chicken Liver Pâté, 126 (PO)
  Country Pâté, 87 (SS)
  Liver Pâté, Cajun, 130 (PK)
  Liver Pâté on Toast Rounds,
    Individual, 73 (FG)
Pecans, Butter Toasted, 19 (SS)
Pecans, Hot Pepper, 103 (SS)
Pecans, Salted, 136 (CE);
  86 (FG)
Pecans, Sherried, 88 (SS)
Pecans, Sugared, 31 (CC)
Pineapple-Rum Bits, 124 (SS)
Pirogi, 136 (BR)
Pizzas, Mini, 80 (CE)
Quiches, Party, 80 (CE)
Red Snapper in Aspic,
  Poached, 94 (SE)
Relish Bowl, 14 (CC)
Rumaki, 81 (CE)

Salmon Mousse, 85 (SE)
Salmon, Smoked, 84 (SE)
Sandwiches, Noisette, 42 (FG)
Sausage Rolls, 13 (CE)
Sausage Swirls, 84 (CC)
Scallop Cocktail, 45 (SE)
Seviche, 45 (SE)

Shrimp Aspic, 87 (SS)
Shrimp, Barbecued, 104 (SS)
Shrimp, Boiled, 46 (SE)
Shrimp Boil, Gulf
  Coast, 47 (SE)
Shrimp, Chilled Pickled, 22 (SP)
Shrimp Cocktail,
  Marinated, 128 (SS)
Shrimp, Dill, 114 (SP)
Shrimp Fritters, 47 (SE)
Shrimp Mold, 135 (CE)
Shrimp Mousse, 51 (SE)
Shrimp on Ice, 109 (CC)
Shrimp, Pickled, 23 (CE);
  51 (SE)
Shrimp Puffs, 79 (CE)
Shrimp Puffs, Curried, 106 (SS)
Shrimp, St. Augustine, 53 (SE)
Shrimp with Cocktail Sauce,
  Boiled, 129 (SP)
Shrimp with Red Sauce,
  Boiled, 91 (FG)

Soups
  Beef Bouillon, 26 (SO)
  Beef Consommé, 28 (SO)
  Broccoli Soup, 18 (SP)
  Clam Madrilene, 30 (SO)
  Cucumber Soup,
    Cold, 21 (CC); 114 (SP)
  Fruit Soup,
    Scandinavian, 43 (SO)
  Iced Bouillon, 26 (SO)
  Indian River Soup, 36 (SO)
  Jellied Consommé, 29 (SO)
  Madrilene, 30 (SO)
  Madrilene à la Russe, 30 (SO)
  Mushroom Broth, 35 (SO)
  Peach-Orange Soup,
    Cold, 41 (SO)
  Tomato Bouillon, 27 (SO)
  Tomato Consommé,
    Herbed, 31 (SP)
  Vegetable Bouillon,
    Old-South, 27 (SO)
  Vegetable Consommé, 29 (SO)
  Wine Consommé, 29 (SO)
Spinach Balls, 23 (SP)
Spinach Puffs, 124 (SS)

Appetizers, *continued*
  Spreads and Fillings
    Bacon and Egg Sandwich
      Spread, 120 (PK)
    Caviar Mold, Layered, 91 (FG)
    Chicken Salad, 105 (CC);
      36 (CE)
    Ham Sandwich
      Spread, 89 (PK)
    Liver Mold, Chopped, 129 (FG)
    Mustard Spread, 104 (SS)
    Olive Spread, Toasted Biscuits
      with, 64 (CE)
    Salmon Mold, 19 (FG)
    Salmon Mold with Bagels,
      Smoked, 97 (FG)
    Salmon Spread,
      Smoky, 129 (SP)
    Shrimp Paste, 51 (SE)
    Spinach Mold, 114 (SP)
  Sweetbreads, Deviled, 80 (CE)
  Sweetbreads Wrapped in
    Bacon, 115 (BE)
  Tortilla Chips, Fried, 34 (CC);
    126 (CE)
  Turkey Rolls, Smoked, 83 (CC)
  Vegetable Bowl, Fresh, 95 (FG)
  Walnuts, Sautéed, 24 (CE)
**Apples**
  Applesauce à la Mode, 34 (SP)
  Aspic, Apple, 55 (CE)
  Baked Apples, 20 (BB); 40 (PO)
  Baked Apples, Harvest, 57 (SS)
  Baked Apples, Stuffed, 36 (DE)
  Baked Ginger Apples, 69 (BB)
  Bars, Apple Spice, 90 (CJ)

Biscuits, Fruit Drop, 96 (BR)
Brown Betty, Apple, 39 (DE)
Butter, Apple, 48 (BB)
Butter, Old-Fashioned
  Apple, 25 (GR)
Cabbage and Apples,
  Red, 21 (FG)
Cabbage with Apples,
  Red, 32 (VE)
Cake, Apple Cider
  Pound, 118 (CA)
Cake, Apple Honey
  Upside-Down, 39 (CA)
Cake, Auntie's Apple, 39 (CA)
Cake, Dried Apple, 38 (CA)
Cake, Fresh Apple, 133 (SP)
Cake, Nobby Apple, 40 (CA)
Cake, Tennessee Apple
  Upside-Down, 70 (CA)
Candied Apples, 104 (CE)
Casserole, Apple, 48 (SP)
Catsup, Apple, 70 (GR)
Charlotte, Classic
  Apple, 37 (DE)
Chutney, Apple, 55 (GR)
Cider, Berkeley Spiced, 116 (CE)
Cider, Mulled, 90 (BB)
Cobbler, Kentucky
  Apple, 33 (PP)
Coffee Cake, Apple, 104 (BB)
Conserve, Apple, 28 (GR)
Cookies, Apple-Molasses
  Drop, 48 (CJ)
Cornbread,
  Sausage-Apple, 131 (BB)
Crab Apples, Spiced, 36 (GR)

Crisp, Apple, 36 (DE)
Crisp, Apple-Cherry, 97 (PK)
Crumble, Apple, 36 (DE)
Ducklings with Apples and
  Raisins, 60 (CC)
Dumplings, Baked
  Apple, 128 (PP)
Dumplings, Boiled
  Apple, 129 (PP)
Fried Apples, 65 (PK)
Fried Apples and Bacon, Carlyle
  House, 119 (PK)
Fried Apples, Breakfast, 12 (BB)
Fried Apples, Glazed, 54 (CC)
Fried Apple Slices, 56 (SP)
Fried Apples, Pork Chops
  with, 29 (PK)
Fritters, Apple, 36 (BB);
  128 (BR)
Fruitcake, Dried Apple, 38 (CA)
Glazed Apples, 104 (CC)
Griddle Cakes,
  Apple-Rice, 114 (BB)
Jelly, Apple, 10 (GR)
Jelly, Apple-Raspberry, 10 (GR)
Jelly, Crab Apple, 10 (GR)
Lemonade, Apple, 86 (CE)
Loaf, Apple-Sausage, 105 (PK)
Muffins, Apple Butter, 31 (SS)
Noodle Kugel, 97 (FG)
Pandowdy, Apple, 39 (DE)
Pie, Apple, 23 (BB)
Pie, Apple-Pecan, 29 (PP)
Pie, Apple Pot, 33 (PP)
Pie, Carolina Apple, 30 (PO)
Pie, Cheese-Apple, 137 (CC)
Pie, Country Apple, 29 (PP)
Pie, Crumb-Topped
  Apple, 31 (PP)
Pie, Duncan Hines
  Apple, 28 (PP)
Pie Goody, Apple, 32 (PP)
Pie, Marion Flexner's Apple
  Custard, 69 (PP)
Pie, Old-Time Apple, 96 (CC)
Pie, Pork and Apple, 38 (PK)
Pie, Praline-Topped
  Apple, 30 (PP)
Pies, Fried Apple, 42 (CC);
  132 (PP)
Pie, Travellers' Rest Skillet
  Apple, 31 (PP)
Pie with Cheese Pastry,
  Apple-Cranberry, 32 (PP)
Pudding, Apple, 18 (DE)
Pudding, Bird's Nest, 53 (DE)
Pudding, Ginger-Apple, 18 (DE)
Pudding, Ozark, 40 (DE)
Punch, Passion, 71 (BB)
Rings, Sherried Apple, 21 (PK)
Roll, Apple, 46 (BB)
Salads, Individual
  Apple, 75 (CC)
Salad, Waldorf, 40 (SS)
Salad with Wine,
  Waldorf, 31 (SP)
Salt Pork and Apples, 124 (PK)
Sausage with Apples, 107 (PK)
Soup, Cold Apple, 38 (SO)
Special, Apples, 112 (FG)

*An overflowing basket elicits a smile of pride, c.1920.*

Brown Brothers

Apples, *continued*
  Spiced Apples, Moravian, 19 (CC)
  Spiced Red Apples, 14 (PK)
  Sticks, Apple Jack, 111 (GR)
  Strudel, Apple, 119 (BR)
  Stuffing, Roast Duckling with
    Apple, 41 (PO)
  Toddy, Hot Apple, 67 (BB)
  Torte, Huguenot, 40 (DE)
  Treats, Dried Apple, 82 (GR)
**Applesauce**
  à la Mode, Applesauce, 34 (SP)
  Aspic, Applesauce, 70 (PK)
  Bread, Casselman Inn
    Applesauce Nut, 103 (BR)
  Cake, Brown
    Applesauce, 37 (CA)
  Cake, Massie Stack, 41 (CA)
  Cake,
    Raisin-Applesauce, 69 (CA)
  Cookies, Applesauce, 48 (CJ)
  Marlow, Applesauce, 106 (DE)
  Muffins, Applesauce, 111 (BR)
  Muffins, Mississippi
    Spice, 102 (BB)
  Squares, Peanut-Apple, 85 (CA)
  Turnovers, Applesauce, 135 (PP)
**Apricots**
  Balls, Apricot, 96 (FG); 80 (GR)
  Blondies, Apricot, 107 (CJ)
  Bread, Apricot Nut, 102 (BB)
  Charlotte, Apricot, 82 (DE)
  Filling, Apricot, 70 (BR);
    107 (CA)
  Fool, Apricot, 32 (DE)
  Ice Cream, Hannah Glasse's
    Apricot, 97 (DE)
  Jam, Christmas, 25 (GR)
  Jewels, Apricot, 49 (CJ)
  Leather, Apricot, 82 (GR)
  Loaf, Frozen Apricot, 111 (DE)
  Marmalade,
    Apricot-Orange, 21 (GR)
  Mustard, Apricot, 73 (GR)
  Pie, Apricot Chiffon, 109 (PP)
  Pies, Fried Apricot, 132 (PP)
  Roll, Apricot Candy, 80 (GR)
  Sauce, Apricot, 75 (DE)
  Sherbet, Apricot, 91 (DE);
    127 (FG)
  Tapioca,
    Apricot-Macaroon, 85 (SS)
  Tarts, Apricot, 116 (PP)
  Tarts, Apricot Cream, 29 (FG)
  Turnovers, Apricot, 65 (CJ)
  Wafers, Dutch Cheese, 68 (CJ)
**Artichokes**
  Dip, Hot Artichoke, 88 (FG)
  Eggs Sardou, 122 (BB)
  Hearts, Artichoke, 9 (VE)
  Hearts, Creamed
    Artichoke, 9 (VE)
  How To Prepare Fresh
    Artichokes, 8 (VE)
  How To Prepare Fresh Jerusalem
    Artichokes, 9 (VE)

Pickled Jerusalem
  Artichokes, 78 (CE)
Pickles, Jerusalem
  Artichoke, 40 (GR)
Quiche, Artichoke, 125 (BB)
Salad, Marinated
  Artichoke, 110 (CC)
Salad with Stilton Dressing,
  Endive, 128 (SS)

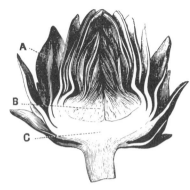

Soup, Cream of
  Artichoke, 60 (SO)
Spiced Jerusalem
  Artichokes, 9 (VE)
Steamed Artichokes,
  Whole, 12 (PO)
Stuffed Artichokes, 8 (VE)
Stuffed Artichokes
  Sicilian, 133 (FG)
**Asparagus**
  Bacon Rings, Fresh Asparagus
    in, 11 (VE)
  Baked Fresh Asparagus, 12 (VE)
  Casserole, Asparagus, 126 (FG)
  Chicken-Cheese Sauce,
    Asparagus with, 132 (BB)
  Chicken Divan, 104 (PO)
  Chilled Asparagus with
    Thousand Island
    Dressing, 44 (SS)
  Dressed Asparagus, 12 (SP)
  Fresh Asparagus, 28 (BB);
    44 (CC)
  Fried Fresh Asparagus, 13 (VE)
  How To Prepare Fresh
    Asparagus, 10 (VE)
  Lemon Butter, Asparagus
    with, 110 (FG)
  Marion Harland's Ambushed
    Asparagus, 12 (VE)
  Meringue, Asparagus, 13 (VE)
  Mushrooms and Cream Sauce,
    Asparagus with, 11 (VE)
  Patties, Baked
    Asparagus, 14 (VE)
  Peas with Egg Sauce, Asparagus
    and, 12 (VE)
  Rolls, Ham-Asparagus, 78 (PK)
  Sandwiches, Rolled
    Asparagus, 51 (SS)

Sauce, Grandmother Flexner's
  Asparagus, 132 (VE)
Scalloped Asparagus with
  Almonds, 14 (VE)
Soufflé, Asparagus, 14 (VE)
Soup, Cream of
  Asparagus, 60 (SO)
Steamed Asparagus,
  Chilled, 103 (FG)
Steamed Asparagus with
  Hollandaise Sauce, 84 (SS)
Veal Loin Chops with
  Asparagus, 67 (BE)
Vidalia Onions, Crunchy
  Asparagus with, 72 (VE)
Vinaigrette, Asparagus, 12 (VE)
**Aspic**
  Apple Aspic, 55 (CE)
  Applesauce Aspic, 70 (PK)
  Cucumber Aspic, 107 (CC)
  Redfish Aspic, 83 (SE)
  Red Snapper in Aspic,
    Poached, 94 (SE)
  Shrimp Aspic, 87 (SS)
  Tomato Aspic, 44 (CC)
  Tomato Aspics,
    Individual, 107 (FG)
  Tomato Aspic, Spicy, 49 (SS)
**Avocados**
  Dip, Guacamole, 34 (CC)
  Dressing with Creamed Chicken,
    Avocado, 63 (CE)
  Guacamole, 37 (BE)
  Guacamole with Pomegranate
    Seeds, 126 (CE)
  Liver with Avocado,
    Sautéed, 110 (BE)
  Mousse, Avocado, 105 (CC)
  Salad, Florida
    Grapefruit-Avocado, 135 (FG)
  Salad,
    Grapefruit-Avocado, 64 (CC)

# B

**Bacon**
  Angels on Horseback, 24 (FG);
    37 (SE)
  Apples and Bacon, Carlyle House
    Fried, 119 (PK)
  Bass with Bacon,
    Baked, 105 (SE)
  Biscuits, Bacon, 49 (FG)
  Canadian Bacon,
    Baked, 131 (BB)
  Canadian Bacon, Baked
    Stuffed, 121 (PK)
  Canadian Bacon
    Special, 78 (FG)
  Canadian Bacon with Port Wine
    Sauce, Baked, 120 (PK)

Bacon, *continued*
  Casserole,
    Bacon-Cheese, 126 (BB)
  Chowder, Bean and
    Bacon, 97 (SO)
  Cornish Hens with
    Bacon, 25 (SS)
  Dip,
    Bacon-Horseradish, 125 (SP)
  Fried Breakfast Bacon with Milk
    Gravy, 119 (PK)
  Green Beans, Bacon and
    Piquant, 119 (PK)
  Green Beans, Country, 11 (FG)
  Grill, Bacon, 132 (BB)
  Hominy, Bacon, 47 (VE)
  Liver with Bacon, Sautéed
    Calves', 20 (BB)
  Muffins, Date-Bacon, 113 (BR)
  Poke Greens, Arkansas, 57 (VE)
  Poke Sallet with Bacon, 56 (VE)
  Potatoes, Ranch-Style, 97 (PK)
  Puffs, Cheese-Bacon, 11 (SS)
  Rings, Fresh Asparagus in
    Bacon, 11 (VE)
  Shad Roe with Bacon, 28 (BB)
  Spread, Bacon and Egg
    Sandwich, 120 (PK)
  Sweetbreads Wrapped in
    Bacon, 115 (BE)
**Bananas**
  Ambrosia, Holiday, 30 (DE)
  Baked Bananas, 23 (BB)
  Baked Bananas with Lemon
    Sauce, 41 (DE)
  Bars, Banana, 90 (CJ)
  Bites, Banana, 105 (GR)
  Bread, Banana Nut, 77 (CC)
  Bread, Corrie Hill's Banana
    Nut, 103 (BR)
  Bread, Old-Fashioned
    Banana, 103 (BB)
  Cake, Banana-Nut, 68 (CA)
  Cake, Delicious Banana
    Layer, 22 (CA)
  Compote, Sunrise, 30 (DE)
  Cookies, Banana Cake,
    49 (CJ)
  Foster, Bananas, 104 (DE)
  Ice Cream,
    Banana-Fruit, 82 (FG)
  Marlow, Banana, 107 (DE)
  Pie, Kentucky Banana
    Cream, 93 (PP)
  Pudding, Banana, 103 (CC)
  Pudding, Banana
    Cream, 55 (DE)
  Pudding, Banana
    Custard, 54 (DE)
  Puffs, Banana, 117 (BB)
  Salad, Banana-Peanut,
    73 (CE)
  Syrup, Banana, 92 (CC)
  Wine, Bananas in, 41 (DE)
**Barbecue**
  Bass, Barbecued, 107 (SE)

Beans, Barbecued Pinto, 72 (SP)
Beef Barbecue, Chafing
  Dish, 36 (CE)
Beef, Barbecued, 34 (SP)
Beef Brisket, Barbecued, 72 (SP)
Bluefish, Grilled, 61 (SE)
Bread, Grilled Garlic, 77,
  90 (SP)
Brisket, Barbecued, 38 (CC)
Brisket, Grilled, 16 (BE)
Brisket of Beef,
  Barbecued, 16 (BE)
Brisket,
  Oven-Barbecued, 16 (BE)
Catfish, Grilled
  Sesame, 111 (SE)
Catfish, Smoked, 112 (SE)
Cheeseburgers, Grilled, 40 (SE)
Chicken, Barbecued, 88 (CE)
Chicken Barbecue, Paper
  Sack, 87 (PO)
Chicken, Basic
  Barbecued, 87 (PO)
Chicken, Grilled, 55 (SP)
Chicken, Marinated
  Grilled, 88 (PO)
Chicken,
  Oven-Barbecued, 87 (PO)
Chicken, Saucy
  Oven-Barbecued, 88 (FG)
Chicken, Savory
  Barbecued, 88 (PO)
Chicken, Spicy Grilled, 87 (PO)
Corn, Grilled, 97 (SP)
Corn Grilled in Husks, 89 (SP)
Crabs, Grilled
  Soft-Shell, 14 (SE)
Duck, Smoked, 40 (SP)
Franks in Barbecue
  Sauce, 111 (PK)
Green Beans,
  Barbecued, 22 (VE)
Grouper, Grilled, 69 (SE)
Grouper Kabobs, 69 (SE)
Ham Steaks, Barbecued, 53 (PK)
Kabobs, Southern
  Tender, 58 (PK)
King Mackerel, Grilled, 73 (SE)
Lamb Chops, Grilled, 94 (BE)
Lamb, Grilled, 86 (BE)
Lamb, Oven-Barbecued, 87 (BE)
Lamb Shanks,
  Barbecued, 97 (BE)
Liver, Grilled Calves', 112 (BE)
Lobster Tails, Grilled, 31 (SE)
Marlin, Barbecued, 106 (SP)
Mixed Grill, 58 (PK)
Mullet, Grilled, 76 (SE)
Mullet, Smoked, 76 (SE)
Oysters, Roasted, 97 (SP)
Oysters, Smokehouse, 37 (SE)
Pig, Barbecued Whole, 45 (PK)
Pork, Barbecued Leg of, 49 (PK)
Pork Barbecue,
  Stove-Top, 22 (PK)
Pork Chops, Barbecued, 52 (PK)

*Fixings for a big barbecue at the LBJ ranch, Texas.*

Pork Chops,
  Country-Pride, 52 (PK)
Pork Chops, Grilled, 51 (PK)
Pork Chops, Hickory-Smoked
  Stuffed, 51 (PK)
Pork Chops, Honey, 51 (PK)
Pork Chops,
  Oven-Barbecued, 27 (PK)
Pork Cubes,
  Oven-Barbecued, 35 (PK)
Pork Kabobs, 58 (PK)
Pork Loin Roast,
  Spit-Roasted, 48 (PK)
Pork Ribs, Barbecued, 88 (CE)
Pork Ribs,
  Hickory-Smoked, 54 (PK)
Pork Ribs, Oven-Barbecued
  Country, 16 (CE)
Pork Roast,
  Louisiana-Style, 48 (PK)
Pork Roast,
  Orange-Basted, 49 (PK)
Pork Shoulder,
  Barbecued, 15 (FG)
Pork Shoulder, Smoked, 50 (PK)
Pork, Sliced Barbecued, 50 (PK)
Pork Steaks, Marinated, 52 (PK)
Pork Tenderloin, 89 (SP)
Potatoes,
  Charcoal-Baked, 97 (SP)
Pot Roast, Barbecued, 100 (CC)
Ribs, Barbecued, 38 (CC)
Ribs, Country-Style, 54 (PK)
Ribs, Deep South
  Oven-Barbecued, 33 (PK)

---

**BB** *Breakfast & Brunch*　**BE** *Beef, Veal & Lamb*　**BR** *Breads*　**CA** *Cakes*　**CC** *Company's Coming*　**CE** *Celebrations*
**CJ** *Cookie Jar*　**DE** *Just Desserts*　**FG** *Family Gatherings*　**GR** *Gift Receipts*　**PK** *All Pork*　**PO** *Plain & Fancy Poultry*
**PP** *Pies & Pastry*　**SE** *Sea & Stream*　**SO** *Soups & Stews*　**SP** *Sporting Scene*　**SS** *Socials & Soirees*　**VE** *Vegetables*

**Barbecue,** *continued*
Ribs, Florida Barbecued
Country-Style, 57 (PK)
Roast, Oven-Barbecued, 19 (BE)
Salmon, Smoked, 84 (SE)
Salmon Steaks, Grilled, 84 (SE)
Sauces
Barbecue Sauce, 16, 126 (BE);
38 (CC); 71 (GR); 45,54 (PK);
34 (PO); 72 (SP); 104 (SS)
Basting Sauce, 34 (SP)
Basting Sauce,
Carolina, 60 (PK)
Basting Sauce,
Tennessee, 60 (PK)
Basting Sauce, Texas, 60 (PK)
Beer Sauce for
Barbecue, 60 (PK)
Bonaventure Barbecue
Sauce, 22 (PK)
Creole Barbecue
Sauce, 127 (BE)
Deep South Barbecue
Sauce, 33 (PK)
Easy Barbecue Sauce, 52 (SP)
Horseradish Barbecue
Sauce, 60 (PK)
Hot Barbecue Sauce, 49 (PK)
LBJ's Barbecue
Sauce, 127 (BE)
Low Country Barbecue
Sauce, 60 (PK)
Molasses Barbecue
Sauce, 60 (PK)
1948 Original Barbecue
Sauce, 87 (PO)
Panhandle Barbecue
Sauce, 16 (BE)
Western Kentucky-Style
Barbecue Sauce, 88 (CE)
Sausage and Cabbage, Grilled
Polish, 59 (PK)
Sausage, Barbecued, 40 (CC)
Shrimp, Barbecued, 104 (SS)
Spareribs, Barbecued, 68 (SP)
Spareribs, Grilled
Sweet-and-Sour, 56 (PK)
Spareribs, Marinated
Smoked, 56 (PK)
Spareribs, Southern
Barbecued, 53 (PK)
Spareribs, Texas, 54 (PK)
Striped Bass, Grilled, 96 (SE)
Swordfish, Grilled, 98 (SE)
Trout, Grilled, 123 (SE)
Trout Ida, Cedarvale
Gardens, 123 (SE)
Trout, Marinated
Grilled, 122 (SE)
Tuna Steaks, Grilled, 100 (SE)
Turkey,
Lemon-Barbecued, 88 (PO)
Turkey,
Oven-Barbecued, 34 (PO)
Turkey, Overnight
Smoked, 23 (CE)
Turkey, Smoked, 34 (PO)
Turkey, Smoked Wild, 62 (SP)
Venison Steaks,
Barbecued, 52 (SP)

**Bass** *See also* Striped Bass.
à la Brin, Bass, 24 (CC)
Bake, Bass, 105 (SE)
Baked Bass, 104 (SE)
Baked Bass Fillets, 106 (SE)
Baked Bass in Wine, 104 (SE)
Baked Bass, Wilmington
Island, 105 (SE)
Baked Bass with
Bacon, 105 (SE)
Barbecued Bass, 107 (SE)
Broiled Black Bass, 106 (SE)
Deep-Fried Bass, 107 (SE)
Orange Steamed Black
Bass, 108 (SE)
Pan-Fried Bass, 106 (SE)
Stew, Otranto Pine
Bark, 108 (SE)

**Beans**
Baked Beans, 75 (FG)
Baked Beans, Southern, 95 (SS)
Black Bean Soup, 35 (CC);
94 (SO)
Black Beans, Refried, 132 (FG)
Casserole, Black Beans and
Rice, 136 (FG)
Chowder, Bean and
Bacon, 97 (SO)
Green
Almonds, Green Beans
with, 124 (CC)
Amandine, Green
Beans, 55 (SP)
Bacon and Piquant Green
Beans, 119 (PK)
Barbecued Green
Beans, 22 (VE)
Buttered Green
Beans, 64 (CE)
Confetti String Beans, 94 (CE)
Country Green Beans, 11 (FG)
Dilly Beans, 40 (GR)
Fresh Green Beans, 96 (CC)
How To Prepare Fresh Green
Beans, 21 (VE)
Italienne, Green
Beans, 55 (FG)
New Potatoes, Green Beans
and, 23 (VE)
New Potatoes, Green Beans
with, 121 (SS)
Onion Slaw, Green Beans
with, 54 (PO)
Pickled Green Beans, 77 (PO)
Pole Beans, Savory, 18 (CC)
Potatoes, Green Beans
with, 48 (CC)
Salad, Piquant Green
Bean, 32 (FG)
Salad, Winter Green
Bean, 98 (CC)
Salt Pork, Green Beans
with, 21 (VE)
Sautéed Green Beans, 23 (VE)
Sour Cream Dressing, Green
Beans with, 98 (SS)
Southern Style, Green
Beans, 78 (CE)
Split Green Beans, 22 (VE)
Stewed Green Beans, 57 (CE)

Sweet-and-Sour
Beans, 22 (VE)
Tarragon, Green
Beans, 23 (VE)
Kidney
Red Beans and
Hamburger, 42 (BE)
Red Beans and Rice, 29 (CC);
110 (PK)
Red Beans and Rice,
Buster's, 133 (SP)
Red Beans and Rice,
Louisiana, 19 (VE)
Red Beans and Sausage,
Lasyone's, 18 (VE)
Red Bean Soup from Avery
Island, 96 (SO)
Salad, Kidney Bean, 69 (SP)
Lima
Butter Beans, 121 (FG)
Butter Beans,
Southern-Cooked, 21 (VE)
Butter Beans, Special, 21 (VE)
Chowder, Lima Bean, 98 (SO)
Cream, Lima Beans
in, 21 (VE)
Creole Lima Beans, 16 (VE)
How To Prepare Fresh Lima
Beans, 20 (VE)
Onion, Lima Beans
with, 20 (VE)
Sausage, Dried Lima Beans
with, 15 (VE)
Southern-Cooked Dried Lima
Beans, 16 (VE)
Succotash, 127 (VE)
Navy Beans, Baked, 16 (VE)
Navy Beans, Leftover, 16 (VE)
Navy Bean Soup,
Senate, 94 (SO)
Navy Beans, Seasoned, 16 (VE)

Beans, *continued*
Pie, Oklahoma Bean, 57 (PP)
Pinto
  Barbecued Pinto
    Beans, 72 (SP)
  Beer Beans, 34 (SP)
  Cake, Fiesta Bean, 54 (CA)
  Chuckwagon Pinto
    Beans, 18 (VE)
  Frijoles, 38 (BB); 18 (VE)
  Pinto Beans, 51 (BE)
  Ranch-Style Pinto
    Beans, 40 (CC)
  Red Beans, 118 (CE)
  Red Beans, Texas, 64 (CC)
  Seasoned Pinto
    Beans, 126 (PK); 18 (VE)
  Soup, Bean, 93 (SO)
  Soup, Frijole-Cheese, 93 (SO)
  Soup, Pinto Bean, 93 (SO)
Pork and Beans, 122 (PK)
Pork and Beans,
  Campfire, 95 (SP)
Salad, Cold Bean, 89 (SP)
Soup, Lentil, 98 (SO)
Soup, Spanish Bean, 97 (SO)

**Beef**
Barbecue, Chafing Dish
  Beef, 36 (CE)
Borscht, Traditional, 99 (SO)
Bouillon, Beef, 26 (SO)
Bowl of Red, Original
  Texas-Style, 53 (BE)
Bratwurst,
  Sauer-Beckman, 102 (PK)
Brisket
  Barbecued Beef, 34 (SP)
  Barbecued Beef
    Brisket, 72 (SP)
  Barbecued Brisket, 38 (CC)
  Barbecued Brisket of
    Beef, 16 (BE)
  Cholent, 129 (FG)
  Grilled Brisket, 16 (BE)
  Oven-Barbecued
    Brisket, 16 (BE)
  Stew, Brisket, 54 (BE)
  Sweet-and-Sour Brisket with
    Sauerkraut, 17 (BE)
  Texas Prize Brisket of
    Beef, 17 (BE)
Burgoo, 135 (SO)
Burgoo, Kentucky, 61 (PO)
Calf Fries, 35 (SP)
Carbonades à la
  Flamande, 129 (SO)
Chili, Alabama, 51 (BE)
Chili con Carne, 110 (SO)
Chili, Home-Style, 64 (CC)
Chili, Prize-Winning
  Spicy, 113 (SO)
Chili, Texas
  Championship, 110 (SO)
Chipped Beef on Toast, 25 (BE)
Clams in Bouillon, 38 (SS)
Consommé, Beef, 28 (SO)

Corned Beef
  Boiled Corned Beef
    Dinner, 43 (CE)
  Corned Beef, 22 (BE)
  Dinner, Maryland Corned
    Beef, 23 (BE)
  Hash, Corned Beef, 129 (BB)
  Sandwiches, Corned
    Beef, 17 (SP)
  Sandwiches, Hero, 69 (FG)
  Sandwich, Meal-in-a-, 74 (SP)
  Savannah Corned Beef
    Dinner, 42 (CE)
Cuts of Beef, 132 (BE)
Frizzled Beef, 129 (BB)
Good to Know, 133-137 (BE)
Gumbo, Beef and
  Ham, 114 (SO)
Hash, Old-Fashioned Chopped
  Southern Beef, 55 (BE)
Hash with Indian Griddle Cakes,
  Beef, 56 (BE)
Jerky, Beef, 25 (BE)
Jerky, Sliced Beef, 44 (FG)
Kidneys in Red Wine,
  Bahama, 108 (BE)
Liver and Dumplings, 114 (BE)
Liver and Onions,
  Smothered, 110 (BE)
Liver, Grilled Calves', 112 (BE)
Liver in Creole Sauce,
  Baked, 113 (BE)
Liver in Sour Cream,
  Calves', 112 (BE)
Liver, Maryland Baked, 112 (BE)
Liver Nips, 114 (BE)
Liver with Avocado,
  Sautéed, 110 (BE)
Liver with Bacon, Sautéed
  Calves', 20 (BB)
Loaf of Beef, Jellied, 57 (BE)
Mold, Cold Beef, 36 (CE)
Pie, Beef Pot, 56 (BE)
Pie, Deep-Dish Beef, 55 (BE)
Pies, Scottish Meat, 134 (SP)
Ragout, Beef, 54 (BE)

Ribs
  Barbecued Ribs, 38 (CC)
  Broth, French, 31 (SO)
  Carrot Tzimmes, 60 (CE)
  Pot-au-Feu, 76 (SO)
Roasts
  à la Mode, Beef, 20 (BE)
  Barbecued Pot
    Roast, 100 (CC)
  Beef Jerky, Sliced, 44 (FG)
  Beef Wellington, Lucie
    County, 12 (BE)
  Boliche with Carrots,
    Spanish, 135 (FG)
  Cholent, 129 (FG)
  Daube Roast, 21 (BE)
  Eye of Round Roast,
    Cold, 120 (SS)
  Fillet of Beef, Mrs. Lyndon B.
    Johnson's, 11 (BE)
  Fillet of Beef, Roast, 85 (BB)
  Fillet of Beef, Turn-of-the
    Century, 11 (BE)
  Gravy, Roast Beef
    with, 57 (CC)
  Oven-Barbecued
    Roast, 19 (BE)
  Pot Roast, 125 (FG)
  Pot Roast and Vegetables,
    German, 21 (BE)
  Pot Roast, Arkansas, 19 (BE)
  Pot Roast, Chuck
    Wagon, 18 (BE)
  Pot Roast, Creole, 20 (BE)
  Pot Roast, Stove-Top, 21 (BE)
  Pot Roast, Sunday
    Dinner, 19 (BE)
  Prime Rib of Beef, North
    Carolina, 12 (BE)
  Rib Roast, Bourbon, 14 (BE)
  Rib Roast of Beef with Madeira
    Sauce, Standing, 121 (CC)
  Rib Roast, Standing, 12 (BE)
  Rolls, Roast Beef, 57 (BE)
  Round of Beef, Pleasant
    Hill, 21 (BE)

**BB** *Breakfast & Brunch*    **BE** *Beef, Veal & Lamb*    **BR** *Breads*    **CA** *Cakes*    **CC** *Company's Coming*    **CE** *Celebrations*
**CJ** *Cookie Jar*    **DE** *Just Desserts*    **FG** *Family Gatherings*    **GR** *Gift Receipts*    **PK** *All Pork*    **PO** *Plain & Fancy Poultry*
**PP** *Pies & Pastry*    **SE** *Sea & Stream*    **SO** *Soups & Stews*    **SP** *Sporting Scene*    **SS** *Socials & Soirees*    **VE** *Vegetables*

Beef, Roasts, *continued*
Round of Beef,
Steamboat, 125 (SS)
Salad, Cold Roast
Beef, 92 (SP)
Sauerbraten, 22 (FG)
Sauerbraten, Quick, 23 (BE)
Sauerbraten,
Salzburger, 23 (BE)
Sirloin of Beef, Greenbrier
Roast, 14 (BE)
Soup, Beef-Vermicelli, 79 (SO)
Soup, German
Beef-Noodle, 79 (SO)
Spiced Beef Round,
Virginia, 25 (BE)
Spiced Round of Beef,
Tennessee, 25 (BE)
Stew from Sunday's
Roast, 55 (BE)
Tenderloin, Marinated
Beef, 11 (SP)
Tenderloin of Beef,
Lobster-Stuffed, 129 (CC)
Tenderloin of Beef with
Béarnaise Sauce,
Roast, 131 (SS)
Tenderloin of Beef with
Mushrooms, Roast, 73 (FG)
Tenderloin with Bordelaise
Sauce, Beef, 10 (BE)
Yorkshire Pudding, Roast Beef
with, 14 (BE)
Slumgullion, 57 (BE)
Soup, Filled Noodle, 79 (SO)
Soup, Homemade
Vegetable-Beef, 105 (SO)
Soup, Macaroni-Beef, 80 (SO)
Soup, Savannah Okra, 101 (SO)
Soup, Sweet-and-Sour
Cabbage, 100 (SO)
Soup with Liver Dumplings,
Beef, 32 (SO)
Spiced Beef Round,
Virginia, 25 (BE)
Spiced Round of Beef,
Tennessee, 25 (BE)
Steaks
à la Pitchfork, Steak, 26 (BE)
Birds, Steak, 34 (BE)
Bourguignon, Bœuf, 36 (BE)
Broiled Brunch
Steaks, 128 (BB)
Broiled Filet Mignon, 60 (BB)
Broiled Filet Mignon,
Pan-, 27 (BE)
Broiled Rib Eyes, 35 (SP)
Broiled Sirloin Steak, 57 (BB)
Broiled Steaks, 112 (CC)
Broiled Steak with
Mushroom-Wine
Sauce, 27 (BE)
Carne Guisada on
Rice, 131 (FG)
Carpetbag Steak, 29 (BE)
Chicken-Fried Steak, 30 (BE)
Country-Fried Steak, 128 (BB)
Country-Fried Steak, On the
Trail, 31 (BE)
Country Steak, 15 (CC)

Cubed Steak with
Onion, 31 (BE)
Diane, Hotel Roanoke
Steak, 27 (BE)
Eggs, Steak and, 22 (BB)
Fajitas, 37 (BE)
Fingers, Steak, 32 (BE)
Flank Steak, New
Orleans, 30 (BE)
Flank Steak,
Oklahoma, 29 (BE)
Madrilene, 30 (SO)
Mexican Steak, 36 (BE)
Planked Steak, 26 (BE)
Pudding, Steak and
Kidney, 109 (BE)
Roll, Fruited Steak, 29 (BE)
Roll, Norwegian Meat, 19 (FG)
Rolls, German Steak, 36 (BE)
Rolls, Greek-Stuffed
Beef, 35 (BE)
Rouladen, Beef, 35 (BE)
Round Steak, Blue
Ribbon, 34 (BE)
Round Steak,
Kentucky, 33 (BE)
Spanish Steak, 27 (BE)
Steak on a Stick, 102 (CE)
Stroganoff, Beef, 36 (BE)
Swiss Steak, Georgia
Tearoom, 32 (BE)
Texas Steak, 26 (BE)
Stew, Baked Beef, 126 (SO)
Stew, Beef, 32 (CC)
Stew, Big-Batch Beef, 78 (SP)
Stew, Brunswick, 135 (SO)
Stew, Camp, 134 (SO)
Stew, Creole Beef, 126 (SO)
Stew, Irish Beef, 44 (CE)
Stew, Kentucky
Mulligan, 135 (SO)
Stew, Old-Fashioned
Beef, 54 (BE)
Stew, Old-Time Beef, 126 (SO)
Stew, Texas Beef, 128 (SO)
Stew with Dumplings, Wine
Beef, 128 (SO)
Stock, Beef, 10 (SO)
Tamales, 36 (CC)
Tenderloin, Marinated
Beef, 11 (SP)
Tenderloin of Beef,
Lobster-Stuffed, 129 (CC)
Tenderloin of Beef with
Béarnaise Sauce,
Roast, 131 (SS)
Tenderloin of Beef with
Mushrooms, Roast, 73 (FG)
Tenderloin, Roast Beef, 130 (SP)
Tenderloin with Bordelaise
Sauce, Beef, 10 (BE)
Tongue, Pickled, 119 (BE)
Tongue,
Sweet-and-Sour, 119 (BE)
Tongue with Raisin Sauce,
German, 120 (BE)
Wellington, Beef, 128 (SS)
**Beef, Ground**
Burgers, Bonfire, 101 (CE)
Cabbage Rolls, 129 (FG)

Cabbage Rolls, Stuffed, 50 (BE)
Cajun Special, 41 (BE)
Cheeseburgers, Grilled, 40 (BE)
Chili
Cold Weather Chili, 113 (SO)
Easy Hearty Chili, 111 (SO)
Meaty Chili, 111 (SO)
Pedernales River
Chili, 51 (BE)
Prize-Winning Spicy
Chili, 113 (SO)
Texas Chili, 110 (SO)
Venison Chili, 113 (SO)
Creole Beef, 42 (BE)
Eggplant, Oaklawn Gardens'
Stuffed, 52 (VE)
Empanadas, Beef, 47 (BE)
Enchiladas, Texas, 48 (BE)
Filet Mignon, Mock, 41 (BE)
Forfar Bridies, 13 (CE)
Green Peppers,
Beef-Stuffed, 50 (BE)
Hamburger, Red Beans
and, 42 (BE)
Hamburger Steak
Deluxe, 40 (BE)
Hash, Texas Ground
Beef, 42 (BE)
Johnnie Marzetti, 43 (BE)
Liver Nips, 114 (BE)
Meatballs
Beef Porcupines, 39 (BE)
Danish Meatballs, 11 (CE)
German-Style
Meatballs, 39 (BE)
Scandinavian
Meatballs, 18 (FG)
Soup, Mexican
Meatball, 77 (SO)
Wine Gravy, Meatballs
in, 91 (FG)
Meat Loaf
Rolled Meat Loaf with Walnuts
and Oranges, 38 (BE)
Shakertown Meat
Loaf, 39 (BE)
Welsh Meat Loaf, 38 (BE)
Mincemeat Pie,
Homemade, 120 (CE)
Minestrone, 106 (SO)
Pastichio, 58 (CE)
Pasties, Beef and Pork, 45 (BE)
Picadillo, 42 (BE)
Pie, Hot Tamale, 46 (BE)

*Meat chopper.*

**Beef, Ground,** *continued*
Pie, Louisiana Meat, 45 (BE)
Pies, Polish Meat, 46 (BE)
Pie, Tony's Italian
Pasta-Meat, 43 (BE)
Sausage, Country Beef, 50 (BE)
Soup, Filled Noodle, 79 (SO)
Steaks, Mock
Chicken-Fried, 41 (BE)
Stew, Campers', 76 (SP)
Stew, Meatball, 129 (SO)
Stew, Pioneer Corn, 130 (SO)
Tacos, 48 (BE)
Tamales, Hot, 48 (BE)
Turnovers, Meat, 73 (CE)

**Beets**
Borscht, 99 (SO)
Borscht, Traditional, 99 (SO)
Buttered Beets, 10 (CC)
Creamed Beets, 25 (VE)
Glazed Fresh Beets, 58 (CC)
Harvard Beets, 25 (VE)
How To Prepare Fresh
Beets, 24 (VE)
Orange Sauce, Beets in, 25 (VE)
Pickles, Beet, 40 (GR)
Relish,
Beet-Horseradish, 75 (GR)
Salad with Pickled Herring,
Beet, 19 (FG)
Sweet-and-Sour Beets, 24 (VE)

**Beverages**
Alcoholic
Absinthe Frappé, 34 (CE)
Andrew Jackson
Cooler, 92 (FG)
Apple Toddy, Hot, 67 (BB)
Bloody Bulls, 117 (SP)
Bloody Mary,
Mexican, 37 (BB)
Bloody Marys, 94 (BB); 16, 34,
63, 76 (CE); 24 (SP)
Bloody Sam, 76 (BB)
Champagne Cocktail,
Mimosa, 104 (CC)
Cherry Bounce, 118 (SS)
Cider, Berkeley
Spiced, 116 (CE)
Claret Cup, 118 (SS)
Eggnog, 21, 136 (CE)
Eggnog, Christmas, 50 (FG)
Eggnog, Morning, 95 (BB)
Gin Fizz, Ramos, 28 (CC)
Hot Irish, 47 (CE)
Lemonade, Claret, 94 (BB)
Margaritas, 93 (BB); 131 (FG)
Martini, 63 (CE)
Mimosa, 93 (BB); 35 (CE)
Mint Julep, Kentucky, 81 (CE)
Mint Juleps, 15 (BB);
89 (CC); 21 (SP)
Morning Call, 93 (BB)
Morning Pick-Up, 62 (BB)
Mulled Claret, 84 (CC)
Negroni, 35 (CE)
Ojen Cocktail, 35 (CE)

Orange Blossom, 93 (BB)
Peach Daiquiri, 78 (FG)
Punch, Champagne, 95 (BB);
118 (FG); 112 (SP); 61 (SS)
Punch, Chatham
Artillery, 126 (SS)
Punch, Fruited
Champagne, 86 (FG)
Punch, Hogmanay, 15 (CE)
Punch, Hot Rum, 12 (CE)
Punch, Jeff Davis, 109 (SS)
Punch, Milk, 94 (BB)
Punch, Mocha Milk, 78 (SS)
Punch, New Orleans
Milk, 35 (CE)
Punch, Passion, 71 (BB)
Punch, Planter's, 92 (FG)
Punch, Queen's, 118 (SS)
Punch, Rose Leaf, 71 (SS)
Punch, Winterthur, 18 (SP)
Rum Tea, Hot, 18 (CE)
Rum Tea, Spiced, 63 (SS)
Salty Dog, 93 (BB)
Sangría, 37 (CC)
Sazerac Cocktail, 28 (CC)
Scarlett O'Hara, 94 (BB)
Syllabub, 123 (CE)
Tea, Five o'Clock, 71 (SS)
Wine Cooler, 25 (BB)
Wine Spritzers, 116 (SP)
Black Cows, 19 (SS)
Café au Lait, 33 (BB)
Café au Lait, Rich, 69 (CC)
Café con Leche, 38 (BB)
Café Noir, 69 (CC)
Chocolate, Afternoon, 71 (SS)
Chocolate Fluff, 92 (BB)
Chocolate, Hot, 87 (BB);
29 (CE); 59 (FG); 113 (SS)
Chocolate, Old-Fashioned
Hot, 92 (BB)
Cider, Mulled, 90 (BB)
Cocoa, Breakfast, 18 (BB)
Coffee, A Good Cup of, 90 (BB)
Coffee for a Crowd, 90 (BB)
Coffee, Iced, 90 (BB)
Coffee, Lovefeast, 50 (CE)
Coffee, Old-Fashioned
Boiled, 73 (CC)
Coffee, Riverbank, 41 (BB)
Cranberry Cooler, 92 (BB)
Cranberry Juice
Cocktail, 105 (FG)
Cranberry Syrup, 113 (SS)
Lemonade, 17 (FG)
Lemonade, Apple, 86 (CE)
Lemonade, Fresh, 123 (SP)
Lemonade, Refreshing, 113 (SS)
Orange Blush, 50 (BB)
Orange Juice, Spiced, 77 (SP)
Pineapple Orangeade, 68 (FG)
Punch
Artillery Punch,
Chatham, 126 (SS)
Champagne Punch, 95 (BB);
118 (FG); 112 (SP); 61 (SS)

Champagne Punch,
Fruited, 86 (FG)
Fruit Punch with Ice
Ring, 26 (SP)
Ginger Ale Punch, 82 (SS)
Hogmanay Punch, 15 (CE)
Jeff Davis Punch, 109 (SS)
Milk Punch, 94 (BB)
Milk Punch, New
Orleans, 35 (CE)
Mint Punch, Golden, 86 (FG)
Mint Punch, Tropical, 73 (CC)
Mint Tea Punch, 126 (SS)
Mocha Milk Punch, 78 (SS)
Mocha Punch, Frosty, 12 (SS)
Passion Punch, 71 (BB)
Planter's Punch, 92 (FG)
Queen's Punch, 118 (SS)
Rose Leaf Punch, 71 (SS)
Rum Punch, Hot, 12 (CE)
Shrub, 26 (CE)
Spiced Punch, Hot, 73 (CC)
Springtime Punch, 71 (CE)
Tea Punch, 82 (CC); 66 (SS)
Tea Punch, Iced, 36 (SS)
Wedding Punch, 118 (FG);
88 (SS)
Winterthur Punch, 18 (SP)
Tea, Fruited Iced, 20 (SP)
Tea, Good, 90 (BB)
Tea, Iced Mint, 33 (SS)
Tea, Russian, 61 (SS)
Tea, Sassafras, 33 (CC)
Tea, Spiced, 90 (BB); 108 (CE)
Tea, Spiced Hot, 29 (FG)
Tomato Juice, Hot
Spiced, 92 (BB)

Brown Brothers

---

**BB** *Breakfast & Brunch*   **BE** *Beef, Veal & Lamb*   **BR** *Breads*   **CA** *Cakes*   **CC** *Company's Coming*   **CE** *Celebrations*
**CJ** *Cookie Jar*   **DE** *Just Desserts*   **FG** *Family Gatherings*   **GR** *Gift Receipts*   **PK** *All Pork*   **PO** *Plain & Fancy Poultry*
**PP** *Pies & Pastry*   **SE** *Sea & Stream*   **SO** *Soups & Stews*   **SP** *Sporting Scene*   **SS** *Socials & Soirees*   **VE** *Vegetables*

*The beverage thermos was an indispensable piece of picnic equipage even in the 1920s.*

Beverages, *continued*
Tomato Juice, Spiced, 14 (CC)
Wassail, 26 (CE)
Witches' Brew, 104 (CE)

**Biscuits**
Angel Food Biscuits, 92 (BR)
Bacon Biscuits, 49 (FG)
Basic Biscuits
  Baking Powder
    Biscuits, 110 (BE); 83 (BR);
    137 (CC)
  Breakfast Biscuits, 84 (BR)
  Buttermilk Biscuits, 56 (FG);
    65 (PK)
  Buttermilk Biscuits,
    Grandma's Best, 96 (BB)
  Buttermilk Biscuits,
    Old-Fashioned, 11 (BB)
  Buttermilk Biscuits,
    Virginia, 85 (BR); 71 (CE)
  Company's Coming
    Biscuits, 96 (CC)
  Country Biscuits, 53 (CC)
  Down Home
    Biscuits, 102 (CC)
  Foolproof Biscuits, 110 (CE)
  How-To, Basic
    Biscuit, 86 (BR)
  Luncheon Biscuits, 39 (SS)
  Self-Rising Biscuits, 31 (BB)
  Self-Rising Buttermilk
    Biscuits, 85 (BR)
  Soda Biscuits, 14 (BB);
    84 (BR)
  Supreme, Biscuits, 35 (FG)

Beaten
  Beaten Biscuits, 68 (BB);
    76 (BR)
  "Bread Brake"
    Biscuits, 76 (BR)
  How-To, Beaten
    Biscuit, 78 (BR)
  Kentucky Beaten
    Biscuits, 77 (BR)
  Maryland Beaten
    Biscuits, 77 (BR)
  Old South Beaten
    Biscuits, 121 (SS)
  Processor Beaten
    Biscuits, 77 (BR)
Benne Seed Biscuits, 93 (BR)
Bran Biscuits, 89 (BR); 51 (SP)
Bran Biscuits, Caraway, 93 (BR)
Buttermilk Drop
  Biscuits, 84 (BR)
Cathead Biscuits, 85 (BR)
Cheddar Biscuits, Tiny, 107 (CE)
Cheese Biscuits, 46 (CC);
  65 (SS)
Cheese Biscuits,
  Cheddar, 97 (BB)
Cheese Biscuit Thins, 94 (BR)
Cheese Rounds, 94 (BR)
Chicken Biscuits, 88 (BR)
Chicken with Biscuits,
  Stewed, 17 (PO)
Cinnamon Biscuit Rolls, 94 (BR)
Cocktail Biscuits, 94 (BR)
Cornmeal Biscuits, 22 (BR)
Cowboy Biscuits, 88 (BR)
Cream Biscuits, 96 (BB)
English Biscuits with Cinnamon
  Butter, 42 (FG)
Fat Rascals, 134 (BR)
Fruit Drop Biscuits, 96 (BR)
Ham Biscuits,
  Smithfield, 91 (PK)
Hot Biscuits, 112 (FG)
Lemon Tea Biscuits, 63 (BB)
Miniature Biscuits, 84 (SS)
Orange Biscuits, 55 (BB)
Orange Biscuits,
  Florida, 97 (BR)
Peanut Biscuits, 89 (BR)
Puffs, Biscuit, 126 (BR)
Raisin Biscuits, 91 (BR);
  14 (SS)
Ring, Biscuit, 124 (PO)
Sesame Seeds, Biscuits
  with, 83 (BR)
Skon Bread, 91 (BR)
Sour Cream Biscuits, 97 (BB)
Sourdough Biscuits, 81 (BR);
  41 (CC)
Sourdough Starter, 81 (BR);
  41 (CC)
Sweet Biscuits, 91 (BR); 28 (SP)
Sweet Potato Biscuits, 97 (BB);
  89 (BR)
Sweet Potato Biscuits with
  Baked Ham, 106 (SS)
Tea Biscuits, Crescent, 96 (BR)
Tiny Biscuits, 87 (BB)
Toasted Biscuits with Olive
  Spread, 64 (CE)

Topping, Biscuit, 41 (SE)
Whipping Cream
  Biscuits, 90 (BR)
Whole Wheat Angel
  Biscuits, 95 (FG)
Whole Wheat Biscuits with
  Honey Butter, 98 (BB)
Yeast
  Angel Biscuits, 73 (BB);
    80 (BR)
  Chuck Wagon Biscuits, 80 (BR)
  Fluffy Yeast Biscuits, 12 (FG)
  Risen Biscuits, 100 (SS)
  Sourdough Biscuits, 81 (BR);
    41 (CC)
  Sourdough Starter, 81 (BR);
    41 (CC)
  Topknot Biscuits, 82 (BR)
  Velvet Biscuits, 82 (BR)
  Whole Wheat Angel
    Biscuits, 95 (FG)

**Bisques**
Clam Bisque, 52 (SO)
Crab Bisque, 52 (SO)
Crayfish Bisque, 26 (SE)
Oyster Bisque, 54 (SO)
Salsify Bisque, 69 (SO);
  100 (VE)
Shrimp Bisque, 56 (SO)
Tomato Bisque, 70 (SO)
White Bisque,
  Charleston, 58 (SO)

**Blackberries**
Berry Roly-Poly, 53 (CC)
Cake, Blackberry, 43 (CA)
Cake, "Little Nanny's" Blackberry
  Jam, 46 (CA)
Cobbler, Berry, 47 (PP)
Cobbler, Deep-Dish
  Blackberry, 48 (PP)
Cobbler, Easy
  Blackberry, 123 (FG)
Cobbler, Quick
  Blackberry, 103 (SP)
Dumplings, Blackberry, 130 (PP)
Jam (*Note*), Blackberry, 23 (GR)
Jelly, Blackberry, 10 (GR)
Pie, Berry, 47 (PP)
Sauce, Blackberry, 104 (FG)
Sherbet, Blackberry, 92 (DE)

**Blueberries**
Buckle, Blueberry, 42 (DE)
Cake, Blueberry Pound, 42 (CA)
Cake, Stars and Stripes
  Blueberry, 85 (CE)
Cobbler, Berry, 47 (PP)
Cobbler Roll, Blueberry, 47 (PP)
Grunt, Blueberry, 42 (DE)
Jam, Blueberry, 23 (GR)
Muffins, Blueberry, 101 (BB);
  112 (BR)
Muffins, Petite
  Blueberry, 80 (BB)
Pancakes, Blueberry, 35 (BB)
Pie, Berry, 47 (PP)
Pudding, Blueberry, 42 (DE)
Sauce, Blueberry, 36 (BB);
  66 (DE)
Soufflé, Blueberry, 66 (DE)
Tarts, Blueberry, 116 (PP)

**Bluefish**
Baked Stuffed Bluefish, 60 (SE)
Capt'n Buddy's Favorite, 60 (SE)
Grilled Bluefish, 61 (SE)
Poached Bluefish,
  Seaside, 61 (SE)
**Bran**
Biscuits, Bran, 89 (BR); 51 (SP)
Biscuits, Caraway Bran, 93 (BR)
Cookies, Bran Drop, 42 (CJ)
Muffins, Bran, 50 (BB);
  127 (FG)
Muffins, Grove Park Inn
  Bran, 110 (BR)
Muffins, Raisin Bran, 115 (BR)
**Brazil Nuts**
Cake, Brazil Nut, 90 (CA)
Logs, Holiday Delight, 119 (GR)
Macaroons, Brazil Nut, 15 (CJ)
**Breads.** *See also* specific types.
Applesauce Nut Bread,
  Casselman Inn, 103 (BR)
Apricot Nut Bread, 102 (BB)
Baking Powder Bread, 100 (BR)
Balls, Bread and Butter, 15 (SO)
Banana Bread,
  Old-Fashioned, 103 (BB)
Banana Nut Bread, 77 (CC)
Banana Nut Bread, Corrie
  Hill's, 103 (BR)
Beer Bread, 117 (PK)
Bishops' Bread, 119 (BR)
Caraway Salt Sticks, 135 (BR)
Cheese Puffs, 136 (BR);
  118 (SP)
Cheese Straws, 136 (BR)
Cheese Wafers, 92 (CC)
Chew Bread,
  Grandma's, 63 (CA)
Chocolate Mandel
  Bread, 130 (FG)
Croûtes, 35 (SO)
Croutons, 18 (SO)
Croutons, Baked, 18 (SO)
Croutons, Butter
  Toasted, 83 (SP)
Croutons, Cheese, 18 (SO)
Date Nut Bread, 77 (CC)
Dressing, Bread, 48 (PO)
Dressing, Breadcrumb, 97 (CC)
Dressing, Onion-Bread, 13 (PK)
Fat Rascals, 134 (BR)
Fry Bread, Indian, 33 (CC)
Garlic Bread, 51 (SP)
Garlic Bread, Grilled, 77,
  90 (SP)
Graham Squares,
  Easy, 134 (BR)
Griddle Cakes
  Apple-Rice Griddle
    Cakes, 114 (BB)
  Corn Griddle Cakes,
    Alabama, 26 (BR)
  Cornmeal Batty Cakes, 25 (BR)
  Cornmeal Cakes, Mrs.
    Paul's, 25 (BR)

Cornmeal Flapjacks,
  Arkansas, 26 (BR)
Cornmeal Patty
  Cakes, 16 (BB)
Hoecakes, Indian, 27 (BR)
Indian Griddle Cakes, 56 (BE)
Lace Cakes,
  Kentucky, 26 (BR)
Potato Griddle Cakes, 35 (BB)
Lemon Bread, 104 (BR)
Marmalade Nut Bread, 104 (BR)
Nut Loaf,
  Old-Fashioned, 105 (BR)
Orange Bread, Florida, 105 (BR)
Pancakes, Breadcrumb, 35 (BB)
Peanut Butter Bread, 105 (BR)
Persimmon Nut Bread, 105 (BR)
Philpy, 103 (BR)
Pirogi, 136 (BR)
Praline Bread, 40 (CE)
Prune Bread, 106 (BR)
Puddings
  Bon Ton's Bread
    Pudding, 12 (DE)
  Bourbon Sauce, Bread and
    Butter Pudding
    with, 15 (SP)
  Caramel Bread
    Pudding, 13 (DE)
  Lemon Sauce, Bread Pudding
    with, 13 (DE)
  Wine Sauce, Bread Pudding
    with, 13 (DE)
Pumpkin Bread, 106 (BR)

Sally Lunn, Quick, 100 (BR)
Scones, Four o'Clock
  Tea, 77 (SS)
Scones, Scotch Soda, 134 (BR)
Scones, Tea, 132 (BR)
Shortbread, 13 (CE)
Short'nin' Bread, 60 (CA)
Sippets, 130 (BR); 18 (SO)
Skon Bread, 91 (BR)
Soda Bread, Irish, 43 (CE)
Soda Bread, Whiskey, 47 (CE)
Sourdough
  Biscuits, Sourdough, 81 (BR)
  Bread, Shaker
    Friendship, 38 (BR)
  Bread, Sourdough, 40 (BR)

Starter Food, 38 (BR)
Starter, Potato-Yeast, 40 (BR)
Starter, Sourdough, 38,
  40 (BR)
Spoonbreads
  Awendaw, 31 (BR)
  Dixie Spoonbread, 35 (BR)
  Egg Bread, 35 (BR)
  Hotel Roanoke
    Spoonbread, 33 (BR)
  Individual
    Spoonbreads, 32 (BR)
  Luncheon
    Spoonbread, 32 (BR)
  Ovendaugh, South
    Carolina, 31 (BR)
  Parmesan
    Spoonbread, 32 (BR)
  Plantation
    Spoonbread, 126 (CC)
  Southern
    Spoonbread, 31 (BR)
  Spider Bread,
    Louisiana, 35 (BR)
  Turkey Spoonbread, 120 (PO)
  Virginia Spoonbread, 14 (BB)
Sweet Potato Bread, 106 (BR)
Sweet Rolls
  Breakfast Puffs,
    French, 112 (BR)
  Cinnamon Biscuit
    Rolls, 94 (BR)
  Cinnamon Rolls, 48 (BB)
  Cinnamon Rolls, Southern
    Kitchen, 68 (BR)
  Cinnamon Rolls, S&S, 79 (CC)
  Herren's Sweet Rolls, 72 (BR)
  Honey Almond Rolls, Anna
    Maude's, 69 (BR)
  Kolaches, 70 (BR)
  Miniature Sweet
    Rolls, 73 (BB)
  Orange Rolls, 108 (BB);
    71 (BR)
  Orange Roll-Ups,
    Sweet, 97 (BR)
  Pan Dulce, 67 (BR)
  Pecan Rolls, Boca
    Raton, 73 (BR)
  Pecan Twists, 73 (BR)
  Sweet Rolls in New
    Dress, 71 (BR)
  Tiny Sweet Rolls, 25 (CE)
Toast
  Anchovy Toast,
    Buttered, 65 (SS)
  Baskets, Toast, 33 (SE)
  Cheese Toast, 19 (SO)
  Cinnamon Glazed
    Toast, 111 (BB)
  Cups, Creamed Eggs in
    Toast, 78 (BB)
  Cups, Toast, 122 (PO)
  French Toast, 112 (BB)
  French Toast,
    Orange, 112 (BB)

---

**BB** *Breakfast & Brunch*   **BE** *Beef, Veal & Lamb*   **BR** *Breads*   **CA** *Cakes*   **CC** *Company's Coming*   **CE** *Celebrations*
**CJ** *Cookie Jar*   **DE** *Just Desserts*   **FG** *Family Gatherings*   **GR** *Gift Receipts*   **PK** *All Pork*   **PO** *Plain & Fancy Poultry*
**PP** *Pies & Pastry*   **SE** *Sea & Stream*   **SO** *Soups & Stews*   **SP** *Sporting Scene*   **SS** *Socials & Soirees*   **VE** *Vegetables*

*A demonstration of kneading bread for a captive audience, c.1915.*

Breads, Toast, *continued*
  Orange-Cinnamon
    Toast, 112 (BB)
  Pain Perdu, 113 (BB)
  Texas Toast, 34 (SP)
  Vasilopeta (Greek Sweet
    Bread), 64 (FG)
  Whole Wheat
    Golden Brown
      Bread, 100 (BR)
    Graham Bread, 53 (BR)
    Honey Bread, Whole
      Wheat, 101 (BR)
    Honey Wheat Bread,
      Winkler, 51 (BR)
    Muffins, Grove Park Inn
      Bran, 110 (BR)
    Muffins, Shirley
      Graham, 110 (BR)
    Quick Bread, Whole
      Wheat, 101 (BR)
    Squares, Whole
      Wheat, 101 (BR)
    Sunflower Seed
      Bread, 55 (BR)
    Wheaten Bread,
      Shaker, 17 (CC)

  Whole Wheat Bread, 51 (BR)
Yeast. *See also* Sweet Rolls
  above.
  Adobe Oven Bread, 45 (BR)
  Amish Cakes, 64 (BR)
  Apple Roll, 46 (BB)
  Beignets, 32 (BB)
  Beignets, French
    Market, 122 (BR)
  Bread Bows, Glazed, 108 (CE)
  Breadsticks,
    Parmesan, 23 (SO)
  Brioche, Basic, 48 (BR)
  Brioche,
    Hermann-Grima, 48 (BR)
  Brioche, Petite, 116 (SS)
  Brioche, Sausage in, 48 (BR)
  Brioche, Traditional, 49 (BR)
  Brioche with Gruyère and
    Parmesan, 48 (BR)
  Calas, 68 (CC)
  Challah, 130 (FG)
  Chocolate Bread,
    1935, 62 (BR)
  Croissants, 44 (BB)
  Crumpets, 132 (BR)
  Cuban Bread, 136 (FG)

  Easy Yeast Bread, 16 (BB)
  Egg Braid, Swiss, 47 (BR)
  Everlasting Bread, 109 (BB)
  French Bread, 39 (FG);
    97 (PK); 32, 59 (SP)
  French Bread, Herbed, 84 (SP)
  French Bread, New
    Orleans, 46 (BR)
  French Bread, Sour, 120 (SP)
  French Breadsticks, 108 (CC)
  Graham Bread, 53 (BR)
  Greek Bread, 63 (FG)
  Greek Holiday Bread, 63 (BR)
  Herb Bread, 20 (SP)
  Homemade Yeast
    Loaves, 45 (FG)
  How-To, Basic White
    Bread, 42 (BR)
  Irish Bread, 45 (BR)
  Light Bread, Egg, 46 (BR)
  Light Bread, Ivy Neck, 45 (BR)
  Monkey Bread,
    Neiman-Marcus, 47 (BR)
  Pecan Loaf, 25 (BB)
  Potato Bread,
    Dunleith, 133 (CC)
  Pumpernickel Bread, 53 (BR)

**Breads, Yeast,** *continued*
Raisin Bread, 110 (BB);
22 (FG)
Raisin Bread,
Salzburger, 63 (BR)
Rice Bread, Brown, 31 (FG)
Rice Bread, Mrs. Yohe's
Original Brown, 55 (BR)
Round Crusty Loaf, 52 (BR)
Rusk, Mr. Paca's, 131 (BR)
Rye Bread, Dark, 17 (SP)
Rye Bread, Swedish, 55 (BR)
Saffron Bread,
Cornish, 62 (BR)
Sally Lunn, 69 (BB);
122 (FG); 133 (SS)
Sally Lunn, Kentucky, 50 (BR)
Sally Lunn, North
Carolina, 50 (BR)
Sally Lunn, Old
Virginia, 30 (PO)
Salt-Rising Bread,
Foolproof, 40 (BR)
Salt-Rising Bread,
Shaker, 39 (BR)
Salt Sticks,
Caraway, 135 (BR)
Salt Sticks, Garlic, 135 (BR)
Salt Sticks,
Parmesan, 135 (BR)
Shaker Daily Loaf, 44 (BR)
Shaker Friendship
Bread, 38 (BR)
Sopaipillas, 123 (BR); 66 (CC)
Sunflower Seed
Bread, 55 (BR)
Sweet Bread, Greek, 58 (CE)
Sweet Potato Bread, 30 (CC)
Wheat Bread, Winkler
Honey, 51 (BR)
White Bread, Basic, 42 (BR)
Whole Wheat Bread, 51 (BR)
Zucchini Bread, 120 (SP)
**Bream**
Beer 'n' Bream, Ole
Timer's, 114 (SE)
Broiled Bream, 114 (SE)
Fried Bream, 114 (SE)
Pan-Fried Bream with
Sauce, 115 (SE)
**Broccoli**
Bake,
Chicken-Broccoli, 133 (BB)
Braised Broccoli in Tomato
Cups, 11 (CC)
Cheese Sauce, Broccoli Baked
with, 26 (VE)
Hollandaise Sauce, Broccoli
with, 111 (CC)
How To Prepare Fresh
Broccoli, 26 (VE)
Lemon Broccoli, 26 (VE)
Lemon Broccoli Spears, 99 (SS)
Parmesan, Broccoli, 27 (VE)
Salad in Lettuce Cups, Fresh
Broccoli, 68 (BB)

Library of Congress

*Butter in the making allows time for a good book, c.1897.*

Soufflé, Broccoli, 27 (VE)
Souffléed Broccoli, 133 (CC)
Soup, Broccoli, 18 (SP)
Soup, Cream of
Broccoli, 60 (SO); 56 (SS)
Southern Broccoli, 30 (PO)
Steamed Broccoli, 61 (CE)
Wine-Butter Broccoli, 27 (VE)
**Brussels Sprouts**
Browned Butter, Brussels
Sprouts in, 29 (VE)
Brussels Sprouts, 116 (SS)
Chestnuts, Brussels Sprouts
and, 29 (VE)
Cream, Brussels Sprouts
with, 29 (VE)
Creamed Brussels Sprouts and
Onions in Acorn
Squash, 118 (CC)
Dill Butter, Brussels Sprouts
with, 116 (CE)

Festive Brussels
Sprouts, 29 (VE)
How To Prepare Fresh Brussels
Sprouts, 28 (VE)
Maître d'Hôtel Sauce, Brussels
Sprouts with, 39 (FG)
Piquant Brussels
Sprouts, 62 (CC)
**Buffalo**
Roast, Buffalo, 52 (SP)
**Butter**
Almond Butter, 132 (VE)
Apple Butter, 48 (BB)
Apple Butter,
Old-Fashioned, 25 (GR)
Beurre Blanc, 128 (SE)
Broccoli, Wine-Butter, 27 (VE)
Browned Butter, Brussels
Sprouts in, 29 (VE)
Cheese Butter, English Muffins
Toasted with, 123 (SP)

**BB** *Breakfast & Brunch*   **BE** *Beef, Veal & Lamb*   **BR** *Breads*   **CA** *Cakes*   **CC** *Company's Coming*   **CE** *Celebrations*
**CJ** *Cookie Jar*   **DE** *Just Desserts*   **FG** *Family Gatherings*   **GR** *Gift Receipts*   **PK** *All Pork*   **PO** *Plain & Fancy Poultry*
**PP** *Pies & Pastry*   **SE** *Sea & Stream*   **SO** *Soups & Stews*   **SP** *Sporting Scene*   **SS** *Socials & Soirees*   **VE** *Vegetables*

20

Butter, *continued*
Cinnamon Butter, 42 (FG)
Clarified Butter, 127 (SE)
Dill Butter, Brussels Sprouts
with, 116 (CE)
Drawn Butter, 132 (VE)
Garlic Butter, Clarified, 43 (SE)
Grape Butter, 26 (GR)
Herb Butter, 47 (SS); 136 (VE)
Herb Butter, Tarragon, 136 (VE)
Honey Butter, 98 (BB); 65 (PK)
Lemon Butter, Asparagus
with, 110 (FG)
Maître d'Hôtel Butter, 29 (BE);
127 (SE)
Orange Butter, 20 (BB)
Parsley Butter, New Potatoes
with, 46 (CC)
Peach Butter,
Old-Fashioned, 27 (GR)
Plum Butter, Spiced, 27 (GR)
Rum-Butter Mixture, 80 (BB)
Sauce au Beurre Noir, 124 (BE)
Sauce, Boiled Chicken with
Butter, 17 (PO)
Sauce, Clarified Butter, 12 (PO)
Sauce, Lemon-Butter, 132 (VE)
Sauce, Rum Butter, 88 (GR)
Sauce, Tangy Butter, 132 (VE)
Steak Butter, 126 (BE)
Whiskey Butter, 47 (CE)
**Butterscotch**
Bars, Hello Dolly, 92 (CJ)
Brownies, Butterscotch, 75 (SP)
Candy, Cathedral, 103 (GR)
Cookies, Butterscotch, 67 (CJ)
Crunchies, Peanut
Butter, 98 (CJ)
Custard, Butterscotch, 52 (DE)
Pie, Pecan-Butterscotch,
101 (PP)
Pie, Smith and Welton's Tea
Room Butterscotch
Meringue, 90 (PP)
Pinwheels,
Butterscotch, 67 (CJ)
Sauce, Butterscotch, 85 (GR)
Sauce, Frances Virginia Tea
Room Butterscotch, 132 (DE)
Sauce, High Hampton
Butterscotch, 132 (DE)
Squares, Butterscotch-Fruit,
91 (CJ)
Suckers, Butterscotch, 116 (GR)

# C

**Cabbage**
Apples, Red Cabbage
and, 21 (FG)
Apples, Red Cabbage
with, 32 (VE)
au Gratin, Cabbage, 31 (VE)
Boiled Cabbage, 30 (VE)
Bubble and Squeak, 31 (VE)
Corned Beef Dinner,
Maryland, 23 (BE)

Fried Cabbage,
Tennessee, 32 (VE)
Grilled Polish Sausage and
Cabbage, 59 (PK)
How To Prepare Fresh
Cabbage, 30 (VE)
Rolls, Cabbage, 129 (FG)
Rolls, Greek Cabbage, 39 (PK)
Rolls, Stuffed Cabbage, 50 (BE)
Salad, Cabbage, 19 (CC)
Salad, Hayden, 12 (FG)
Salad, Perfection, 76 (FG)
Sauerkraut, German, 33 (VE)
Sauerkraut, Wine, 33 (VE)
Sausage Dish,
German, 108 (PK)
Scalloped Cabbage, 30 (VE)
Slang Jang, 44 (SP)
Slaws
Almond Coleslaw, 74 (SP)
Cabbage Slaw, 16 (FG)
Cold Slaw, 65 (CE)
Cole Slaw, 44 (CE)
Coleslaw, 61, 89 (SP)
German Slaw, 97 (PK)
Marinated Cole Slaw, 77 (PO)
Mustard Cole Slaw, 47 (PK)
Salad, Cabbage, 19 (CC)
Summer Slaw, 106 (SP)
Sweet-and-Sour
Slaw, 119 (CE)
Texas Coleslaw, 40 (CC)
Smothered Red
Cabbage, 32 (VE)
Soup, Sweet-and-Sour
Cabbage, 100 (SO)
Southern-Cooked
Cabbage, 31 (VE)
**Cakes.**
*See also* Breads, Cookies.
Ambrosia Cake, 20 (CE)
Angel Food
Basic Angel Food
Cake, 112 (CA)
Bridal Cake, Angel
Food, 85 (SS)
Chocolate Angel Food
Cake, 112 (CA)
Coffee Angel Food
Cake, 113 (CA)
Ice Cream Balls, Angel Food
Cake with, 77 (FG)
Lemon Angel Food
Cake, 112 (CA)
Mock Angel Food
Cake, 113 (CA)
Pineapple Angel Food
Cake, 112 (CA)
Self-Frosting Angel
Cake, 112 (CA)
Apple Cake, Auntie's, 39 (CA)
Apple Cake, Dried, 38 (CA)
Apple Cake, Fresh, 133 (SP)
Apple Cake, Nobby, 40 (CA)
Applesauce Cake,
Brown, 37 (CA)
Banana Layer Cake,
Delicious, 22 (CA)
Banana-Nut Cake, 68 (CA)
Bar Mitzvah Cake, 101 (FG)

Bars and Squares
Bon Bons, Bunco, 93 (SS)
Cake Fingers, 85 (CA)
Chess Bars,
Lemon-Glazed, 90 (SP)
Chew Bread,
Grandma's, 63 (CA)
Chocolate Delights, 89 (FG)
Coconut Squares,
Toasted, 77 (SP)
Coffee Cake Squares, 12 (SS)
Coming-Out Cakes, 82 (SS)
Confederate Soldiers, 65 (CA)
Gingerbread, Hot
Water, 65 (CA)
Gingerbread,
Lafayette, 89 (CC)
Gingerbread,
Old-Fashioned, 65 (CA)
Gingerbread with Lemon
Sauce, 54 (SS)
Lemon Squares, 26 (FG)

Mississippi River Stage
Planks, 66 (CA)
Molasses Spice Bars, 17 (SP)
Peach Cake, South Carolina
Fresh, 44 (CA)
Peanut-Apple
Squares, 85 (CA)
Petits Fours, 109 (CA);
91 (CC)
Petits Fours,
Monogrammed, 13 (SP)
Spice Bars, Frosted, 32 (FG)
Wine Bars, 121 (SP)
Beer Cakes, 61 (CA)
Birthday Cake,
Coconut, 103 (CA)
Birthday Cake, Miss
Arintha's, 104 (CA)
Birthday Cake, Mother
Ann's, 105 (CA)
Birthday Cake, Sweet
Sixteen, 70 (FG)
Birthday Layer Cake,
77 (FG)
Blackberry Cake, 43 (CA)
Blackberry Jam Cake, "Little
Nanny's," 46 (CA)
Blueberry Cake, Stars and
Stripes, 85 (CE)
Bride's Cake, 107 (CA);
117 (FG)
Caraway Cakes, New
Year's, 96 (CA)

Cakes, *continued*
Cheesecakes
  Best-Ever
    Cheesecake, 128 (DE)
  Chocolate-Mocha
    Cheesecakes, 23 (SS)
  Cream Cheesecake, Jennie
    Selligman's, 80 (PP)
  German Cheesecake, 81 (PP)
  Mocha Cheesecake, 79 (PP)
  Old-Fashioned Cheesecake,
    "The Original," 78 (PP)
  Orange Cheesecake, Blue
    Ribbon, 82 (PP)
  Pineapple Cheesecake, 83 (PP)
  Praline Cheesecake, 84 (PP)
  Pumpkin Cheesecake, 85 (PP)
Chocolate
  Angel Food Cake,
    Chocolate, 112 (CA)
  Brownstone Front
    Cake, 63 (CA)
  Bûche de Noël, 94 (CA)
  Checkerboard Cake, 24 (CA)
  Chiffon, Chocolate, 114 (CA)
  Chocolate Cake, 116 (CA)
  Choo-Choo Chocolate
    Cake, 67 (FG)
  Date Fudge Cake,
    Halloween, 102 (CA)
  Delights, Chocolate, 89 (FG)
  Devil's Food Cake, 26,
    117 (CA); 13 (FG)
  "Failure" Cake,
    Chocolate, 80 (CA)
  Fudge Cake,
    Maryland, 67 (CE)
  Fudge Cake, Old-Fashioned
    Chewy, 83 (CA)
  German Sweet Chocolate
    Cake, 27 (CA)
  Groom's Cake,
    Chocolate, 108 (CA)
  Groom's Cake,
    Spirited, 89 (SS)
  Hot Water Chocolate
    Cake, 82 (CA)
  Jiffy Chocolate Cake, 83 (CA)
  Mahogany Cake, 28 (CA)
  Marble Loaf Cake, 31 (SS)
  Midgets, Chocolate, 80 (CA)
  Mississippi Mud Cake, 82 (CA)
  Mocha Cheesecakes,
    Chocolate-, 23 (SS)
  Mocha Layer Cake, 29 (CA)
  Mocha Pound Cake, 121 (CA)
  Neapolitan Halloween
    Cake, 101 (CA)
  Pound Cake,
    Chocolate, 121 (CA)
  Pound Cake, Pecan-Topped
    Chocolate, 118 (CA)
  Ribbon Cake,
    Chocolate, 25 (CA)
  Sheath Cake,
    Chocolate, 81 (CA)

Sour Cream-Cocoa
  Cake, 54 (SS)
Sponge Cake, Passover
  Chocolate, 100 (CA)
Syrup Cake, Busy
  Day, 84 (CA)
Wacky Cake, 84 (CA)
Whipped Cream Roll,
  Gertrude's
  Chocolate, 125 (CA)
Yeast Cake,
  Chocolate, 27 (CA)
Cider Cake, October, 59 (CC)
Coconut
  Ambrosia Cake, 22 (CA)
  Birthday Cake,
    Coconut, 103 (CA)
  Cream Cake,
    Coconut, 124 (CE)
  Moss Rose Cake, 23 (CA)
  Orange Coconut Cake,
    Easter, 100 (CA)
  Pound Cake,
    Coconut, 121 (CA); 89 (FG)
  Rocky Mountain Coconut
    Cake, 15 (CA)
  Snowball Cake, 95 (CA)
  Toasted Coconut
    Cake, 74 (CA)
  White Mountain Cake, 21 (CA)

Coffee Cakes
  Almond Puff Coffee
    Cake, 77 (BB)
  Amish Cakes, 64 (BR)
  Apple Coffee Cake, 104 (BB)
  Apple Roll, 46 (BB)
  Apple Strudel, 119 (BR)
  Bishops' Bread, 119 (BR)
  Black Coffee Cake, 105 (BB)
  Braided Coffee Cake, 110 (BB)
  Cinnamon Ring,
    Glazed, 118 (BR)
  City Hall Coffee Cake, 64 (CA)
  Crumb Topping, Coffee Cake
    with, 117 (BR)
  Honey-Crisp Coffee
    Cake, 64 (CA)
  Huckleberry Coffee
    Cake, 105 (BB)

Jingle Bread Coffee
  Cake, 51 (FG)
Morning Coffee
  Cake, 104 (BB)
Oatmeal-Coconut Coffee
  Cake, 103 (BB)
Old-South Coffee
  Cake, 117 (BR)
Overnight Kaffee
  Kuchen, 64 (BR)
Pecan Loaf, 25 (BB)
Prize-Winning Coffee
  Cake, 66 (BR)
Raisin Coffee Cake,
  1860, 64 (BR)
Rum-Butter Coffee
  Cake, 80 (BB)
Sophie's Coffee
  Cake, 118 (BR)
Squares, Coffee Cake, 12 (SS)
Sugar Cake,
  Moravian, 65 (BR)
Swedish Tea Ring, 47 (BB)
Swirl Coffee Cake, 110 (BB)
Cracker Cake,
  Gretchen's, 75 (CA)
Cream Cake, Italian, 90 (SP)
Cupcakes
  Black Cat Cupcakes, 104 (CE)
  Brownie Cupcakes, 86 (CA)
  Carrot Cupcakes, 73 (SP)
  Chocolate Gems, 71 (CE)
  Christmas Cakes, 136 (CE)
  Delicate Cupcakes, 86 (CA)
  Funeral Cakes,
    Stellar's, 60 (CA)
  Kossuth Cakes, 125 (DE)
  Mix-Easy Cupcakes, 86 (CA)
  Orange Cupcakes, 86 (CA)
  Orange Tea Cakes, 65 (SS)
  Spice Cupcakes, 44 (CE)
  Sponge Drop Cakes, 82 (CC)
  Wine Cakes, 95 (CA)
Dolly Varden Cake, 20 (CA)
Easter Dawn Cake, 49 (CC)
Fig Layer Cake, Fresh, 44 (CA)
Fig Preserves Cake, 45 (CA);
  15 (SS)
Fruitcakes
  Apple Fruitcake,
    Dried, 38 (CA)
  Bourbon Cake, 13 (CC)
  Brazil Nut Cake, 90 (CA)
  Dundee Cake, 15 (CE)
  Groom's Cake, 118 (FG)
  Holiday Fruitcake, 128 (CE)
  Individual Fruitcakes,
    Shenandoah, 92 (CA)
  Irish Festive Cake, 47 (CE)
  James K. Polk
    Fruitcake, 91 (CA)
  Japanese Fruitcake, 25 (CA);
    57 (FG)
  Martha Washington's Great
    Cake, 90 (CA)
  Southern Fruitcake, 93 (CA)

---

**BB** *Breakfast & Brunch*   **BE** *Beef, Veal & Lamb*   **BR** *Breads*   **CA** *Cakes*   **CC** *Company's Coming*   **CE** *Celebrations*
**CJ** *Cookie Jar*   **DE** *Just Desserts*   **FG** *Family Gatherings*   **GR** *Gift Receipts*   **PK** *All Pork*   **PO** *Plain & Fancy Poultry*
**PP** *Pies & Pastry*   **SE** *Sea & Stream*   **SO** *Soups & Stews*   **SP** *Sporting Scene*   **SS** *Socials & Soirees*   **VE** *Vegetables*

*The Ingram family of Arkansas poses with their favorite cakes, c.1880.*

Cakes, Fruitcakes, *continued*
Tutti-Frutti Cake, 31 (CA)
Twelfth Night Cake, 26 (CE)
Wedding Fruitcake,
    Traditional, 109 (CA)
White Fruitcake, 92 (CA)
Fruit Cocktail Cake, 76 (CA)
Gâteau aux Amandes, 136 (SS)
General Robert E. Lee
    Cake, 18 (CA)
Grape Cake, Mayflower, 30 (CA)
Hasty Cake, 74 (CA)
Hickory Nut Cake, East
    Texas, 49 (CA)
Huckleberry Cake, 43 (CA)
Ice Cream Cake, 67 (CA);
    121 (SP)
Irish Tea Brack, 43 (CE)
Jam Cake, 95 (CE)
Jam Cake, Brown's
    Church, 46 (CA)
Jam Cake, Heritage, 45 (CA)
Jam Cake, Tennessee, 17 (FG)
John Garner Cake, 76 (CA)
Jumbles, Mamaw's
    Confederate, 85 (CA)
Karethopeta (Walnut
    Cake), 58 (CE)
King Cake, 99 (CA); 38 (CE)
Lady Baltimore Cake, 12 (CA)
Lane Cake, 14 (CA)
La Reine Cake (The
    Queen), 17 (CA)
Lazy-Dazy Cake, 66 (CA)
Lemon Gold Cake, 115 (CA);
    84 (FG)

Lemon Pecan Cake, 49 (CA)
Lemon Sheet Cake, 127 (SP)
Little Fancy Cakes, 42 (FG)
Lord Baltimore Cake, 13 (CA)
Macaroons, Cake-Crumb, 14 (CJ)
Mincemeat Cake,
    Thanksgiving, 102 (CA)
Minnehaha Cake, 19 (CA)
Molasses Cake, Marble, 77 (CA)
Mount Vernon Cake, 98 (CA)
Mystery Cake, First, 29 (CA)
Oatmeal Cake with Coconut
1-2-3-4 Cake, 117 (CA)
    Topping, 70 (SP)
Orange Cake,
    Williamsburg, 21 (CA)
Orange Coconut Cake,
    Easter, 100 (CA)
Orange-Date Cake, 68 (CA)
Orange Icebox Cake, 86 (DE)
Orange-Walnut Cake, 50 (CA)
Peach Cake, Fresh, 81 (SP)
Peach Cake, South Carolina
    Fresh, 44 (CA)
Peanut Cake, Harvest, 51 (CA)
Pear Preserves Cake, 47 (CA)
Pecan Cake, Bringhurst, 48 (CA)
Pecan Cake, Texas, 48 (CA)
Pecan Torte, 98 (SS)
Persimmon Cake, 44 (CA)
Pineapple Cake, 123 (FG)
Pineapple Icebox Cake, 86 (DE)
Pineapple Meringue
    Cake, 77 (CA)
Pineapple Pecan Cake, 124 (CE)
Poppy Seed Cake, 99 (CC)

Pork Cake,
    Williamsburg, 62 (CA)
Pound
Apple Cider Pound
    Cake, 118 (CA)
Blueberry Pound
    Cake, 42 (CA)
Brandy Pound Cake,
    Texas, 118 (CA)
Brown Sugar Pound
    Cake, 120 (CA)
Chocolate Pound
    Cake, 121 (CA)
Chocolate Pound Cake,
    Pecan-Topped, 118 (CA)
Coconut Pound
    Cake, 121 (CA); 89 (FG)
Cream Cheese Pound
    Cake, 120 (CA); 18 (CE)
Eggs on Toast, 75 (CA)
Geranium Pound
    Cake, 118 (CA)
Ginger Pound Cake, 122 (SS)
Lemon Pound Cake, 123 (SP)
Mocha Pound Cake, 121 (CA)
Pecan Pound Cake,
    Orange-Glazed, 98 (SP)
Pineapple Pound
    Cake, 12 (CC)
Pound Cake, 91 (CE)
Sweet Potato Pound
    Cake, 56 (CA)
Praline Cake, 78 (CA)
Praline Chiffon Cake, 115 (CA)
Prune Cake, 69 (CA)
Prunella Cake, 69 (CA)

Cakes, *continued*
Pumpkin Cake, 102 (CE)
Quick Cake, 78 (CA)
Raisin-Applesauce Cake, 69 (CA)
Rum Cake, Jennie
    Benedict's, 13 (CA)
Sauerkraut Cake, 67 (CA)
Scripture Cake, 61 (CA)
Shortbread, 13 (CE)
Shortcakes
    Orange Shortcakes,
        Fresh, 53 (CA)
    Pastry, Shortcake, 53 (CA)
    Peach Shortcakes,
        Individual, 53 (CA)
    Strawberry
        Shortcake, 52 (CA);
        55 (CE); 13 (PO); 28 (SP)
    Strawberry Shortcake,
        Old-Fashioned, 52 (CA)
Short'nin' Bread, 60 (CA)
Silver Anniversary Cake, 83 (FG)
Silver Cake, 117 (CA)
Spice Cake, 116 (CA)
Spice Cake, Scotch, 78 (CA)
Sponge
    Almond Sponge Cake, 122 (CA)
    Chocolate Sponge Cake,
        Passover, 100 (CA)
    Chocolate Whipped Cream
        Roll, Gertrude's, 125 (CA)
    Delicate Sponge
        Cake, 124 (CA)
    Drop Cakes, Sponge, 82 (CC)
    How-To, Sponge
        Cake, 122 (CA)
    Lemon Roll, 127 (CA)
    Lemon Sponge Roll,
        Tender, 126 (CA)
    Orange Jellyroll, 126 (CA)
    Tipsy Cake, 125 (CA)
    Tipsy Cake, Tarboro, 60 (DE)
Stack Cake, Massie, 41 (CA)
Stack Cake, Tennessee, 41 (CA)
Sugar Cake, Moravian, 50 (CE)
Tea Cakes, Gram's, 122 (FG)
Tea Cakes, Moravian, 19 (CC)
Tea Cakes, Orange, 65 (SS)
Tea Cakes, Victorian, 70 (SS)
Upside-Down
    Apple Honey Upside-Down
        Cake, 39 (CA)
    Apple Upside-Down Cake,
        Tennessee, 70 (CA)
    Cherry Upside-Down
        Cake, 70 (CA)
    Pecan Upside-Down
        Cake, 49 (CA)
    Pineapple-Ambrosia
        Upside-Down Cake, 71 (CA)
    Pineapple Upside-Down
        Cake, 70 (CA)
Valentine Cake, Creole, 97 (CA)
Valentine Cake, Red, 96 (CA)
Vasilopeta (Greek Sweet
    Bread), 64 (FG)

Vegetable
    Bean Cake, Fiesta, 54 (CA)
    Carrot Cake,
        Cottonwood, 55 (CA)
    Carrot Cake,
        Traditional, 55 (CA)
    Potato Cake, Mashed, 57 (CA)
    Pumpkin Cake, 57 (CA)
    Sweet Potato Cake, 56 (CA)
    Sweet Potato Pound
        Cake, 56 (CA)
Walnut Spice Cake,
    Black, 50 (CA)
Watermelon Cake, Red, 79 (CA)
Wedding Cake,
    Heritage, 107 (CA)
Welcome Cake, 62 (CA)
Whipped Cream Cake, 32 (CA)
Whiskey Cake,
    Hootenholler, 62 (CA)
White and Yellow Cake, 33 (CA)
White Cake, Blue
    Ribbon, 93 (CA)
White Cake, Sam
    Houston, 16 (CA)
White Layer Cake, 117 (CA)
White Wonder Cake, 33 (CA)
Yellow Cake, Basic, 116 (CA)

**Candies**
Almond Acorns, 91 (GR)
Almonds, Candied, 91 (GR)
Apple Jack Sticks, 111 (GR)
Apple Treats, Dried, 82 (GR)
Apricot Balls, 80 (GR)
Apricot Candy Roll, 80 (GR)
Apricot Leather, 82 (GR)
Banana Bites, 105 (GR)
Bonbons, Bourbon, 134 (GR)
Bonbons, Creamy
    Pastel, 30 (CE)
Bonbons, Orange, 134 (GR)
Buttercream Easter
    Eggs, 135 (GR)

Butterscotch Suckers, 116 (GR)
Candied Pansies, Mint Leaves,
    and Rose Petals, 97 (GR)
Caramels, Ribbon, 118 (GR)
Caramelts, 117 (GR)
Cathedral Candy, 103 (GR)
Chocolate Caramels, 118 (GR)
Chocolate-Covered
    Cherries, 31 (CE); 133 (GR)
Chocolate-Covered
    Mints, 132 (GR)

Chocolate Cream
    Candy, 21 (CE)
Chocolate Cream Drops, 63 (SS)
Chocolate Creams, 133 (GR)
Chocolate-Pecan
    Brittle, 113 (GR)
Chocolate Pecan Logs, 134 (GR)
Chocolate Peppermint
    Dainties, 73 (CC)
Citrus Peel, Candied, 89 (GR);
    71 (SS)

Citrus Peel,
    Chocolate-Covered, 89 (GR)
Coconut Brittle, 113 (GR)
Cracker Jacks, 114 (GR)
Cream Candy,
    Kentucky, 110 (GR)
Crystallized Rose Petals and Mint
    Leaves, 73 (CC)
Date Kisses, 30 (CE)
Date-Nut Roll, 80 (GR)
Divinity, Coffee, 101 (GR)
Easter Eggs, Homemade
    Candy, 52 (CE)
Figs, Holiday Stuffed, 81 (GR)
Fruit Glacé, 90 (GR)
Fruit Sweets, 81 (GR)
Fudge
    Angel Fudge, 122 (GR)
    Blond Pecan Fudge, 125 (GR)
    Chocolate Fudge, 120 (GR)
    Chocolate Fudge,
        Dark, 122 (GR)
    Chocolate Fudge,
        Favorite, 121 (GR)
    Chocolate-Pecan
        Fudge, 122 (GR)
    Coconut Fudge, 73 (CE);
        124 (GR)
    College Fudge, 120 (GR)
    Divinity Fudge, 100 (GR)
    Festive Fudge, 122 (GR)
    Homemade Fudge, 25 (CE)
    Orange Fudge, 124 (GR)
    Peanut Butter
        Fudge, 125 (GR)
    Quick Fudge, 120 (GR)
    Sour Cream Fudge, 125 (GR)
Georgia Nuggets, 128 (GR)
Holiday Delight Logs, 119 (GR)
Honey-Pistachio
    Nougat, 102 (GR)
Horehound Candy, 111 (GR)
How to Pull Taffy, 107 (GR)
Hunky Dories, 136 (GR)
Lollipops, 111 (GR)

**Candies,** *continued*
Marshmallows, 103 (GR)
Marshmallows, Mint, 73 (CE)
Marzipan, 20 (CE); 92 (GR)
Meringues, Brown
  Sugar, 128 (CE)
Millionaires, Texas, 136 (GR)
Mint Roses, 84 (FG)
Mints, Pastel, 12 (SS)
Mints, Pulled Sugar, 109 (SS)
Mint Twists, 115 (FG)
Molasses Caramels, 116 (GR)
Nuts, Holiday, 96 (GR)
Nuts, Minted, 31 (CE)
Nuts, Sugar and Spice, 97 (GR)
Nuts, Sugared, 25 (CE)
Orange and Lemon Peel,
  Candied, 25 (CE)
Oriental Delight, 105 (GR)
Peach Leather, 82 (CE)
Peanut Brittle, 73 (CE)
Peanut Brittle Wreath, 112 (GR)
Peanut Butter Cups, 136 (GR)
Peanut Clusters,
  Double, 136 (GR)
Peanut Patties, 130 (GR)
Pecan Brittle, 112 (GR)
Pecan Caramels,
  Creamy, 117 (GR)
Pecan Crunch, 112 (GR)
Pecans, Citrus-Candied, 92 (GR)

Pecans, Coffee, 92 (GR)
Pecans, Frosted, 93 (GR)
Pecans, Minted, 92 (GR)
Pecans, Orange-
  Candied, 93 (GR)
Pecan Toffee, 116 (GR)
Penuche, President
  Street, 126 (GR)
Peppermint Drops, 71 (SS)
Pineapple and Cherries,
  Candied, 90 (GR)
Popcorn Balls, 114 (GR)
Praline Drops, 95 (GR)
Pralines, Buttermilk, 128 (GR)
Pralines, Coconut, 130 (GR)
Pralines, Creole, 127 (GR)
Pralines, Maple, 130 (GR)
Pralines, Peanut, 92 (FG)
Pralines, Plantation, 128 (GR)
Raisin Penuche, 126 (GR)
Raspberry Truffles, 132 (GR)
Seafoam Candy, 101 (GR)
Secrets, 30 (CE)
Strawberry Turkish
  Paste, 104 (GR)

Sweet Potato Candy,
  Mexican, 127 (GR)
Syrup Stages in Candy
  Making, 108 (GR)
Taffy, 106 (GR)
Truffles, Solger's, 132 (GR)
Turkish Delight, 104 (GR)
Walnut Brittle, Black, 111 (GR)
Walnuts, Cinnamon, 96 (GR)
Walnuts, Coffee, 96 (GR)
Walnuts, Sugared, 95 (GR)
Whiskey Kisses, 131 (CE)
**Capon**
Gravy, Capon, 94 (CC)
Oven-Roasted Capon, 94 (CC)
Roast Capon with Virginia
  Oyster Stuffing, 37 (PO)
**Caramel**
Caramelts, 117 (GR)
Chocolate Caramels, 118 (GR)
Cookies, Caramel Press, 86 (CJ)
Custard Petit Arnaud,
  Caramel, 64 (DE)
Fingers,
  Chocolate-Caramel, 103 (CJ)
Flan, Caramel, 63 (DE)
Frosting, Caramel, 22, 49,
  84 (CA)
Frosting, Caramel Cream, 43,
  102 (CA)
Frosting, Caramelized, 130 (CA)
Frosting, Heritage
  Caramel, 47 (CA)
Frosting, Sorghum
  Caramel, 136 (CA)
Fruit, Hot Caramel, 85 (BB)
How-To, Caramelized
  Frosting, 130 (CA)
Ice Cream, Caramel, 99 (DE);
  81 (FG)
Icing, Brown Sugar
  Caramel, 56 (CA)
Millionaires, Texas, 136 (GR)
Molasses Caramels, 116 (GR)
Pecan Caramels,
  Creamy, 117 (GR)
Pie, Damson Caramel, 75 (PP)
Pie, Old-Fashioned Caramel
  Cream, 91 (PP)
Pudding, Caramel
  Bread, 13 (DE)
Pudding, Caramel
  Sponge, 23 (DE)
Ribbon Caramels, 118 (GR)
Sauce, Caramel, 75, 132 (DE);
  85 (GR)
Soufflé of Caramel, 105 (CC)
Tarts, Caramel Cream, 119 (PP)
**Carrots**
Balls, Carrot, 35 (VE)
Boliche with Carrots,
  Spanish, 135 (FG)
Cake, Cottonwood
  Carrot, 55 (CA)
Cake, Traditional
  Carrot, 55 (CA)
Candied Carrots in Orange
  Rings, 35 (VE)
Cookies, Carrot-Orange, 51 (CJ)
Cupcakes, Carrot, 73 (SP)

Fried Carrots, 36 (VE)
Fritters, Carrot, 36 (VE)
Ginger Carrots, 55 (FG)
How To Prepare Fresh
  Carrots, 34 (VE)
Lemon-Glazed Carrots,
  Shaker, 35 (VE)
Medley, Parsley Potato, 94 (CC)
Mold, Carrot Ring, 22 (CC)
Pickled Carrots, 41 (GR)
Pickles, Carrot, 16 (CC)

Pickles, Mixed
  Vegetable, 46 (GR)
Pot o' Gold, 98 (VE)
Relish, Carrot, 50 (GR)
Ring, Carrot, 36 (VE)
Sandwiches, Carrot, 77 (SS)
Soufflé, Carrot, 118 (SP)
Soup, Cream of Carrot, 62 (SO)
Spicy Carrots, 129 (FG)
Sweet-and-Sour
  Carrots, 64 (SP); 36 (VE)
Tzimmes, Carrot, 60 (CE)
**Casseroles**
Apple Casserole, 48 (SP)
Bacon-Cheese
  Casserole, 126 (BB)
Beans and Rice Casserole,
  Black, 136 (FG)
Beans, Baked, 75 (FG)
Beans, Southern Baked, 95 (SS)
Chicken Casserole,
  Plantation, 119 (PO)
Chile-Cheese Rice, 38 (BB)
Egg and Mushroom Casserole,
  Stuffed, 124 (BB)
Egg Casserole, 118 (SP)
Egg Casserole, Baked
  Creole, 123 (BB)
Egg Casserole, Cheesy, 127 (BB)
Egg Casserole, Jo's, 110 (CE)
Grits, Baked, 55 (BB); 65 (PK)
Grits Soufflé, Cheese, 72 (BB)
Grits, Southern Cheese, 50 (BB)
Haddock, Scalloped, 71 (SE)

Casseroles, *continued*
 Johnnie Marzetti, 43 (BE)
 Macaroni au Gratin, 40 (FG)
 Macaroni Pudding, 122 (CC)
 Noodle Kugel, 97 (FG)
 Pastitsio, 104 (BE)
 Pork
  Beans, Pork and, 122 (PK)
  Corn Casserole, Pork
   and, 37 (PK)
  Ham au Gratin, 79 (PK)
  Ham Casserole, 85 (PK)
  Ham, Creamed, 79 (PK)
  Ham Jambalaya, 85 (PK)
  Ham, Macaroni and Cheese
   with, 80 (PK)
  Macaroni Casserole, Pork
   and, 38 (PK)
  Sausage and Egg
   Casserole, 76 (BB)
  Sausage Casserole, 131 (BB)
  Sausage-Cheese
   Casserole, 105 (PK)
 Rice and Cheese Casserole,
  Wild, 42 (SP)
 Rice, Baked Wild, 127 (FG)

 Riced Eggs, 112 (FG)
 Rice, Wild, 133 (CC); 48 (FG)
 Salmon, Creamed, 84 (SE)
 Seafood
  Crab Imperial, 18 (SE)
  Crabmeat with Curried
   Rice, 22 (SE)
  Low Country Seafood
   Casserole, 54 (SE)
  Scallops au Gratin, 44 (SE)
  Scallops, Virginia
   Baked, 44 (SE)
  Shrimp Pie, 48 (SE)
  Shrimp Pilau, Pirates'
   House, 48 (SE)
 Slumgullion, 57 (BE)
 Tuna Casserole, 101 (SE)
 Turkey-Sausage
  Casserole, 119 (PO)
 Veal Chops in
  Casserole, 67 (BE)
 Vegetable
  Asparagus Casserole, 126 (FG)
  Asparagus Meringue, 13 (VE)
  Brussels Sprouts and
   Chestnuts, 29 (VE)

 Cauliflower, Creole, 39 (VE)
 Celery and Pecan
  Casserole, 40 (VE)
 Celery Casserole,
  Creamy, 118 (CC)
 Corn Casserole,
  Fresh, 45 (VE)
 Corn Pudding,
  Southern, 114 (CE)
 Eggplant, Baked, 51 (VE)
 Green Peas, Baked, 78 (VE)
 Onions, Baked
  Curried, 69 (VE)
 Potato Casserole,
  Creamy, 57 (CC)
 Potatoes, Escalloped, 88 (VE)
 Spinach au Gratin, 103 (VE)
 Spinach Casserole, 55 (CE)
 Spinach Soufflé, 76 (CC)
 Squash Casserole, 16, 76 (FG)
 Squash Casserole,
  Crunchy, 107 (VE)
 Squash Casserole,
  Pattypan, 109 (VE)
 Squash Casserole, Smith
  House, 107 (VE)
 Squash, Mississippi Style
  Chayote, 112 (VE)
 Sweet Potato
  Casserole, 96 (VE)
 Sweet Potato Casserole,
  Virginia, 96 (VE)
 Sweet Potatoes,
  Company, 119 (CE)
 Sweet Potatoes,
  Holiday, 96 (VE)
 Sweet Potato Soufflé, 54 (CC)
 Tomato Casserole,
  Green, 121 (VE)
 Tomatoes, Baked, 110 (CC)
 Tomatoes, Parmesan
  Scalloped, 51 (SP)
 Tomatoes, Scalloped, 121 (FG)
 Tomatoes, Summertime
  Stewed, 120 (VE)
 Turnip Casserole,
  Baked, 123 (VE)
 Vegetable Casserole, 93 (SP)
 Vegetable Casserole,
  Summer, 124 (VE)
 Vegetables, Mixed
  Garden, 124 (VE)
 Yam Variation, 126 (CC)
 Zucchini and Tomatoes,
  Baked, 110 (VE)
**Catfish**
 Broiled Catfish, 109 (SE)
 Broiled Catfish, Zippy, 109 (SE)
 Country-Fried Catfish with Hush
  Puppies, 111 (SE)
 Dinner, Catfish, 112 (SE)
 Étouffée, Catfish, 112 (SE)
 Fried Catfish, 61 (SP)
 Fried Catfish and Hush Puppies,
  Daphne Lodge, 111 (SE)
 Fried Catfish Fillets, 40 (BB)

 Fried Fish, Ogeechee
  River, 96 (CE)
 Grilled Sesame
  Catfish, 111 (SE)
 Mushroom Cream Sauce, Catfish
  in, 113 (SE)
 Pan-Fried Catfish,
  Alabama, 110 (SE)
 Sandwiches, Fried
  Catfish, 111 (SE)
 Smoked Catfish, 112 (SE)
 Stew, Catfish, 112 (SE)
 Stew, Georgia Catfish, 97 (CE)
 Stew, Pine Bark, 136 (SO)
**Catsup**
 Apple Catsup, 70 (GR)
 Tomato Catsup, 70 (GR)
**Cauliflower**
 à la Vinaigrette,
  Cauliflower, 39 (FG)
 au Gratin, Cauliflower, 37 (VE)
 Baked Cauliflower, 39 (VE)
 Creole Cauliflower, 39 (VE)
 Duchesse, Cauliflower, 38 (VE)
 Fried Cauliflower, 39 (VE)
 Hollandaise, Cauliflower
  with, 44 (SS)
 How To Prepare Fresh
  Cauliflower, 37 (VE)
 Maître d'Hôtel,
  Cauliflower, 38 (VE)
 Pickles, Cauliflower, 41 (GR)
 Soup, Cauliflower, 62 (SO)
**Caviar**
 Canapés, Caviar, 79 (CE);
  37 (SS)
 Dip, Caviar, 94 (SE)
 Mold, Layered Caviar, 91 (FG)
 Ring, Caviar, 11 (SP)
 Salad, Tomato Caviar, 131 (CC)
 Texas Caviar, 129 (SP)
**Celery**
 Casserole, Celery and
  Pecan, 40 (VE)
 Casserole, Creamy
  Celery, 118 (CC)
 Colle, Celery, 42 (VE)
 Dressing, Celery Seed, 100 (SS)
 French Fried Celery, 42 (VE)
 How To Prepare Fresh
  Celery, 40 (VE)
 Mushrooms, Celery with, 40 (VE)
 Pickles, French, 44 (GR)
 Pickles, Mixed
  Vegetable, 46 (GR)
 Pimiento Cheese Stuffed
  Celery, 69 (CE)
 Relish, Tart Celery, 136 (VE)
 Roll, Stuffed Celery, 131 (CE)
 Sandwiches, Celery-Nut, 62 (SS)
 Sauce, Creole Celery, 15 (BR)
 Simmered Celery,
  Florida, 42 (VE)
 Soup, Cream of Celery, 129 (CE)
 Stuffed Celery, 121 (FG);
  75 (SP)

Celery, *continued*
  Stuffing, Colonial Roast Chicken
    with Celery, 35 (PO)
**Cheese**
  Appetizers and Dips
    Ball, Pecan Cheese, 92 (SP)
    Bells, Cheese, 115 (FG)
    Blue Cheese Mousse,
      97 (SS)
    Blue Cheese Whip, 88 (SS)
    Brambles, Cheese, 103 (SS)
    Butter, English Muffins
      Toasted with
      Cheese, 123 (SP)
    Celery, Pimiento Cheese
      Stuffed, 69 (CE)
    Celery, Stuffed, 121 (FG)
    Cream Cheese Dip, 16 (SS)
    Crescents, Cheese, 68 (SS)
    Dates, Cheese, 12 (CE)
    Dreams, Cheese, 23 (SP)
    Eggs au Gratin, 46 (SS)
    Flambé, Fried Cheese, 62 (FG)
    Ham and Cheese
      Appetizers, 124 (SS)
    Heart, Herbed Cheese, 80 (SP)

  Herbed Party
    Triangles, 68 (SS)
  Log, Cheddar Cheese, 57 (SS)
  Mold, Horseshoe
    Cheese, 10 (SP)
  Mound, Caraway
    Cheese, 83 (CC)
  Mounds, Cheddar
    Cheese, 129 (SP)
  Puffs, Cheese, 118 (SP)
  Puffs, Cheese-Bacon, 11 (SS)
  Puffs, Chicken Salad in
    Cheese, 74 (SS)
  Roquefort Roll, 103 (SS)
  Sandwiches,
    Cucumber-Cheese, 87 (CC)
  Sandwiches, Cucumber-Cream
    Cheese, 28 (FG)
  Sandwiches, Heart and
    Diamond, 72 (CC)
  Sandwich Loaf,
    Ribbon, 71 (CC)
  Sausage-Cheese Dip, 107 (PK)
  Sticks, Cheese, 49 (SS)
  Strata, Cheese, 36 (SS)
  Straws, Cheese, 12 (SP);61 (SS)

  Straws, Old-Fashioned
    Cheese, 125 (FG)
  Toast Rounds, Ham and
    Cheese, 115 (SS)
  Triangles, Ginger
    Cream, 69 (CE)
  Triangles, Shrimp and Cream
    Cheese, 81 (SS)
Breads
  Biscuits, Cheddar
    Cheese, 97 (BB)
  Biscuits, Cheese, 46 (CC);
    65 (SS)
  Biscuits, Tiny
    Cheddar, 107 (CE)
  Biscuit Thins,
    Cheese, 94 (BR)
  Breadsticks,
    Parmesan, 23 (SO)
  Brioche with Gruyère and
    Parmesan, 48 (BR)
  Cornbread, Ranch, 16 (BR)
  Croutons, Cheese, 18 (SO)
  Pirogi, 136 (BR)
  Puffs, Cheese, 136 (BR);
    118 (SP)

*The pressure of a cheese press is checked by a class at Hampton Institute, Virginia, in 1900.*

Cheese, Breads, *continued*
Rolls, Quick-Fried
Cheese, 19 (SO)
Rounds, Cheese, 94 (BR)
Salt Sticks,
Parmesan, 135 (BR)
Spoonbread,
Luncheon, 32 (BR)
Spoonbread, Parmesan, 32 (BR)
Straws, Cheese, 136 (BR)
Toast, Cheese, 19 (SO)
Wafers, Cheese, 98 (BB);
92 (CC)
Wafers, Cream Cheese, 98 (BB)
Wafers, Dutch Cheese, 68 (CJ)
Brownies, German Cream
Cheese, 104 (CJ)
Cake, Cream Cheese
Pound, 120 (CA); 18 (CE)
Casseroles
Bacon-Cheese
Casserole, 126 (BB)
Chile-Cheese Rice, 38 (BB)
Egg Casserole,
Cheesy, 127 (BB)
Grits Soufflé, Cheese, 72 (BB)
Grits, Southern
Cheese, 50 (BB)
Macaroni and Cheese with
Ham, 80 (PK)
Macaroni au Gratin, 40 (FG)
Parmesan Scalloped
Tomatoes, 51 (SP)
Sausage-Cheese
Casserole, 105 (PK)
Wild Rice and Cheese
Casserole, 42 (SP)
Cheesebits, 20 (SO)
Cheesecake, Best-Ever, 128 (DE)
Cheesecake, Blue Ribbon
Orange, 82 (PP)
Cheesecake, German, 81 (PP)
Cheesecake, Jennie Selligman's
Cream, 80 (PP)
Cheesecake, Mocha, 79 (PP)
Cheesecake, "The Original"
Old-Fashioned, 78 (PP)
Cheesecake, Pineapple, 83 (PP)
Cheesecake, Praline, 84 (PP)
Cheesecake, Pumpkin, 85 (PP)
Cheesecakes,
Chocolate-Mocha, 23 (SS)
Cooked Cheese, 45 (FG)
Cookies, Cream Cheese
Thumbprint, 63 (CJ)
Dressing, Creamy Blue
Cheese, 114 (CC)
Dressing, Stilton, 128 (SS)
Eggs, Cheese Nest, 127 (BB)
Enchiladas, Green, 35 (CC)
Fingers, Cheese, 19 (SO)
Frosting, Cream Cheese, 25,
51 (CA); 85 (CE)
Glaze, Cream Cheese, 102 (CE)
Grits and Sausage,
Country, 131 (BB)

Grits, Cheese, 26 (SP)
Grits, Chile-Cheese, 127 (BB)
Grits Soufflé, Cheese, 72 (BB)
Grits, Southern Cheese, 50 (BB)
Horns, Cream Cheese, 63 (CJ)
Mint Roses, 84 (FG)
Omelet, Cheese, 121 (BB)
Pancakes, Cottage
Cheese, 113 (BB)
Parmesan Rosettes, 23 (SO)
Parmigiana, Veal, 70 (BE)
Pastries, Cream
Cheese, 135 (PP)
Pastry, Cheddar Cheese, 16 (PP)
Pastry, Cheese, 137 (CC)
Pastry, Cream Cheese, 123 (PP);
126 (SS)
Pastry, Double-Crust
Cheese, 32 (PP)
Pastry Shell, Cream
Cheese, 20 (PP)
Pastry Shells, Cheese, 114 (PO)
Pie, Cheese-Apple, 137 (CC)
Pie, Kleeman's Cottage
Cheese, 78 (PP)

Pie, Picnic, 82 (PK)
Pie, Pineapple-Cottage
Cheese, 82 (PP)
Pudding, Cheese, 74 (CC)
Salad, Pineapple
Cheddar, 96 (CC)
Sandwiches, Anne's Pimiento
Cheese, 16 (SS)
Sandwiches, Calla Lily, 68 (SS)
Sandwiches, Cream Cheese and
Pineapple, 52 (SS)
Sandwiches,
Cucumber-Cheese, 87 (CC)
Sandwiches, Cucumber-Cream
Cheese, 28 (FG)
Sandwiches, Heart and
Diamond, 72 (CC)
Sandwiches, Hero, 69 (FG)
Sandwiches, Noisette, 42 (FG)
Sandwiches,
Olive-Cheese, 21 (SS)
Sandwiches, Pimiento
Cheese, 29 (CE); 100 (SP)
Sandwiches, Ribbon, 88 (SS)
Sandwich Loaf, Ribbon, 71 (CC)

Sauces
Broccoli Baked with Cheese
Sauce, 26 (VE)
Cheese Sauce, 114 (PO);
133 (VE)
Chicken-Cheese Sauce,
Asparagus with, 132 (BB)
Creamy Cheese
Sauce, 115 (PO)
Sauce Rochambeau, 106 (PO)
Seafood au Gratin,
Baked, 55 (SE)
Soufflé, Cheese, 82 (BB)
Soufflé, Easy Cheese, 126 (BB)
Soups
Beer Cheese Soup, 47 (SO)
Driskill Hotel Cheese
Soup, 46 (SO)
Emergency Cheese
Soup, 47 (SO)
Frijole-Cheese Soup, 93 (SO)
Jalapeño Cheese
Soup, 47 (SO)
Onion Soup,
Huguenot, 35 (SO)
Tortilla Soup, Rio
Grande, 86 (SO)
Tartlets, Cheese, 122 (PP)
Tarts, Orange-Cheese, 118 (PP)
Vegetables
Broccoli Parmesan, 27 (VE)
Cabbage au Gratin, 31 (VE)
Cauliflower au Gratin,
37 (VE)
Chiles Rellenos with
Cheese, 82 (VE)
Hominy, Chili, 47 (VE)
Onions au Gratin, 69 (VE)
Potatoes, Cheese, 55 (SP)
Sauce, Broccoli Baked with
Cheese, 26 (VE)
Spinach au Gratin, 103 (VE)
Waffles, Cheese, 114 (BB)
Welsh Rarebit on Toast
Points, 39 (SS)
**Cheesecakes.** *See* Cakes, Cheese.
**Cherries**
Bachelor Buttons, Thomas
Jefferson's, 33 (CJ)
Bars, Cherry-Coconut, 120 (CJ)
Bounce, Cherry, 118 (SS)
Cake, Cherry
Upside-Down, 70 (CA)
Cake, Creole Valentine, 97 (CA)
Cake, Mount Vernon, 98 (CA)
Candied Pineapple and
Cherries, 90 (GR)
Chocolate-Covered
Cherries, 31 (CE); 133 (GR)
Crisp, Apple-Cherry, 97 (PK)
Delights, Cherry, 115 (CJ)
Filling, Cherry, 98 (CA)
Frosting, Cherry, 29 (CE)
Glaze, Cherry, 104 (BB)
Ice, Cherry, 80 (CC)
Jam, Christmas, 25 (GR)

---

**BB** *Breakfast & Brunch*   **BE** *Beef, Veal & Lamb*   **BR** *Breads*   **CA** *Cakes*   **CC** *Company's Coming*   **CE** *Celebrations*
**CJ** *Cookie Jar*   **DE** *Just Desserts*   **FG** *Family Gatherings*   **GR** *Gift Receipts*   **PK** *All Pork*   **PO** *Plain & Fancy Poultry*
**PP** *Pies & Pastry*   **SE** *Sea & Stream*   **SO** *Soups & Stews*   **SP** *Sporting Scene*   **SS** *Socials & Soirees*   **VE** *Vegetables*

Cherries, *continued*
  Jubilee, Cherries, 104 (DE)
  Maraschino Cream, 75 (CC)
  Pie, Cherry, 114 (CC)
  Pie, Coconut-Cherry
    Cream, 94 (PP)
  Pie, Mount Vernon Red
    Cherry, 34 (PP)
  Pie, Royal Anne Cherry, 35 (PP)
  Preserves, Cherry, 17 (GR)
  Roll, Tutti-Frutti
    Icebox, 129 (DE)
  Sauce, Cherry, 70 (CA); 21 (DE)
  Soup, Cold Cherry, 40 (SO)
  Squares, Cherry, 59 (SP)
  Tarts, Cherry, 78 (SS)
  Tarts, Petite Cherry, 121 (PP)
  Winks, Cherry, 116 (CJ)
**Chestnuts**
  Brussels Sprouts and
    Chestnuts, 29 (VE)
  Cream, Chestnut, 73 (DE)
  Soufflé, Chestnut, 67 (DE)
  Soup, Cream of
    Chestnut, 49 (SO)
  Stuffing, Chestnut, 29 (PO)
**Chicken**
  à la King, Chicken, 71 (BB);
    122 (PO)
  à la Marengo, Chicken, 101 (PO)
  Arroz con Pollo, Hearty, 67 (PO)
  Bake, Chicken-
    Broccoli, 133 (BB)
  Baked Chicken, 97 (CC)
  Baked Chicken, Basic, 35 (PO)
  Baked Chicken in Scuppernong
    Wine, 37 (PO)
  Baked Chicken with Wine and
    Mushrooms, 109 (FG)
  Barbecued
    Barbecued Chicken, 88 (CE)
    Basic Barbecued
      Chicken, 87 (PO)
    Grilled Chicken, 55 (SP)
    Marinated Grilled
      Chicken, 88 (PO)
    Oven-Barbecued
      Chicken, 87 (PO)
    Oven-Barbecued Chicken,
      Saucy, 88 (FG)
    Paper Sack Chicken
      Barbecue, 87 (PO)
    Savory Barbecued
      Chicken, 88 (PO)
    Spicy Grilled Chicken, 87 (PO)
  Biscuits, Chicken, 88 (BR)
  Bisque, Charleston
    White, 58 (SO)
  Boiled Chicken with Butter
    Sauce, 17 (PO)
  Bouchées à la Reine, 133 (SO)
  Braised Chicken, Texas, 23 (PO)
  Breasts of Chicken,
    Stuffed, 42 (SS)
  Broiled Chicken Deluxe, 96 (PO)
  Broth, French, 31 (SO)
  Burgoo, 135 (SO)
  Burgoo, Kentucky, 61 (PO)
  Burgoo, Old-Fashioned
    Kentucky, 15 (SP)

  Canapés, Hot Chicken, 123 (SP)
  Casserole, Plantation
    Chicken, 119 (PO)
  Cavatoni Chicken Eggplant
    Francesca, 95 (PO)
  Coliseum, Chicken, 93 (PO)
  Country Captain, 102 (PO)
  Country Ham, Maryland Chicken
    and, 104 (PO)
  Cranberry Baked Chicken
    Breasts, 60 (CE)
  Creamed Chicken, 133 (BB);
    76 (CC); 63, 130 (CE)
  Creamed Chicken in Patty
    Shells, 104 (FG)
  Creamed Chicken,
    Virginia, 122 (PO)
  Croquettes, Chicken, 124 (PO);
    120 (SS)
  Curried Chicken, 103 (PO)
  Dirty Rice, 129 (PO)
  Divan, Chicken, 104 (PO)
  Dumplings, Carolina Chicken
    and Drop, 18 (PO)
  Dumplings, Chicken
    and, 121 (FG)
  Dumplings, Chicken and
    Plump, 21 (PO)
  Dumplings, Chicken and
    Rolled, 20 (PO)
  Dumplings, Chicken and
    Slick, 20 (PO)
  Dumplings, Chicken and
    Slippery, 19 (PO)
  Dumplings, Stewed Chicken
    with Light, 18 (PO)
  Dumplings, Texas-Style, Chicken
    and Drop, 18 (PO)
  Edwards House
    Chicken, 105 (PO)
  Escalloped Chicken,
    Georgia-Style, 97 (PO)
  Étouffée, Chicken, 25 (PO)
  Fiesta, Chicken, 125 (PO)

  Fricassee, A Brown, 14 (PO)
  Fricassee, A White, 16 (PO)
  Fricassee, Eliza Pinckney's
    Chicken, 13 (PO)
  Fricassee, Marion
    Harland's, 15 (PO)
  Fricassee, Stew-Hole
    Chicken, 15 (PO)
  Fricassee, Thomas
    Jefferson's, 16 (PO)
  Fricassee, White Wine, 16 (PO)
  Fried
    Batter Fried Chicken, 81 (PO)
    Buttermilk Fried
      Chicken, 82 (PO); 82 (SP)
    Buttermilk Fried Chicken,
      Crusty, 80 (PO)
    Buttery Fried
      Chicken, 80 (PO)
    Coastal Fried Chicken with
      Brown Crumb
      Gravy, 84 (PO)
    Country-Fried
      Chicken, 81 (PO)
    Crumb-Coated Fried
      Chicken, 79 (PO)
    Deep-Fat Fried
      Chicken, 79 (PO)
    Fried Chicken, 94 (SS)
    Garlic Fried Chicken, 80 (PO)
    Golden Fried Chicken, 84 (CE)
    Homestead Fried Chicken,
      The, 97 (PO)
    Maryland Fried Chicken with
      Cream Gravy, 83 (PO)
    Neshoba County Fried
      Chicken, 93 (CE)
    Nuggets, Golden
      Chicken, 79 (PO)
    Nuggets, Spicy
      Chicken, 125 (SP)
    Old Dominion Fried Chicken
      with Gravy, 84 (PO)
    Oven-Fried Chicken, 86 (PO)

Chicken, Fried, *continued*
  Oven-Fried Chicken,
    Crisp, 99 (SP)
  Oven-Fried Chicken,
    Herbed, 86 (PO)
  Oven-Fried Chicken,
    Pecan, 86 (PO)
  Oven-Fried Chicken,
    Texas, 86 (PO)
  Savannah Fried
    Chicken, 81 (PO)
  Saw Mill Gravy, Fried Chicken
    with, 84 (PO)
  Skillet-Fried Chicken,
    Tennessee, 15 (FG)
  Southern Fried
    Chicken, 52 (CC); 77 (PO)
  Texas Fried Chicken, 75 (FG)
  Texas-Style Fried
    Chicken, 82 (PO)
Good to Know, 130-137 (PO)
Gumbo, Cajun, 120 (SO)
Gumbo, Chicken, 62 (PO)
Gumbo,
  Chicken-Andouille, 113 (PK)
Gumbo, Chicken and
  Oyster, 62 (PO)

Gumbo, Creole
  Chicken, 114 (SO)
Gumbo, Easy Chicken, 63 (PO)
Gumbo Filé, 30 (CC)
Gumbo Filé, Chicken, 116 (SO)
Gumbo, Oyster, 118 (SO)
Gumbo, Savannah
  Chicken, 62 (PO)
Hash, Chicken, 116 (PO)
How to Debone a Chicken
  Breast, 134 (PO)
How to Fry Chicken, 137 (PO)
How to Truss a Bird, 136 (PO)
Jambalaya,
  Chicken-Sausage, 109 (PK)
Jambalaya, Ham and
  Chicken, 69 (PO)

Jambalaya of Chicken, 122 (SO)
Lemon Chicken Breasts, 18 (SP)
Livers
  Appetizers, Chicken
    Liver, 126 (PO)
  Dirty Rice, 129 (PO)
  Eggs Chausseur, 47 (SP)
  Financière, Chicken Livers
    and, 128 (PO)
  Mold, Chopped Liver, 129 (FG)
  Omelet, Chicken
    Liver, 129 (PO)
  Pâté, Chicken Liver, 126 (PO)
  Pâté on Toast Rounds,
    Individual Liver, 73 (FG)
  Rumaki, 81 (CE)
  Sautéed Chicken
    Livers, 134 (BB)
  Spaghetti Caruso, 127 (PO)
  Wine, Chicken Livers
    in, 127 (PO)
Loaf, Symphony
  Chicken, 59 (PO)
Loaf with Almond-Mushroom
  Sauce, Chicken, 134 (BB)
Marengo, Chicken, 101 (PO)
Minestrone, 106 (SO)
Mole, Chicken, 105 (PO)
Mousse, Chicken, 112 (PO)
Omelet, Chicken, 122 (PO)
Oyster Sauce, Chicken
  with, 98 (PO)
Oyster-Stuffed Breast of
  Chicken, 98 (PO)
Paella, 56 (SE)
Paella Valenciana, 68 (PO)
Paprika, Chicken, 106 (PO)
Piccata, Chicken, 99 (PO)
Pie, Chicken and Country Ham
  Deep Dish, 18 (CC)
Pie, Golden Chicken
  Pot, 56 (PO)
Pie, Grandmother's
  Chicken, 53 (PO)
Pie, Real Chicken, 55 (PO)
Pie with Sweet Potato Crust,
  Chicken, 56 (PO)
Pilaf, Charleston
  Chicken, 69 (PO)
Pilau, Turn-of-the-Century
  Chicken, 69 (PO)
Pudding, Maryland
  Chicken, 58 (PO)
Pudding, Mary Randolph's
  Chicken, 59 (PO)
Pudding, Virginia
  Chicken, 58 (PO)
Quenelles, 15 (SO)
Rice, Chicken and
  Yellow, 67 (PO)
Ring Around Chicken, 124 (PO)
Roasted
  Celery Stuffing, Colonial Roast
    Chicken with, 35 (PO)
  Lemon-Roasted
    Chicken, 44 (CC)

Pot-Roasted Chicken, 23 (PO)
Roast Chicken, 126 (FG)
Sausage Stuffing, Festive
  Roast Chicken with
  Tennessee Country, 36 (PO)
Shrimp Stuffing, Roast
  Chicken with, 36 (PO)
Salads
  Amandine, Chicken
    Salad, 113 (PO)
  Baked Chicken
    Salad, 114 (PO)
  Cheese Puffs, Chicken Salad
    in, 74 (SS)
  Chicken Salad, 105 (CC);
    36 (CE)
  Curried Chicken
    Salad, 112 (PO)
  Luncheon Salad,
    Normandy, 56 (SS)
  Maryland Chicken
    Salad, 113 (PO)
  Mousse, Chicken, 112 (PO)
  Patty Shells, Chicken Salad
    in, 114 (PO)
  Pies, Chicken Salad, 114 (PO)
  Sandwiches, Chicken
    Salad, 29 (CE)
  Sandwiches, Highland Park
    Chicken Salad, 111 (PO)
  Tart Shells, Chicken Salad
    in, 80 (SS)
Sandwiches, Amandine
  Chicken, 87 (CC); 11 (SS)
Sandwiches, Chicken, 71 (CC);
  27 (FG)
Sandwiches,
  Chicken-Almond, 51 (SS)
Sandwiches, Highland Park
  Chicken Salad, 111 (PO)
Sandwiches, Hot
  Chicken, 114 (PO)
Sandwiches, Louisville Hot
  Brown, 115 (PO)
Sandwiches, Princess, 21 (SS)

Brown Brothers

---

**BB** *Breakfast & Brunch*    **BE** *Beef, Veal & Lamb*    **BR** *Breads*    **CA** *Cakes*    **CC** *Company's Coming*    **CE** *Celebrations*
**CJ** *Cookie Jar*    **DE** *Just Desserts*    **FG** *Family Gatherings*    **GR** *Gift Receipts*    **PK** *All Pork*    **PO** *Plain & Fancy Poultry*
**PP** *Pies & Pastry*    **SE** *Sea & Stream*    **SO** *Soups & Stews*    **SP** *Sporting Scene*    **SS** *Socials & Soirees*    **VE** *Vegetables*

*In 1905, feeding the chickens was a farm chore even the youngest could do.*

Chicken, *continued*
Sandwich, The Duke of
Windsor, 115 (PO)
Sauce, Asparagus with
Chicken-Cheese, 132 (BB)
Sauté, Mexicaine,
Chicken, 99 (PO)
Scallop, Georgia
Chicken, 117 (PO)
Shell, Chicken in a, 119 (PO)
Shortcake, Chicken, 130 (CE)
Shortcake, Dixie
Chicken, 123 (PO)
Simmered Chicken,
Old-Fashioned, 17 (PO)
Smothered Chicken and
Gravy, 25 (PO)
Smothered Chicken,
Virginia, 25 (PO)
Soups
Avgolemono Soup, 33 (SO)
Corn Soup, Chicken
and, 82 (SO)
Cream of Chicken
Soup, 59 (SO)
Filled Dumplings, Chicken
Soup and, 84 (SO)
Golden Chicken Soup, 81 (SO)
Hearty Chicken Soup, 22 (PO)
Matzo Balls, Chicken Soup
with, 59 (CE)
Mulligatawny,
Chicken, 82 (SO)
Noodle Soup,
Chicken, 22 (PO); 83 (SO)
Rich Chicken Soup, 59 (SO)
Stock, Chicken, 11 (SO)
Tortilla Soup, 84 (SO)
Tortilla Soup, Rio
Grande, 86 (SO)
Vegetable Soup,
Chicken, 81 (SO)
Velvet Soup, Chicken, 104 (CC)
White Bisque,
Charleston, 58 (SO)

Sour Cream, Chicken
with, 84 (SS)
Spaghetti, Alabama
Chicken, 71 (PO)
Spaghetti, Mother's
Chicken, 71 (PO)
Spaghetti, Panhandle
Chicken, 72 (PO)
Spaghetti, Party
Chicken, 72 (PO)
Steamed Chicken and
Gravy, 100 (CC)
Stew, Brunswick, 65 (PO);
135 (SO)
Stew, Carolina
Brunswick, 47 (PK)
Stew, Chicken, 132 (SO)
Stewed Chicken with
Biscuits, 17 (PO)
Stew, Farmer's Chicken,
66 (PO)
Stew, Fresh Vegetable and
Chicken, 66 (PO)
Stew, Hopkins County, 61 (PO)
Stew, Kentucky
Mulligan, 135 (SO)
Stew, Old South, 133 (SO)
Tetrazzini, Chicken, 73 (PO)
Wiggle, Chicken, 69 (PO)
Wings, Sesame Chicken, 87 (SS)

**Chili**
Alabama Chili, 51 (BE)
Bowl of Red, Original
Texas-Style, 53 (BE)
Cold Weather Chili, 113 (SO)
con Carne, Chili, 110 (SO)
Easy Hearty Chili, 111 (SO)
Home-Style Chili, 64 (CC)
Hominy, Chili, 47 (VE)
Meaty Chili, 111 (SO)
Pedernales River Chili, 51 (BE)
Sauce, Chili, 71 (GR)
Spicy Chili,
Prize-Winning, 113 (SO)
Texas Championship
Chili, 110 (SO)
Texas Chili, 110 (SO)
Venison Chili, 113 (SO)

**Chocolate**
Bars and Cookies
Bitter Chocolate
Cookies, 61 (CJ)
Bourbon Cookies,
Kentucky, 78 (CJ)
Brownie Drop
Cookies, 39 (CJ)
Brownie Grahams, 106 (CJ)
Brownies, 100 (CJ)
Brownies, Bar
Mitzvah, 99 (FG)
Brownies, Chewy, 107 (SP)
Brownies, Chocolate
Chip, 105 (CJ)
Brownies, Chocolate
Dream, 100 (CJ)
Brownies, Chocolate
Syrup, 102 (CJ)
Brownies, Franklin, 102 (CJ)
Brownies, German
Chocolate, 103 (CJ)

Brownies, German Cream
Cheese, 104 (CJ)
Brownies, Glazed
Orange-Frosted, 75 (SS)
Brownies, Lady Bird's
Texas, 100 (CJ)
Brownies,
Mint-Frosted, 75 (SS)
Brownies, Peanut, 106 (CJ)
Brownie Squares, 74 (BB)
Caramel Fingers,
Chocolate-, 103 (CJ)
Chocolate Chip Forgotten
Cookies, 11 (CJ)
Chocolate Chip Cookies, Sour
Cream, 86 (CE)
Cocoa-Nut Cookies, 78 (CJ)
Congo Bars, 74 (BB)
Cream Cookies,
Chocolate, 40 (CJ)
Crisps, Chocolate, 74 (CJ)
Defense Cookies, 39 (CJ)
Delta Bars, 105 (CJ)
Double-Chocolate
Cookies, 40 (CJ)
Fudge Bars,
Heavenly, 104 (CJ)
Hello Dolly Bars, 92 (CJ)
Icebox Cookies,
Chocolate, 68 (CJ)
Jack O'lantern
Cookies, 104 (CE)
Mint Surprise Cookies,
Starlight, 82 (CJ)
Mocha Jumbles, 23 (CJ)
Nut Fingers,
Double-Dip, 86 (CJ)
Nut Kisses,
Chocolate-, 10 (CJ)

Oatmeal-Chocolate Chip
Cookies, 45 (CJ)
Oatmeal Cookies, No-Bake
Chocolate-, 44 (CJ)
Peanut Blossoms, 81 (CJ)
Peanut Butter Bars,
No-Bake, 98 (CJ)
Peanut Butter
Crunchies, 98 (CJ)
Peanut Butter
Squares, 107 (CJ)
Pinwheel Cookies,
Chocolate, 68 (CJ); 15 (SS)
Rocks, Chocolate, 40 (CJ)
Sandwich Cookies,
Chocolate, 62 (CJ)

*Decorating a chocolate Easter egg was still a craftsman's job in 1902.*

Chocolate, Bars and Cookies,
  *continued*
    Spritz Cookies,
      Chocolate, 27 (SS)
    Toffee Bars, 106 (CJ)
    Toll House Cookies,
      Original, 38 (CJ)
    Walnut Christmas Cookies,
      Chocolate-, 115 (CJ)
    Walnut Refrigerator Cookies,
      Chocolate-, 68 (CJ)
  Beverages
    Afternoon Chocolate, 71 (SS)
    Breakfast Cocoa, 18 (BB)
    Fluff, Chocolate, 92 (BB)
    Hot Chocolate, 87 (BB);
      29 (CE); 59 (FG); 113 (SS)
    Hot Chocolate,
      Old-Fashioned, 92 (BB)

Bread, 1935 Chocolate, 62 (BR)
Bread, Chocolate
  Mandel, 130 (FG)
Cakes and Tortes
  Angel Food Cake,
    Chocolate, 112 (CA)
  Brownie Cupcakes, 86 (CA)
  Brownstone Front
    Cake, 63 (CA)
  Bûche de Noël, 94 (CA)
  Checkerboard Cake, 24 (CA)
  Cheesecakes,
    Chocolate-Mocha, 23 (SS)
  Chiffon, Chocolate, 114 (CA)
  Chocolate Cake, 116 (CA)
  Chocolate Torte, 119 (DE)
  Choo-Choo Chocolate
    Cake, 67 (FG)
  Cupcakes, Black Cat, 104 (CE)

Date Fudge Cake,
  Halloween, 102 (CA)
Delights, Chocolate, 89 (FG)
Devil's Food Cake, 26,
  117 (CA); 13 (FG)
"Failure" Cake,
  Chocolate, 80 (CA)
Fudge Cake,
  Maryland, 67 (CE)
Fudge Cake, Old-Fashioned
  Chewy, 83 (CA)
Gems, Chocolate, 71 (CE)
German Sweet Chocolate
  Cake, 27 (CA)
Groom's Cake,
  Chocolate, 108 (CA)
Groom's Cake, Spirited, 89 (SS)
Hot Water Chocolate
  Cake, 82 (CA)

---

**BB** *Breakfast & Brunch*  **BE** *Beef, Veal & Lamb*  **BR** *Breads*  **CA** *Cakes*  **CC** *Company's Coming*  **CE** *Celebrations*
**CJ** *Cookie Jar*  **DE** *Just Desserts*  **FG** *Family Gatherings*  **GR** *Gift Receipts*  **PK** *All Pork*  **PO** *Plain & Fancy Poultry*
**PP** *Pies & Pastry*  **SE** *Sea & Stream*  **SO** *Soups & Stews*  **SP** *Sporting Scene*  **SS** *Socials & Soirees*  **VE** *Vegetables*

Chocolate, Cakes and Tortes,
*continued*
    Jiffy Chocolate Cake, 83 (CA)
    Mahogany Cake, 28 (CA)
    Marble Loaf Cake, 31 (SS)
    Midgets, Chocolate, 80 (CA)
    Mississippi Mud
      Cake, 82 (CA)
    Mocha Cheesecake, 79 (PP)
    Mocha Layer Cake, 29 (CA)
    Mocha Pound Cake, 121 (CA)
    Neapolitan Halloween
      Cake, 101 (CA)
    Pound Cake,
      Chocolate, 121 (CA)
    Pound Cake, Pecan-Topped
      Chocolate, 118 (CA)
    Ribbon Cake,
      Chocolate, 25 (CA)
    Roll, Gertrude's Chocolate
      Whipped Cream, 125 (CA)
    Sheath Cake,
      Chocolate, 81 (CA)
    Sour Cream-Cocoa
      Cake, 54 (SS)
    Sponge Cake, Passover
      Chocolate, 100 (CA)
    Syrup Cake, Busy
      Day, 84 (CA)
    Wacky Cake, 84 (CA)
    Yeast Cake, Chocolate, 27 (CA)
Candies
    Almond Acorns, 91 (GR)
    Bourbon Bonbons, 134 (GR)
    Buttercream Easter
      Eggs, 135 (GR)
    Caramels, Chocolate, 118 (GR
    Caramels, Ribbon, 118 (GR)
    Cherries, Chocolate-Covered,
      31 (CE); 133 (GR)
    Citrus Peel,
      Chocolate-Covered, 89 (GR)
    Cream Candy,
      Chocolate, 21 (CE)
    Cream Drops,
      Chocolate, 63 (SS)
    Creams, Chocolate, 133 (GR)
    Fudge, Angel, 122 (GR)
    Fudge, Chocolate, 120 (GR)
    Fudge,
      Chocolate-Pecan, 122 (GR)
    Fudge, Coconut, 73 (CE);
      124 (GR)
    Fudge, Dark
      Chocolate, 122 (GR)
    Fudge, Favorite
      Chocolate, 121 (GR)
    Fudge, Festive, 122 (GR)
    Fudge, Homemade, 25 (CE)
    Fudge, Quick, 120 (GR)
    Hunky Dories, 136 (GR)
    Millionaires, Texas, 136 (GR)
    Mints,
      Chocolate-Covered, 132 (GR)
    Orange Bonbons, 134 (GR)
    Peanut Butter Cups, 136 (GR)
    Peanut Clusters,
      Double, 136 (GR)
    Pecan Brittle,
      Chocolate-, 113 (GR)

    Pecan Logs,
      Chocolate, 134 (GR)
    Pecan Toffee, 116 (GR)
    Peppermint Dainties,
      Chocolate, 73 (CC)
    Truffles, Raspberry, 132 (GR)
    Truffles, Solger's, 132 (GR)
Charlotte, Chocolate, 83 (DE)
Charlotte, Chocolate
    Mint, 85 (DE)
Charlotte, Chocolate
    Rum, 83 (DE)
Cream Puffs Deluxe,
    Chocolate-Filled, 122 (DE)
Custard, Creamy
    Chocolate, 52 (DE)
Dessert, Frozen
    Chocolate, 100 (SS)
Éclairs, 124 (DE)
Frostings, Fillings, and Toppings
    Bourbon Frosting,
      Chocolate-, 99 (FG)
    Bourbon Frosting,
      Chocolate, 89 (SS)
    Butter Frosting,
      Chocolate, 24 (CA);
      124 (DE)
    Chocolate Frosting, 74 (BB);
      16, 82, 83, 125, 137 (CA);
      82 (CC); 125 (DE); 67 (FG)
    Chocolate Icing, 27 (CA)
    Chocolate Pastry
      Cream, 122 (DE)
    Cocoa Cream
      Frosting, 104 (CE)
    Creamy Chocolate
      Filling, 40 (CJ)
    Easy Chocolate
      Frosting, 84 (CA)
    Fluffy Filling, 63 (CA)
    Fudge Frosting,
      Chocolate, 101 (CA)
    Fudge Frosting, Dark, 82 (CA)
    Fudge Frosting,
      Quick, 78 (CA)
    Glaze, Chocolate, 29 (CJ);
      75 (SS)
    Glossy Chocolate
      Frosting, 137 (CA)

Mocha Frosting, 29 (CA)
Mocha Icing, Creamy, 29 (CA)
Peanut Frosting,
    Chocolate-, 81 (CA)
Quick Chocolate
    Frosting, 137 (CA)
Rich Chocolate
    Frosting, 137 (CA)

Sour Cream Chocolate
    Frosting, 28 (CA)
Special Chocolate
    Frosting, 108 (CA)
Ice Cream, Chocolate, 90 (CE);
    98 (DE)
Marlow, Chocolate, 107 (DE)
Marshmallow Icebox Dessert,
    Chocolate, 85 (DE)
Mousse, Chocolate, 78, 108 (DE)
Piecrust, Chocolate
    Crumb, 104 (PP)
Piecrust, Chocolate
    Wafer, 22 (PP)
Pies and Tarts
    Angel Pie, Chocolate, 92 (PP)
    Black Bottom Pie,
      Delta, 105 (PP)
    Bourbon Chocolate Pecan
      Pie, 54 (PP)
    Chess Pie, Chocolate, 73 (PP)
    Chip Pie, Chocolate, 70 (SP)
    Chocolate Pie, 110 (CE)
    Cream Pie, Chocolate, 92 (PP)
    French Huguenot Chocolate
      Pie, 68 (PP)
    French Silk Chocolate
      Pie, 112 (PP)
    Fudge Pie, 127 (SP)
    Fudge Pie, Chocolate
      Lover's, 67 (PP)
    Fudge Pie, No-Crust, 68 (PP)
    Icebox Pie,
      Chocolate, 112 (PP)
    Jockey's Reward Pie, 78 (CE)
    Meringue Pie,
      Chocolate, 51 (CC); 91 (PP)
    Morsel Pie, Pleasant Hill
      Chocolate, 68 (PP)
    Pecan Pie, Chocolate, 53 (PP)
    Refrigerator Pie,
      Chocolate, 43 (SP)
    Rum Cream Pie,
      Chocolate, 104 (PP)
    Swiss Chocolate
      Tarts, 50 (SS)
Pots de Crème au
    Chocolat, 65 (DE)
Pudding, Chocolate
    Sponge, 24 (DE)
Pudding, Steamed
    Chocolate, 24 (DE)
Roll, Famous Chocolate
    Refrigerator, 86 (DE)
Sauces
    Chocolate Sauce, 105,
      133 (DE); 82 (FG); 86 (GR)
    Fudge Sauce, 105 (DE);
      111 (PO)
    Fudge Sauce, Hot, 133 (DE);
      86 (GR)
    Raisin-Chocolate
      Sauce, 86 (GR)
    Rich Chocolate
      Sauce, 102 (DE)
    Sherried Chocolate
      Sauce, 133 (DE)
    Whipped Cream-Chocolate
      Sauce, 16 (DE)
S'Mores, 95 (SP)

Chocolate, *continued*
  Soufflé, Dixie
    Chocolate, 65 (DE)
  Strawberries, Chocolate
    Dipped, 129 (SS)
**Chowders**
  Bean and Bacon
    Chowder, 97 (SO)
  Clam Chowder, 12 (SE); 88 (SO)
  Clam Chowder,
    Manhattan-Style, 91 (SO)
  Clam Chowder, Marion
    Harland's, 89 (SO)
  Clam Chowder, New
    England, 91 (SO)
  Cod Chowder, 88 (SO)
  Conch Chowder, Key
    West, 13 (SE)
  Corn Chowder, Creole, 46 (SS)
  Corn-Peanut Chowder, 101 (SO)
  Fish Chowder, Florida, 87 (SO)
  Lima Bean Chowder, 98 (SO)
  Marlin Chowder, 104 (SP)
  Mushroom and Barley
    Chowder, 102 (SO)
  Oyster Chowder,
    Statehouse, 91 (SO)
  Trout Chowder, 88 (SO)
  Turkey Chowder, 66 (PO)
**Clams**
  Bisque, Clam, 52 (SO)
  Bouillon, Clams in, 38 (SS)
  Casino, Clams, 10 (SE)
  Chowder, Clam, 12 (SE);
    88 (SO)
  Chowder, Manhattan-Style
    Clam, 91 (SO)
  Chowder, Marion Harland's
    Clam, 89 (SO)
  Chowder, New England
    Clam, 91 (SO)
  Fried Chesapeake Bay Soft-Shell
    Clams, 11 (SE)
  Fritters, Clam, 11 (SE)
  Madrilene, Clam, 30 (SO)
  Paella, 56 (SE)
  Sauce, Linguine with White
    Clam, 11 (SE)
  Steamed Clams, 10 (SE)
  Stuffed Clams, 80 (CE)
**Coconut**
  Ambrosia, 30 (DE); 57 (FG)
  Ambrosia, Holiday, 30 (DE)
  Balls, Coconut, 78 (CJ)
  Bars, Cherry-Coconut, 120 (CJ)
  Bars, Coconut Pie, 92 (CJ)
  Bars, Hello Dolly, 92 (CJ)
  Brittle, Coconut, 113 (GR)
  Cake, Ambrosia, 22 (CA)
  Cake, Coconut
    Birthday, 103 (CA)
  Cake, Coconut Cream, 124 (CE)
  Cake, Coconut Pound, 121 (CA);
    89 (FG)
  Cake, Easter Orange
    Coconut, 100 (CA)

Cake, Italian Cream, 90 (SP)
Cake, Moss Rose, 23 (CA)
Cake, Rocky Mountain
  Coconut, 15 (CA)
Cake, Self-Frosting
  Angel, 112 (CA)
Cake, Snowball, 95 (CA)
Cake (The Queen), La
  Reine, 17 (CA)
Cake, Toasted Coconut, 74 (CA)
Cake, White Mountain, 21 (CA)
Caramels, Ribbon, 118 (GR)
Coffee Cake,
  Oatmeal-Coconut, 103 (BB)
Cookies, Ambrosia, 112 (CJ)
Cookies, Coconut, 92 (CJ)
Cookies, Coconut
  Icebox, 70 (CJ)
Cookies, Crunchy Skillet, 79 (CJ)
Cream with Caramel Sauce,
  Coconut, 75 (DE)
Crunch,
  Lemon-Coconut, 127 (DE)
Custard, Baked Coconut
  Cup, 56 (DE)
Filling,
  Almond-Coconut, 117 (FG)
Filling, Coconut, 25 (CA)
Filling, Coconut-Pecan, 27 (CA)
Filling, Orange Coconut, 22 (CA)
Filling, Rocky
  Mountain, 15 (CA)
Fingers, Double-Dip
  Nut, 86 (CJ)
Frosting, Cooked
  Cream, 33 (CA)
Frosting, Custard
  Cream, 124 (CE)
Fudge, Coconut, 73 (CE);
  124 (GR)
Glaze,
  Coconut-Pineapple, 92 (PK)
Ice Cream, Coconut, 130 (CC)
Jumbles, Coconut, 23 (CJ)
Logs, Raspberry Jam, 99 (CJ)
Macaroons, Coconut, 15 (CJ);
  108 (SS)
Macaroons,
  Oatmeal-Coconut, 15 (CJ)
Pie, Allison's Little Tea House
  Coconut Cream, 94 (PP)
Pie, Coconut-Cherry
  Cream, 94 (PP)
Pie, Coconut Meringue, 95 (PP)
Pie, Coconut-Pineapple
  Cream, 95 (PP)
Piecrust, Coconut, 23 (PP)
Piecrust, Coconut-
  Graham, 21 (PP)
Pie, Fresh Coconut
  Cream, 96 (PP)
Pie, Moonshine, 90 (PP)
Pie, Old-Fashioned Coconut
  Custard, 71 (PP)
Pie, Sweet Potato-
  Coconut, 58 (PP)

Porcupines, 79 (CJ)
Pralines, Coconut, 130 (GR)
Pudding, Tyler, 127 (CC)
Snowballs, 111 (PO); 33 (SS)
Squares,
  Coconut-Orange, 93 (CJ)
Squares, Toasted
  Coconut, 77 (SP)
Tarts, Miniature
  Coconut, 37 (CE)
Topping, Coconut, 70 (SP)
Torte, Coconut
  Crunch, 127 (DE)
Vanities, Coconut, 93 (CJ)
**Coffee**
A Good Cup of Coffee, 90 (BB)
Bavarian, Coffee, 72 (DE)
Boiled Coffee,
  Old-Fashioned, 73 (CC)
Café au Lait, 33 (BB)
Café au Lait, Rich, 69 (CC)

Café con Leche, 38 (BB)
Café Noir (*Note*), 69 (CC)
Cake, Black Coffee, 105 (BB)
Cake, Coffee Angel
  Food, 113 (CA)
Cake, Mocha Layer, 29 (CA)
Cake, Mocha Pound, 121 (CA)
Cheesecake, Mocha, 79 (PP)
Cheesecakes,
  Chocolate-Mocha, 23 (SS)
Custard, Mocha
  Macaroon, 58 (DE)
Dessert, Mocha
  Macaroon, 102 (DE)
Divinity, Coffee, 101 (GR)
For a Crowd, Coffee, 90 (BB)
Frosting, Mocha, 29 (CA);
  54 (SS)

---

**BB** *Breakfast & Brunch*   **BE** *Beef, Veal & Lamb*   **BR** *Breads*   **CA** *Cakes*   **CC** *Company's Coming*   **CE** *Celebrations*
**CJ** *Cookie Jar*   **DE** *Just Desserts*   **FG** *Family Gatherings*   **GR** *Gift Receipts*   **PK** *All Pork*   **PO** *Plain & Fancy Poultry*
**PP** *Pies & Pastry*   **SE** *Sea & Stream*   **SO** *Soups & Stews*   **SP** *Sporting Scene*   **SS** *Socials & Soirees*   **VE** *Vegetables*

Coffee, *continued*
   Ice Cream, Coffee, 98 (DE)
   Iced Coffee, 90 (BB)
   Icing, Creamy Mocha, 29 (CA)
   Lovefeast Coffee, 50 (CE)
   Mousse, Coffee, 79 (DE)
   Pecans, Coffee, 92 (GR)
   Petits Pots de Crème au
     Café, 65 (DE)
   Pie, Coffee-Almond
     Cream, 93 (PP)
   Punch, Frosty Mocha, 12 (SS)
   Punch, Mocha Milk, 78 (SS)
   Riverbank Coffee, 41 (BB)
   Roll, Mocha Ice Cream, 102 (DE)
   Walnuts, Coffee, 96 (GR)
**Coleslaw.** *See* Cabbage, Salads.
**Conch**
   Chowder, Key West
     Conch, 13 (SE)
   Fried Conch, 13 (SE)
   Fritters, Conch, 13 (SE)
   Stew, Conch, 13 (SE)
**Conserves**
   Apple Conserve, 28 (GR)
   Citrus Conserve, 31 (GR)
   Cranberry Conserve, 28 (GR)
   Fruit Conserve, Fresh, 30 (GR)
   Peach Conserve, 29 (GR)
   Pear Conserve, 29 (GR)
   Plum Conserve, 29 (GR)
   Rhubarb-Pineapple
     Conserve, 29 (GR)
   Strawberry-Pineapple
     Conserve, 30 (GR)
**Cookies**
   Bars and Squares
     Almond Shortbread, 17 (CJ)
     Apple Spice Bars, 90 (CJ)
     Apricot Blondies, 107 (CJ)
     Banana Bars, 90 (CJ)
     Brownie Grahams, 106 (CJ)
     Brownies, 100 (CJ)
     Brownies, Bar Mitzvah, 99 (FG)
     Brownies,
       Butterscotch, 75 (SP)
     Brownies, Chewy, 107 (SP)
     Brownies, Chewy
       Blonde, 107 (CJ); 95 (SS)
     Brownies, Chocolate
       Chip, 105 (CJ)
     Brownies, Chocolate
       Dream, 100 (CJ)
     Brownies, Chocolate
       Syrup, 102 (CJ)
     Brownies, Franklin, 102 (CJ)
     Brownies, German
       Chocolate, 103 (CJ)
     Brownies, German Cream
       Cheese, 104 (CJ)
     Brownies, Glazed
       Orange-Frosted, 75 (SS)
     Brownies, Lady Bird's
       Texas, 100 (CJ)
     Brownies,
       Mint-Frosted, 75 (SS)
     Brownies, Peanut, 106 (CJ)
     Brownie Squares, 74 (BB)
     Brownies, Sasso's
       Blonde, 47 (PK)

Butter Chews, 108 (CJ)
Butter Cookies,
   Dutch, 17 (CJ)
Butter Crisps, 90 (CJ)
Butterscotch-Fruit
   Squares, 91 (CJ)
Cherry-Coconut
   Bars, 120 (CJ)
Chews, Sheffield, 108 (CJ)
Chocolate-Caramel
   Fingers, 103 (CJ)
Cinnamon Cookies,
   Glazed, 91 (CJ)
Coconut Cookies, 92 (CJ)
Coconut-Orange
   Squares, 93 (CJ)
Coconut Pie Bars, 92 (CJ)
Coconut Vanities, 93 (CJ)
Congo Bars, 74 (BB)
Date Bars, Dixie, 95 (CJ)
Date-Nut Squares, 48 (SP)
Date Squares, 81 (CC)
Delta Bars, 105 (CJ)
Dream Bars, 95 (CJ)
Fruit Bars, Gottlieb's
   Bakery, 94 (CJ)
Fruit Logs,
   Brandied, 119 (CJ)
Fudge Bars,
   Heavenly, 104 (CJ)
Gumdrop Cookies, 120 (CJ)
Hello Dolly Bars, 92 (CJ)
Honey Cookies, Hard, 95 (CJ)
Lemon Bars, 98 (FG)
Lemon Squares, 96 (CJ);
   26 (FG)
London Bars, 95 (CJ)
Meringue Bars, 72 (CC)
Mud Hens, 96 (CJ)

Orange-Nut Squares,
   Swedish, 96 (CJ)
Orange Slice Bars, 97 (CJ)
Peanut Bar Cookies,
   Crunchy, 97 (CJ)
Peanut Butter Bars,
   No-Bake, 98 (CJ)
Peanut Butter
   Crunchies, 98 (CJ)

Peanut Butter
   Squares, 107 (CJ)
Pecan Bars, 136 (CE)
Pecan Strips, Kathleen
   Danielson's, 98 (CJ)
Raspberry Jam Logs, 99 (CJ)
Rum Bars, 99 (CJ)
Scotch Hermits, 131 (CE)
Shortbread Squares, 136 (SP)
Toffee Bars, 106 (CJ)
Wax Cookies, 108 (CJ)

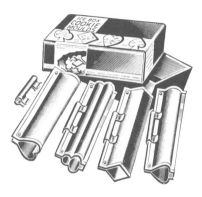

Christmas
   Almond Christmas
     Cookies, 112 (CJ)
   Butter Cookies,
     Christmas, 115 (CJ)
   Candy Cane Cookies, 135 (CJ)
   Chocolate-Walnut Christmas
     Cookies, 115 (CJ)
   Christmas Cookies, 45 (FG)
   Fruit Cookies,
     Christmas, 117 (CJ)
   Gingerbread Bears,
     Holiday, 136 (CJ)
   Italian Christmas
     Cookies, 124 (CJ)
   White Christmas
     Cookies, 136 (CJ)
   Wreath Cookies,
     Scandinavian, 127 (CJ)
Drop
   Almond Cookies,
     Greek, 53 (CJ)
   Almond Lace Wafers, 84 (SP)
   Ambrosia Cookies, 112 (CJ)
   Apple-Molasses Drop
     Cookies, 48 (CJ)
   Applesauce Cookies, 48 (CJ)
   Apricot Jewels, 49 (CJ)
   Bachelor Buttons, Thomas
     Jefferson's, 33 (CJ)
   Banana Cake Cookies, 49 (CJ)
   Benne Seed Wafers, 127 (CE)
   Benne Wafers, Rolled, 46 (CJ)
   Black Pepper Cookies,
     Maryland, 37 (CJ)
   Bourbon Cookies, Aiken's
     Row, 113 (CJ)
   Bran Drop Cookies, 42 (CJ)
   Brownie Drop
     Cookies, 39 (CJ)
   Buttermilk Drop
     Cookies, 32 (CJ)

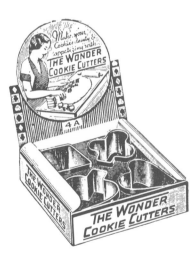

General Electric Company

*The new electric mixer simplified cookie making in 1938.*

Cookies, Kisses, *continued*
  Chocolate Chip Forgotten
    Cookies, 11 (CJ)
  Chocolate-Nut Kisses, 10 (CJ)
  Pecan Kiss Cakes, 10 (CJ)
  Praline Kisses, 10 (CJ)
Macaroons
  Almond Macaroons, New
    Bern, 14 (CJ)
  Brazil Nut Macaroons, 15 (CJ)
  Cake-Crumb
    Macaroons, 14 (CJ)
  Coconut Macaroons, 15 (CJ);
    108 (SS)
  Date-Nut Macaroons, 15 (CJ)
  Macaroons, 123 (CC); 66 (SS)
  Mary Randolph's
    Macaroons, 13 (CJ)
  Monticello Macaroons, 13 (CJ)
  Oatmeal-Coconut
    Macaroons, 15 (CJ)
  Passover Macaroons, 14 (CJ)
No-Bake
  Bourbon Cookies,
    Kentucky, 78 (CJ)
  Chocolate-Oatmeal Cookies,
    No-Bake, 44 (CJ)
  Crunchy Skillet
    Cookies, 79 (CJ)
  Peanut Bar Cookies,
    Crunchy, 97 (CJ)
  Peanut Butter Bars,
    No-Bake, 98 (CJ)
  Peanut Butter
    Crunchies, 98 (CJ)
Nürnberger
  Lebkuchen, 128 (CJ)
Pfeffernüsse, 130 (CJ); 46 (FG)
Pressed
  Basic Pressed
    Cookies, 86 (CJ)
  Caramel Press
    Cookies, 86 (CJ)
  Chocolate Spritz
    Cookies, 27 (SS)
  Nut Fingers,
    Double-Dip, 86 (CJ)
  Spritz Cookies, 86 (CJ)
  Sugar 'n Spice Cookies,
    Old-Fashioned, 87 (CJ)
Refrigerator
  Almond Icebox
    Cookies, 66 (CJ)
  Butterscotch Cookies, 67 (CJ)
  Butterscotch
    Pinwheels, 67 (CJ)
  Cheese Wafers, Dutch, 68 (CJ)
  Chocolate Icebox
    Cookies, 68 (CJ)
  Chocolate Pinwheel
    Cookies, 68 (CJ); 15 (SS)
  Chocolate-Walnut Refrigerator
    Cookies, 68 (CJ)
  Citrus Wafers, 69 (CJ)
  Coconut Icebox
    Cookies, 70 (CJ)
  Date Pinwheel
    Cookies, 70 (CJ)
  Honey Cookies, 71 (CJ)
  Icebox Cookies, 82 (FG)

Lebkuchen, 46 (FG)
Peanut Butter Refrigerator
  Cookies, 71 (CJ)
Pecan Cookies,
  German, 71 (CJ)
Pecan Icebox Cookies, 23 (SP)
Petticoat Tails, 70 (SS)
Swedish Cookies, 67 (CJ)
Vanilla Cookies,
  Shaker, 66 (CJ)
Vanilla Nut Icebox
  Cookies, 66 (CJ)
Rolled
  Almond Christmas
    Cookies, 112 (CJ)
  Almond Meringue
    Cookies, 23 (SS)
  Apricot Turnovers, 65 (CJ)
  Bizcochos, 124 (CJ)
  Butter Cookies, St. Augustine
    Fiesta, 125 (CJ)
  Chocolate Cookies,
    Bitter, 61 (CJ)
  Chocolate Sandwich
    Cookies, 62 (CJ)
  Cream Cheese Horns, 63 (CJ)
  Cream Cheese Thumbprint
    Cookies, 63 (CJ)
  Cream Cheese Wafers, 98 (BB)
  Date Rolls, Grecian, 65 (CJ)
  Derby Cakes, Mary
    Telfair's, 28 (CJ)
  Exposition Cookies, Susan G.
    Cooke's, 61 (CJ)
  Fattigmands
    Bakkelse, 126 (CJ)
  Gingerbread Bears,
    Holiday, 136 (CJ)
  Ginger Cakes,
    Winkler's, 20 (CJ)
  Ginger Cookies,
    Moravian, 20 (CJ)
  Gingersnaps, 94 (CE); 23 (FG)
  Greek Holiday
    Cookies, 122 (CJ)
  Half-Moons, 127 (CJ)
  Hamantaschen, 123 (CJ)
  Highland Cookies, 42 (FG)
  Italian Christmas
    Cookies, 124 (CJ)
  Italian Pillows, 65 (CJ)
  Jack O'lantern
    Cookies, 104 (CE)
  Jumbles, Sotterly, 24 (CJ)
  Lemon Cookies, 59 (CJ);
    45 (FG)
  Linzer Cookies, 63 (CJ)
  Mocha Jumbles, 23 (CJ)
  Molasses Cookies, 60 (CJ)
  Monogrammed
    Cookies, 118 (FG)
  Orange-Mincemeat Filled
    Cookies, 119 (CJ)
  Pastel Cream Wafers, 77 (SS)
  Pecan Shortbreads, 84 (CC)
  Rye Cookies, Swedish, 18 (CJ)
  Sand Dollars, 60 (CJ)
  Shrewsbury Cakes, 12 (CE);
    60 (CJ)
  Sour Cream Cookies, 62 (CJ)

Spook Cookies, 134 (CJ)
Springerle, 130 (CJ)
Sugar Cookies, 45, 100 (SP)
Sugar Cookies, Brittle
  Brown, 88 (CE)
Sugar Cookies,
  Decorator, 58 (CJ)
Sugar Cookies, Oma's, 59 (CJ)
Sugar Cookies,
  Valentine, 29 (CE)
Sugar Cookies, Walden's Ridge
  Toll House, 58 (CJ)
Sugar Crisps, 18 (CE)
Symbol Cookies, 132 (CJ)
Tea Cakes, Butter, 25 (CJ)
Tea Cakes, Gram's, 122 (FG)
Tea Cakes, Moravian, 19 (CC);
  27 (CJ)
Tea Cakes, North
  Carolina, 27 (CJ)
Tea Cakes,
  Old-Fashioned, 97 (CE)
Tea Party Cakes,
  Edenton, 26 (CJ)
Valentine Cookies,
  To-My-, 133 (CJ)
Vanilla Wafers, 113 (SS)
Zimtkränze, 128 (CJ)
Zimtsterne, 130 (CJ)

Shaped
  Arkansas Travelers, 32 (FG)
  Bird's Nest Cookies, 79 (CJ)
  Bourbon Cookies,
    Kentucky, 78 (CJ)
  Buñuelo Rosettes, 84 (CJ)
  Butter Cookies,
    Christmas, 115 (CJ)
  Butter Cookies,
    Fruit-Shaped, 133 (CJ)
  Butter Fingers, 77 (CJ)
  Candy Cane Cookies, 135 (CJ)
  Cheese Wafers, 98 (BB)
  Cherry Delights, 115 (CJ)
  Cherry Winks, 116 (CJ)
  Chocolate Crisps, 74 (CJ)
  Christmas Cookies,
    White, 136 (CJ)
  Cinnamon Cookies,
    Greek, 74 (CJ)
  Cinnamon Tea Cakes, 25 (CJ)
  Cinnamon Wafers, Mrs. B. C.
    Howard's, 83 (CJ)

Cookies, Shaped, *continued*
  Cocoa-Nut Cookies, 78 (CJ)
  Coconut Balls, 78 (CJ)
  Coconut Jumbles, 23 (CJ)
  Crunchy Skillet
    Cookies, 79 (CJ)
  Date Surprises, 82 (CJ)
  Easter Cookies, New
    Smyrna, 122 (CJ)
  French Cookies, 84 (CJ)
  Ginger Cookies, Tryon
    Palace, 18 (CJ)
  Gingersnaps, 94 (CE);
    108 (SS)
  Ginger Snaps,
    Old-Fashioned, 19 (CJ)
  Guess-Again Cookies, 76 (CJ)
  Jumbles, 66 (SS)
  Jumbles, Waverly, 24 (CJ)
  Ladyfingers, 29 (CJ)
  Lebkuchen,
    Nürnberger, 128 (CJ)
  Lemon Praline
    Cookies, 76 (CJ)
  Lucky Leaves, 132 (CJ)
  Madeleines, 29 (CJ)
  Melting Dreams, 72 (CC)
  Mint Surprise Cookies,
    Starlight, 82 (CJ)
  Oatmeal-Coconut
    Macaroons, 15 (CJ)
  Oatmeal Crinkles, 76 (CJ)
  Peanut Blossoms, 81 (CJ)
  Peanut Cookies, Early
    American, 81 (CJ)
  Pecan Delights, 77 (CJ)
  Pecan Sandies, 77 (CJ)
  Pfeffernüsse, 130 (CJ)
  Plum Cookies,
    Alsatian, 128 (CJ)
  Porcupines, 79 (CJ)
  Pretzel Cookies, 81 (CJ)
  Sand Tarts, 63 (SS)
  Scandinavian Wreath
    Cookies, 127 (CJ)
  Snickerdoodles, 74 (CJ)
  Speculaas, 121 (CJ)
  Spice Cookies, Sea
    Island, 75 (CJ)
  Sugar-Raisin Cookies, Mother
    Kearney's, 82 (CJ)
  Swedish Rose
    Cookies, 12 (SS)
  Sweet Wafers, Rolled, 84 (CJ)
  Tea Cakes, Texas, 27 (CJ)
  Tuilles with Almonds, 83 (CJ)
  Vanilla Crescents, 96 (FG)
  Walk-to-School
    Cookies, 75 (CJ)
Shortbread
  Almond Shortbread, 17 (CJ)
  Butter Cookies,
    Dutch, 17 (CJ)
  Fans, Shortbread, 16 (CJ)
  Pecan Shortbreads, 84 (CC)
  Rye Cookies, Swedish, 18 (CJ)

Shortbread, 13 (CE); 16 (CJ)
Shortbread Cookies, 17 (CJ)
Squares, Shortbread, 136 (SP)
Surprise Cookies,
  Shortbread, 18 (CJ)
**Corn**
Bread, Fresh Corn, 15 (BR)
Casserole, Fresh Corn, 45 (VE)
Casserole, Pork and
  Corn, 37 (PK)
Chowder,
  Corn-Peanut, 101 (SO)
Chowder, Creole Corn, 46 (SS)
Cornbread with Corn, 15 (BR)
Corn-on-the-Cob, 112 (CC);
  84 (CE); 11 (FG); 43 (VE)
Fried Corn, Southern, 44 (VE)
Fritters, Corn, 128 (BR);
  46 (VE)
Grilled Corn, 97 (SP)
Grilled in Husks, Corn, 89 (SP)
How To Prepare Fresh
  Corn, 43 (VE)
Maque Chou, 44 (VE)
Muffins, Richmond
  Corn, 113 (BR)
Omelet, Corn, 121 (BB)
Oysters, Corn, 50 (CC)
Oysters, Fresh Corn, 46 (VE)
Pancakes, Corn, 46 (VE)
Pudding, Corn, 133 (CE)
Pudding, Plantation Corn, 46 (VE)
Pudding, Southern
  Corn, 114 (CE)
Relish, Corn, 49 (GR)
Ring Tum Diddy, 127 (VE)
Roasted Corn in the
  Husk, 98 (CE)
Salad, Corn Relish, 69 (SP)
Sautéed Corn, 94 (CE)
Sautéed White Corn, 44 (VE)
Soup, Chicken and
  Corn, 82 (SO)
Soup, Cream of Corn, 62 (SO)
Stewed Corn,
  Tennessee, 44 (VE)
Stew, Pioneer Corn, 130 (SO)
Succotash, 127 (VE)
**Cornbreads**
Awendaw, 31 (BR)
Basic Cornbreads
  Buttermilk Cornbread, 122 (FG)
  Cornbread, 95 (SS)
  Deep South
    Cornbread, 13 (BR)
  Egg Cornbread,
    Cassie's, 14 (BR)
  Kentucky Cornbread, 18 (CE)
  Mississippi
    Cornbread, 94 (CE)
  Old-Fashioned Cornbread,
    16 (BB); 13 (BR)
  Ranch Cornbread, 16 (BR)
  Skillet Cornbread, 13 (BR)
  Skillet Cornbread,
    Old-Fashioned, 47 (PK)

Southern Cornbread,
  123 (PO); 42 (SP)
Batty Cakes, Cornmeal, 25 (BR)
Biscuits, Cornmeal, 22 (BR)
Cakes, Mrs. Paul's
  Cornmeal, 25 (BR)
Chicken Shortcake, 130 (CE)
Corn Bread, Fresh, 15 (BR)
Corn, Cornbread with, 15 (BR)
Corn Dodgers, Marion
  Harlands's, 21 (BR)
Corn Light Bread, 17 (BR);
  12 (FG)
Corn Light Bread, Mother
  Thomas', 96 (BB)
Corn Pone, 33 (CC); 56 (SP)
Corn Pones, Cherokee, 23 (BR)
Corn Pones, Kentucky, 24 (BR)
Corn Pones, Ozark
  Pumpkin, 24 (BR)
Corn Pones, Sweet
  Potato, 24 (BR)
Corn Pones, Virginia, 23 (BR)
Corn Sticks, 76 (FG); 30 (PO);
  15 (SP)
Corn Sticks, Alabama, 22 (BR)
Corn Sticks, Crisp, 22 (CC)
Corn Sticks, Crunchy, 96 (BB)
Corn Sticks, Golden, 22 (BR)
Crackling Bread, Mock, 15 (BR)
Crackling Cornbread, 78 (SP)
Crackling Cornbread,
  Oklahoma, 14 (BR)
Crackling Pones,
  Tennessee, 24 (BR)
Crisps, Cornmeal, 102 (CC)
Crisps, North Carolina
  Cornmeal, 21 (BR)
Dressing, Mushroom
  Cornbread, 64 (SP)
Dressing,
  Sausage-Cornbread, 31 (PO)
Dressing, Wild Turkey with
  Cornbread, 132 (CE)
Egg Bread, 35 (BR)
Fiesta Cornbread, 125 (PO)
Flapjacks, Arkansas
  Cornmeal, 26 (BR)
Griddle Cakes, Alabama
  Corn, 26 (BR)
Griddle Cakes, Indian, 56 (BE)
Griddle Cakes, Potato, 35 (BB)
Hoecakes, Hot Water, 27 (BR)
Hoecakes, Indian, 27 (BR)
Hush Puppies, 97 (CE); 26 (FG);
  110, 111 (SE); 61 (SP)
Hush Puppies, Boone
  Tavern, 30 (BR)
Hush Puppies, Cross
  Creek, 28 (BR)
Hush Puppies, Golden, 41 (BB)
Hush Puppies, Stagecoach
  Inn, 29 (BR)
Jalapeño Cornbread, 16 (BR)
Johnny Cake, 13 (BR)
Johns Island Cornbread, 14 (BR)

---

**BB** *Breakfast & Brunch*  **BE** *Beef, Veal & Lamb*  **BR** *Breads*  **CA** *Cakes*  **CC** *Company's Coming*  **CE** *Celebrations*
**CJ** *Cookie Jar*  **DE** *Just Desserts*  **FG** *Family Gatherings*  **GR** *Gift Receipts*  **PK** *All Pork*  **PO** *Plain & Fancy Poultry*
**PP** *Pies & Pastry*  **SE** *Sea & Stream*  **SO** *Soups & Stews*  **SP** *Sporting Scene*  **SS** *Socials & Soirees*  **VE** *Vegetables*

*Checking a crop of corn before harvesting in Virginia, c.1927.*

Cornbreads, *continued*
  Lace Cakes, Kentucky, 26 (BR)
  Mexican Cornbread, 23 (SO)
  Muffins, Cornbread, 56 (CC)
  Muffins, Cornmeal, 29 (BB);
    103 (SP)
  Muffins, Crackling
    Cornbread, 18 (BR)
  Muffins, Sausage Corn, 18 (BR)
  Muffins, Tennessee
    Cornmeal, 18 (BR)
  Mush, Fried, 31 (BB)
  Mush, Maryland Fried, 30 (BR)
  Ovendaugh, South
    Carolina, 31 (BR)
  Pancakes, Cornmeal, 35 (BB)
  Patty Cakes, Cornmeal, 16 (BB)
  Rolls, Oklahoma
    Cornmeal, 23 (BR)
  Sally Lunn, Cornmeal, 17 (BR)
  Sausage-Apple
    Cornbread, 131 (BB)
  Sausage Cornbread
    Sticks, 134 (SP)
  Scratch Backs, 21 (BR)

  Sesame Crisps, 20 (SO)
  Sippets, Cornmeal, 18 (SO)
  Special Cornbread, 16 (BR)
  Spider Bread,
    Louisiana, 35 (BR)
  Spoonbread, Dixie, 35 (BR)
  Spoonbread, Hotel
    Roanoke, 33 (BR)
  Spoonbread, Luncheon, 32 (BR)
  Spoonbread, Parmesan, 32 (BR)
  Spoonbread, Plantation, 126 (CC)
  Spoonbreads, Individual, 32 (BR)
  Spoonbread, Southern, 31 (BR)
  Spoonbread, Virginia, 14 (BB)
  Stuffing, Roast Ducklings with
    Cornbread, 42 (PO)
  Stuffing, Rock Cornish Hens
    with Oyster
    Cornbread, 39 (PO)
  Tortillas, Corn, 129 (BR)
  Waffles, Corn, 115 (BB)
  Waffles, Cornmeal, 77 (CE)
**Cornish Hens**
  Bacon, Cornish Hens with, 25 (SS)
  Broiled Cornish Hens, 25 (BB)

  Fried Rock Cornish
    Hens, 82 (PO)
  Herb Gravy, Roast Cornish Hens
    with, 39 (PO)
  Oyster Cornbread Stuffing, Rock
    Cornish Hens with, 39 (PO)
  Raisin Pecan Stuffing,
    Spit-Roasted Cornish Hens
    with, 38 (PO)
  Sage Stuffing, Roast Cornish
    Hens with, 38 (PO)
  Sausage Stuffing, Rock Cornish
    Hens with, 39 (PO)
  Sherried Cornish Hens,
    99 (PO)
**Crab**
  au Gratin, Crabmeat, 18 (SE)
  Baked Crab in Shells, 18 (SE)
  Bisque, Crab, 52 (SO)
  Busters Béarnaise, 15 (SE)
  Cakes, Chesapeake House
    Crab, 20 (SE)
  Cakes, Maryland Crab, 98 (CE)
  Cakes, Old Durham Church
    Crab, 65 (CE)

Crab, *continued*
    Casserole, Low Country
      Seafood, 54 (SE)
    Creamed Lump Crab on Toast
      Points, 116 (CC)
    Croquettes, Crab, 115 (SS)
    Croquettes, Ybor City
      Crab, 21 (SE)
    Deviled Crab, 20 (SE)
    Dip, Chafing Dish Crab, 96 (SS)
    Flounder Fillets, Broiled
      Stuffed, 65 (SE)
    Flounder Stuffed with
      Crab, 62 (SE)
    Gumbo, Crab, 118 (SO)
    How to Crack into a
      Crab, 16 (SE)
    Imperial, Commander's Palace
      Crabmeat, 18 (SE)
    Imperial, Crab, 18 (SE)
    Imperial, Crabmeat, 37 (CE)
    Louis, Crab, 23 (SE)
    Mold, Crabmeat, 11 (CE)
    Mousse, Shrimp and
      Crabmeat, 103 (FG)
    Mushroom Caps,
      Crabmeat-Stuffed, 78 (BB)
    Norfolk, Crab, 17 (SE)
    Paella, 56 (SE)
    Pompano en Papillote, 77 (SE)
    Rice, Crabmeat with
      Curried, 22 (SE)
    Royal, Crab, 107 (CC)
    Salad, Bayley's Original West
      Indies, 23 (SE)
    Sandwiches, Chesapeake Bay
      Crab Cake, 28 (SP)
    Sandwiches, Crabmeat, 77 (SS)

    Sandwiches, Crab
      Salad, 16 (SS)
    Sauce Lorenzo, Crab, 22 (SE)
    Seafood au Gratin,
      Baked, 55 (SE)
    Seafood Boil, Bluffton, 55 (SE)
    Seafood Newburg, 54 (SE)
    Soft-Shell Crabs,
      Broiled, 14 (SE)
    Soft-Shell Crabs, Fried, 14 (SE)
    Soft-Shell Crabs,
      Grilled, 14 (SE)
    Soft-Shell Crabs,
      Sautéed, 14 (SE)

    Soufflé, Crabmeat, 20 (SE)
    Soup, Beaufort Cream of
      Crab, 54 (SO)
    Soup, She-Crab, 23 (SE)
    Soup, Spinach and
      Crabmeat, 52 (SO)
    Steamed Blue Crabs, 17 (SE)
    Steamed Crabs, 98 (CE);
      92 (SP)
    Stuffing, Shrimp and
      Crabmeat, 78 (SE)

**Crackers**
    Cake, Gretchen's
      Cracker, 75 (CA)
    Cheesebits, 20 (SO)
    Cheese Wafers, 98 (BB); 92 (CC)
    Cream Cheese Wafers, 98 (BB)
    Date-Nut Squares, 48 (SP)
    Deviled Wafers, 57 (SS)
    Garnish for Cream
      Soups, 20 (SO)
    Moonshine Crackers,
      Maryland, 130 (BR)
    Sesame Crisps, 20 (SO)
    Sippets, 130 (BR); 18 (SO)
    Soda Crackers, 20 (SO)
    Soda Crackers,
      Homemade, 130 (BR)
    Souffléed Crackers, 20 (SO)
    Wheat Crackers, 23 (SO)

**Cranberries**
    Acorn Squash with
      Cranberries, 29 (PO)
    Chicken Breasts, Cranberry
      Baked, 60 (CE)
    Chutney, Hot
      Cranberry, 55 (GR)
    Cocktail, Cranberry
      Juice, 105 (FG)
    Compote, Cranberry, 43 (DE)
    Conserve, Citrus, 31 (GR)
    Conserve, Cranberry, 28 (GR)
    Cooler, Cranberry, 92 (BB)
    Frappé, Cranberry, 114 (CE)
    Glaze, Cranberry, 90 (BE);
      92 (PK)
    Glaze, Cranberry-Raisin, 92 (PK)
    Ham Slice,
      Cranberry-Glazed, 76 (PK)
    Ice, Cranberry, 90 (DE)
    Muffins, Robert Morris Inn
      Cranberry, 101 (BB)
    Pie, Cranberry, 48 (PP)
    Pies, Southern Fried
      Cranberry, 134 (PP)
    Pie with Cheese Pastry,
      Apple-Cranberry, 32 (PP)
    Pork Chops,
      Cranberry-Glazed, 27 (PK)
    Pudding,
      Cranberry-Molasses, 25 (DE)
    Relish, Cranberry-Orange, 56 (FG);
      75 (GR); 43 (SP)
    Salad, Cranberry, 136 (CC)
    Sauce,
      Cranberry-Cumberland, 38 (FG)

    Sherbet, Cranberry, 92 (DE)
    Shrub, 26 (CE)
    Syrup, Cranberry, 113 (SS)
**Crappie**
    Baked Crappie, 115 (SE)
    Creole Fried Crappie, 116 (SE)
    Fried Crappie, 115 (SE)
    Paysanne, Crappie, 116 (SE)
    Skillet Crappie, 116 (SE)
**Crayfish**
    Bisque, Crayfish, 26 (SE)
    Boiled Crayfish, 57 (BB);
      24 (SE)
    Bouillabaisse, New
      Orleans, 55 (SE)

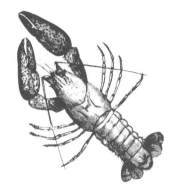

    Étouffée, Crayfish, 25 (SE);
      124 (SO)
    Fried Crayfish, 24 (SE)
    Jambalaya, Crayfish, 24 (SE)
    Pie, Crayfish, 25 (SE)
    Stew, Crayfish, 136 (SO)
    Stuffed Crayfish Heads, 26 (SE)
**Crêpes**
    Basic Dessert Crêpes, 121 (DE)
    Crêpes, 120, 122 (DE)
    Fitzgerald, Crêpes, 121 (DE)
    Soufflé, Crêpes, 122 (DE)
    Suzette, Crêpes, 120 (DE)
**Croquettes**
    Chicken Croquettes, 124 (PO);
      120 (SS)
    Crab Croquettes, 115 (SS)
    Crab Croquettes, Ybor
      City, 21 (SE)
    Dough, Croquette, 21 (SE)
    Ham Croquettes, 89 (PK)
    Okra Croquettes, 66 (VE)
    Riz Isle Brevelle, 25 (CC)
    Salmon Croquettes, 85 (SE);
      46 (SS)
    Sweet Potato
      Croquettes, 96 (VE)
    Veal Croquettes, 80 (BE)
**Croutons**
    Butter-Toasted
      Croutons, 83 (SP)
    Croutons, 130 (BR); 18 (SO)
    Croutons, Baked, 18 (SO)
    Croutons, Cheese, 18 (SO)

---

**BB** *Breakfast & Brunch*  **BE** *Beef, Veal & Lamb*  **BR** *Breads*  **CA** *Cakes*  **CC** *Company's Coming*  **CE** *Celebrations*
**CJ** *Cookie Jar*  **DE** *Just Desserts*  **FG** *Family Gatherings*  **GR** *Gift Receipts*  **PK** *All Pork*  **PO** *Plain & Fancy Poultry*
**PP** *Pies & Pastry*  **SE** *Sea & Stream*  **SO** *Soups & Stews*  **SP** *Sporting Scene*  **SS** *Socials & Soirees*  **VE** *Vegetables*

## Cucumbers

Aspic, Cucumber, 107 (CC)
Braised Cucumbers, 50 (VE)
Canapés, Cucumber
  Ring, 11 (CE)
Combo, Cucumber, 125 (VE)
Dill Chips, 44 (GR)
Dressed Cucumbers, 88 (CE)
Dressed Cucumbers with
  Tomatoes, 116 (SS)
Fried Cucumbers,
  Oklahoma-Style, 49 (VE)
How To Prepare Fresh
  Cucumbers, 48 (VE)
Pickles, Bread and
  Butter, 20 (FG); 43 (GR)
Pickles, Mixed
  Vegetable, 46 (GR)
Pickles, Sweet
  Cucumber, 43 (GR)
Relish, Cucumber, 50 (GR)
Rings, Sweet
  Cucumber, 43 (GR)
Sandwiches, Cucumber, 81 (SS)
Sandwiches, Cucumber and
  Watercress, 52 (SS)

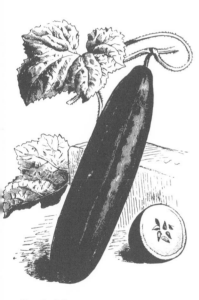

Sandwiches,
  Cucumber-Cheese, 87 (CC)
Sandwiches, Cucumber-Cream
  Cheese, 28 (FG)
Sauce, Cucumber, 31, 127 (SE)
Sautéed Cucumbers,
  Florida, 50 (VE)
Soup, Cold Cucumber, 21 (CC);
  114 (SP)
Soup, Cream of
  Cucumber, 63 (SO)
Sour Cream, Cucumbers
  in, 52 (CC)
Stuffed Cucumbers, 49 (VE)

## Custards

Baked Cup Custard, 56 (DE)
Baked Custard,
  Connemara, 56 (DE)
Baked Custard with Rum
  Sauce, 94 (PO)
Banana Cream
  Pudding, 55 (DE)
Banana Custard
  Pudding, 54 (DE)
Bird's Nest Pudding, 53 (DE)
Boiled Custard, 119 (CE); 50,
  60, 62 (DE); 117 (SS)
Boiled Custard, Easy, 51 (DE)
Boiled Custard, Soft, 50 (DE)
Butterscotch Custard, 52 (DE)
Caramel Custard Petit
  Arnaud, 64 (DE)
Caramel Flan, 63 (DE)
Chocolate Custard,
  Creamy, 52 (DE)
Coconut Cup Custard,
  Baked, 56 (DE)
Crème Brûlée, 63 (DE)
Filling, Creamy
  Custard, 125 (CA)
Flan, Spanish, 136 (FG)
Floating Island,
  Grand, 60 (DE)
Floating Islands, 119 (CC)
Fried Custard, 64 (DE)
Frosting, Custard
  Cream, 124 (CE)
Frozen Custard, 97 (DE);
  93 (SP)
Hen's Nest, A, 59 (DE)
Kiss Pudding, 53 (DE)
Lemon Custard,
  Frozen, 112 (DE)
Mango Custard, 132 (FG)
Mocha Macaroon
  Custard, 58 (DE)
Mushroom-Onion
  Custard, 49 (FG)
Orange Custard, 55 (DE)
Orange Custard Cream, 73 (DE)
Peach Custard, 55 (DE)
Pie, Buttermilk
  Custard, 95 (CE)
Pie, Dewberry Custard, 70 (PP)
Pie, Egg Custard, 54 (PO)
Pie, Egg Custard
  Meringue, 67 (PP)
Pie, Florida Lime
  Custard, 70 (PP)
Pie, Marion Flexner's Apple
  Custard, 69 (PP)
Pie, Mrs. Doc's Egg
  Custard, 67 (PP)
Pie, Old-Fashioned Coconut
  Custard, 71 (PP)
Pie, Sweet Potato
  Custard, 103 (CC); 23 (FG)
Raisin Custard, Baked, 58 (DE)
Royal Custard, 16 (SO)
Sauce, Custard, 70, 76 (DE)
Sauce over Strawberries and
  Raspberries, Chilled
  Custard, 84 (SP)
Sauce, Wine Custard, 137 (DE)
Soft Custard, 59 (DE)
Tipsy Parson, 62 (DE)
Trifle, Classic English, 62 (DE)
Vanilla Custard, 50, 120 (DE)

## Dates

Bars, Dixie Date, 95 (CJ)
Bread, Date Nut, 77 (CC)
Cake, Halloween Date
  Fudge, 102 (CA)
Cake, Orange-Date, 68 (CA)
Cheese Dates, 12 (CE)
Cookies, Alsatian
  Plum, 128 (CJ)
Cookies, Christmas
  Fruit, 117 (CJ)
Cookies, Crunchy
  Skillet, 79 (CJ)
Cookies, Date Drop, 50 (CJ)
Cookies, Date Pinwheel, 70 (CJ)
Cookies, Stuffed Date, 50 (CJ)
Kisses, Date, 30 (CE)
Macaroons, Date-Nut, 15 (CJ)
Muffins, Date-Bacon, 113 (BR)
Porcupines, 79 (CJ)
Pudding, Bishop
  Whipple, 20 (DE)
Pudding, Date, 127 (FG)
Pudding, Date Tapioca, 17 (DE)
Pudding with Cherry Sauce,
  Date, 21 (DE)
Roll, Date-Nut, 80 (GR)
Rolls, Grecian Date, 65 (CJ)
Roll, Tutti-Frutti
  Icebox, 129 (DE)
Sandwiches, Date Roll, 61 (SS)
Sandwiches, Open-Face
  Date-Nut, 81 (SS)
Squares, Date, 81 (CC)
Squares, Date-Nut, 48 (SP)
Stuffed Dates, 73 (CC)
Surprises, Date, 82 (CJ)
Tarts, Miniature
  Date-Pecan, 124 (PP)
Triangles, Date, 136 (PP)

## Desserts. *See also* specific types.

Amaretto Mousse, 13 (SP)
Apple Brown Betty, 39 (DE)
Apple Casserole, 48 (SP)
Apple-Cherry Crisp, 97 (PK)
Apple Crisp, 36 (DE)
Apple Crumble, 36 (DE)
Apple Pandowdy, 39 (DE)
Applesauce à la Mode, 34 (SP)
Apples, Baked Ginger, 69 (BB)
Apples, Harvest Baked, 57 (SS)
Apple Slices, Fried, 56 (SP)
Apples, Moravian
  Spiced, 19 (CC)
Apples, Stuffed Baked, 36 (DE)
Apricot Balls, 96 (FG)
Apricot Fool, 32 (DE)
Apricot-Macaroon
  Tapioca, 85 (SS)
Bananas, Baked, 23 (BB)
Bananas Foster, 104 (DE)
Bananas in Wine, 41 (DE)
Bananas with Lemon Sauce,
  Baked, 41 (DE)
Berry Roly-Poly, 53 (CC)

*New Orleans public school officials pose in the midst of dessert, 1912.*

Desserts, *continued*

Blancmange, 123 (CC); 59 (DE)

Blancmange with
Strawberries, 76 (DE)

Blueberry Buckle, 42 (DE)

Blueberry Grunt, 42 (DE)

Blueberry Soufflé, 66 (DE)

Bourbon Soufflé, The Greenbrier
Cold, 80 (DE)

Buñuelos, 59 (FG)

Caramel Flan, 63 (DE)

Charlottes

Apple Charlotte,
Classic, 37 (DE)

Apricot Charlotte, 82 (DE)

Chocolate Charlotte, 83 (DE)

Chocolate Mint
Charlotte, 85 (DE)

Chocolate Rum
Charlotte, 83 (DE)

Orange Charlotte, 84 (DE);
92 (SS)

Pumpkin-Almond
Charlotte, 63 (CC)

Russe, Charlotte, 82 (DE)

Strawberry Charlotte, 84 (DE)

Cherries Jubilee, 104 (DE)

Cherry Squares, 59 (SP)

Chestnut Cream, 73 (DE)

Chestnut Soufflé, 67 (DE)

Chocolate

Charlotte, Chocolate, 83 (DE)

Charlotte, Chocolate
Mint, 85 (DE)

Charlotte, Chocolate
Rum, 83 (DE)

Cream Puffs Deluxe,
Chocolate-Filled, 122 (DE)

Éclairs, 124 (DE)

Frozen Chocolate
Dessert, 100 (SS)

Marlow, Chocolate, 107 (DE)

Marshmallow Icebox Dessert,
Chocolate, 85 (DE)

Mousse, Chocolate, 78,
108 (DE)

Pots de Crème au
Chocolat, 65 (DE)

Pudding, Chocolate
Sponge, 24 (DE)

Roll, Famous Chocolate
Refrigerator, 86 (DE)

S'Mores, 95 (SP)

Soufflé, Dixie
Chocolate, 65 (DE)

Strawberries, Chocolate
Dipped, 129 (SS)

Torte, Chocolate, 119 (DE)

Coconut Cream with Caramel
Sauce, 75 (DE)

Coffee Bavarian, 72 (DE)

Coffee Mousse, 79 (DE)

Compote Amulet, 26 (CC)

Cranberry Compote, 43 (DE)

Cream Puffs, Basic, 122 (DE)

Cream Puffs, Miniature, 40 (CE)

Desserts, *continued*
  Cream Puff Swan
    Variation, 122 (DE)
  Crème Brûlée, 63 (DE)
  Crêpes, Basic Dessert, 121 (DE)
  Crêpes Fitzgerald, 121 (DE)
  Crêpes Soufflé, 122 (DE)
  Crêpes Suzette, 120 (DE)
  Diples (Rolled Honey
    Pastry), 64 (FG)
  Filbert Cream with Apricot
    Sauce, 75 (DE)
  Flan, Spanish, 136 (FG)
  Floating Island, Grand, 60 (DE)
  Floating Islands, 119 (CC)
  Frozen
    Almond Parfait, Burnt, 111 (DE)
    Applesauce Marlow, 106 (DE)
    Apricot Loaf, Frozen, 111 (DE)
    Banana Marlow, 107 (DE)
    Biscuit Glace aux
      Marrons, 44 (SS)
    Biscuit Tortoni, 112 (DE)
    Chocolate Dessert,
      Frozen, 100 (SS)
    Chocolate Marlow, 107 (DE)
    Chocolate Mousse, 108 (DE)
    Ice Cream Cups, 104 (DE)
    Ice Cream Pie, Mile
      High, 105 (DE)
    Ice Cream
      Sandwiches, 93 (SS)
    Lemon Custard,
      Frozen, 112 (DE)
    Lemon Dessert,
      Frozen, 112 (DE)
    Maple Parfait, 111 (DE)
    Mocha Ice Cream
      Roll, 102 (DE)
    Orange Marlow, 107 (DE)
    Orange Mousse, 108 (DE)
    Parfait with Raspberry Sauce,
      Angel, 111 (DE)
    Peach Mousse, 109 (DE)
    Pecan Balls with Fudge Sauce,
      Neiman-Marcus
      Toasted, 105 (DE)
    Pineapple Delight,
      Frozen, 112 (DE)
    Raspberry Mousse, 109 (DE)
    Strawberry Mousse, 109 (DE)
    Strawberry Surprise, 47 (SS)
  Fruit
    Ambrosia, 30 (DE); 57 (FG)
    Ambrosia, Holiday, 30 (DE)
    Cantaloupe Melon
      Cups, 32 (DE)
    Compote, Hot Spiced, 32 (SP)
    Compote, Sunrise, 30 (DE)
    Sauce, Tropical
      Fruit, 135 (DE)
    Strudel, Fruit, 101 (FG)
    Timbales, Dessert, 120 (DE)
    Watermelon Bowl, 32 (DE)
    Wine Jelly Mold, 70 (DE)
  Gâteau aux Amandes, 136 (SS)

Gorp, 78 (SP)
Hen's Nest, A, 59 (DE)
Honey Flummery, 75 (DE)
Kossuth Cakes, 125 (DE)
Krum Kake, 20 (FG)
Lemon Charlotte Russe, 15 (PK)
Lemon-Coconut
  Crunch, 127 (DE)
Lemon Curd Trifle, 61 (CE)
Lemon Soufflé, Hot, 67 (DE)
Maids of Honour, 119 (CC)
Mango Flameador, 44 (DE)
Maraschino Cream, 75 (CC)
Meringue Hearts with Pastel
  Sherbets, Pale Green, 110 (FG)
Mocha Macaroon
  Dessert, 102 (DE)
Nectarines, Brandied, 47 (DE)
Orange Custard Cream, 73 (DE)
Oranges, Ambrosial, 31 (DE)
Oranges in Wine Sauce, 20 (SP)
Parfaits
  Almond Parfait,
    Burnt, 111 (DE)
  Angel Parfait with Raspberry
    Sauce, 111 (DE)
  Crème de Menthe
    Parfaits, 111 (CC); 103 (DE)
  Grapefruit Parfait,
    Texas, 81 (DE)
  Lemon Parfait, 116 (SP)
  Maple Parfait, 111 (DE)
  Strawberry Rum
    Parfait, 133 (CC)
Peach Crisp, 44 (DE)
Peaches, Baked, 44 (DE)
Peaches, Bourbon, 131 (SP)
Peaches, Brandied, 123 (CC)
Peaches over Frozen Custard,
  Bourbon-Blazed, 93 (SP)
Peaches with Raspberries,
  Fresh, 33 (DE)
Pear Crumble, 46 (DE)
Pears, Gorgonzola, 134 (FG)
Pears Julianne,
  Poached, 93 (PO)
Pears, Poached, 46 (DE)
Pecan Delight, Wyatt's, 128 (DE)
Peppermint Bavarian, 71 (DE)
Petits Pots de Crème au
  Café, 65 (DE)
Prune Whip, 47 (DE)
Rainbow Alaska, 103 (DE)
Raspberry Fool, 46 (CC)
Rhubarb Crumble, 47 (DE)
Rosettes, 20 (FG)
Rum Bavarian Cream, 72 (DE)
Rum Mousse, Snowden
  House, 79 (DE)
Sauces
  Apricot Sauce, 75 (DE)
  Blackberry Sauce, 104 (FG)
  Blueberry Sauce, 36 (BB);
    66 (DE)
  Bourbon Sauce, 136 (DE);
    44 (PP); 15 (SP)

  Brandy Sauce, 24 (DE)
  Brown Sugar Sauce, 20 (DE)
  Butterscotch Sauce, 85 (GR)
  Butterscotch Sauce, Frances
    Virginia Tea Room, 132 (DE)
  Butterscotch Sauce, High
    Hampton, 132 (DE)
  Caramel Sauce, 75, 132 (DE);
    85 (GR)
  Cherry Sauce, 70 (CA);
    21 (DE)
  Chocolate Sauce, 105,
    133 (DE); 82 (FG); 86 (GR)
  Chocolate Sauce,
    Rich, 102 (DE)
  Chocolate Sauce,
    Sherried, 133 (DE)
  Custard Sauce, 70, 76 (DE)
  Custard Sauce over Strawberries
    and Raspberries,
    Chilled, 84 (SP)
  Eggnog Sauce,
    Irma's, 136 (DE)

  Fig Sauce, 88 (GR)
  Fruit Sauce,
    Tropical, 135 (DE)
  Fruit Starter,
    Brandied, 135 (DE)
  Fudge Sauce, 105 (DE);
    111 (PO)
  Fudge Sauce, Hot, 133 (DE);
    86 (GR)
  Grape Wine Sauce, 13 (DE)
  Hard Sauce, 116 (CE);
    135 (DE); 49 (FG)
  Hard Sauce,
    Brandied, 37 (CA)
  Hard Sauce, Sherried,
    12 (CC); 40 (FG)
  Lemon Cream Sauce, Mary
    Randolph's, 86 (GR)
  Lemon Hard Sauce, 36 (DE)
  Lemon Sauce, 13, 18,
    41 (DE); 54 (SS)
  Lemon Sauce,
    Creamy, 136 (DE)
  Lemon Sauce, Old-Fashioned
    Golden, 137 (DE)
  Lemon Sauce, Tangy, 65 (CA)
  Lemon Sauce, Tart, 137 (DE)
  Orange-Pineapple
    Sauce, 134 (DE)

---

**BB** *Breakfast & Brunch*  **BE** *Beef, Veal & Lamb*  **BR** *Breads*  **CA** *Cakes*  **CC** *Company's Coming*  **CE** *Celebrations*
**CJ** *Cookie Jar*  **DE** *Just Desserts*  **FG** *Family Gatherings*  **GR** *Gift Receipts*  **PK** *All Pork*  **PO** *Plain & Fancy Poultry*
**PP** *Pies & Pastry*  **SE** *Sea & Stream*  **SO** *Soups & Stews*  **SP** *Sporting Scene*  **SS** *Socials & Soirees*  **VE** *Vegetables*

Desserts, Sauces, *continued*
    Orange Sauce, 137 (DE);
      88 (GR)
    Peach Sauce, 133 (DE)
    Peanut Butter Sauce, 82 (FG)
    Plum Pudding Sauce, 26 (DE)
    Raisin-Chocolate
      Sauce, 86 (GR)
    Raspberry Sauce, 111 (DE)
    Rum Butter Sauce, 88 (GR)
    Rum Sauce, 25 (DE); 94 (PO)
    Sabayon Sauce, 40 (SS)
    Sherry Sauce, 88 (GR)
    Sherry Sauce, Hot, 137 (DE)
    Strawberry Sauce,
      Brandied, 134 (DE)
    Strawberry Sauce,
      Fresh, 134 (DE)
    Strawberry Sauce over Vanilla
      Ice Cream, 56 (SP)

    Tutti-Frutti, 84 (GR)
    Vanilla Sauce,
      Creamy, 22 (DE)
    Vanilla Sauce,
      Greenbrier, 136 (DE)
    Whipped Cream-Chocolate
      Sauce, 16 (DE)
    Whiskey Sauce, 12 (DE)
    Wine Custard Sauce, 137 (DE)
    Wine Sauce, 27, 137 (DE)
    Wine Sauce, Oranges in, 20 (SP)
Snowballs, 111 (PO); 33 (SS)
Snowy Nests with Pineapple and
  Spun Sugar, 133 (SS)
Sopaipillas, 123 (BR); 66 (CC)
Soups
    Apple Soup, Cold, 38 (SO)
    Cantaloupe Soup,
      Cold, 38 (SO)
    Champagne-Lemon
      Soup, 38 (SO)
    Cherry Soup, Cold, 40 (SO)
    Fruit Soup, Dried, 43 (SO)
    Fruit Soup,
      Scandinavian, 43 (SO)
    Papaya Soup, Cold, 40 (SO)
    Peach-Orange Soup,
      Cold, 41 (SO)
    Peach Soup, Cold, 41 (SO)
    Raspberry Soup,
      Chilled, 42 (SO)
    Strawberry Soup, 42 (SO)

    Strawberry Soup,
      Marilyn's, 42 (SO)
    Strawberries à la Mode, 34 (DE)
    Strawberries, Chocolate
      Dipped, 129 (SS)
    Strawberries, Frosted, 34 (DE)
    Strawberries in Wine, 34 (DE)
    Strawberries, Rose Hill, 33 (DE)
    Strawberries with Crème
      Fraîche, 37 (CE)
    Strawberries with Rich
      Cream, 23 (SP)
    Strawberry Bavarian
      Cream, 71 (DE)
    Strawberry Delight, 81 (DE);
      107 (FG)
    Strawberry Flambé, 136 (SS)
    Strawberry Roulage, 87 (DE)
    Syllabub, 123 (CE)
    Syllabub, Deep South, 134 (CE)
    Timbales, Dessert, 120 (DE)
    Tipsy Parson, 62 (DE)
    Tortes
      Almond Brittle
        Torte, 126 (DE)
      Bars, Torte, 18 (SS)
      Blitz Torte, 126 (DE)
      Chocolate Torte, 119 (DE)
      Coconut Crunch
        Torte, 127 (DE)
      Huguenot Torte, 123 (CE);
        40 (DE)
      Opa's Torte, 125 (DE)
      Schaum Torte, 118 (DE)
      Strawberry Meringue
        Torte, 118 (DE)
    Trifle, Classic English, 62 (DE)
    Trifle, Mrs. Howard's, 117 (SS)
    Tutti-Frutti Icebox
      Roll, 129 (DE)
    Wine Jelly Mold, 70 (DE)
    Wine Jelly with Sabayon
      Sauce, 40 (SS)
**Dewberries**
    Cobbler, Dewberry, 37 (SP)
    Pie, Dewberry Custard, 70 (PP)
**Doughnuts**
    a Yankee Cake,
      Doughnuts—, 122 (BR)
    Banana Puffs, 117 (BB)
    Beignets, 32 (BB)
    Beignets, French
      Market, 122 (BR)
    Biscuit Puffs, 126 (BR)
    Breakfast Puffs, 61 (BB)
    Cake Doughnuts, 124 (BR)
    Calas "Tout" Chaud, 127 (BR)
    Crullers, 116 (BB)
    Doughnuts, 134 (CE)
    Glazed Doughnuts, 45 (BB)
    Holes, Doughnut, 126 (BR)
    Molasses Doughnuts, 124 (BR)
    Non de Scripts, 127 (BR)
    Orange Doughnuts, 124 (BR)
    Orange Doughnuts,
      Fredericksburg, 117 (BB)

    Potato Doughnuts, 126 (BR)
    Sopaipillas, 123 (BR); 66 (CC)
    Toasted Doughnuts, 82 (BB)
    Twists, Doughnut, 123 (BR)
**Dove**
    Plantation Dove, 50 (SP)
**Duck and Duckling**
    à la Carte, Duckling, 42 (PO)
    Apples and Raisins, Ducklings
      with, 60 (CC)

    Dressing, Wild Duck, 42 (SP)
    Fried Duckling, Creole, 83 (PO)
    Garlic-Roasted
      Duckling, 45 (PO)
    Gumbo, Duck, 63 (PO);
      116 (SO); 59 (SP)
    Roast Ducklings
      Bigarade, 44 (PO)
    Roast Ducklings
      Supreme, 43 (PO)
    Roast Ducklings with Cornbread
      Stuffing, 42 (PO)
    Roast Duckling,
      Virginia, 42 (PO)
    Roast Duckling with Apple
      Stuffing, 41 (PO)
    Roast Duckling with Orange
      Sauce, 43 (PO)
    Roast Duck, Southern
      Style, 132 (CC)
    Rosy Duckling, 100 (PO)
    Smoked Duck, 40 (SP)
**Dumplings**
    Apple Dumplings,
      Baked, 128 (PP)
    Apple Dumplings,
      Boiled, 129 (PP)
    Beef Stew with Dumplings,
      Wine, 128 (SO)
    Blackberry Dumplings, 130 (PP)
    Chicken and
      Dumplings, 121 (FG)
    Cooking Dumplings, 133 (PO)
    Cornmeal Dumplings, Ham
      Hocks with, 124 (PK)
    Cornmeal Dumplings, Turnip
      Greens and, 54 (VE)
    Danish Dumplings, 13 (SO)

---

**BB** *Breakfast & Brunch*   **BE** *Beef, Veal & Lamb*   **BR** *Breads*   **CA** *Cakes*   **CC** *Company's Coming*   **CE** *Celebrations*
**CJ** *Cookie Jar*   **DE** *Just Desserts*   **FG** *Family Gatherings*   **GR** *Gift Receipts*   **PK** *All Pork*   **PO** *Plain & Fancy Poultry*
**PP** *Pies & Pastry*   **SE** *Sea & Stream*   **SO** *Soups & Stews*   **SP** *Sporting Scene*   **SS** *Socials & Soirees*   **VE** *Vegetables*

Dumplings, *continued*
  Drop Dumplings, Carolina
    Chicken and, 18 (PO)
  Drop Dumplings, Green Peas
    and, 78 (VE)
  Drop Dumplings, Texas-Style,
    Chicken and, 18 (PO)
  Filled Dumplings, 84 (SO)
  Light Dumplings, Stewed
    Chicken with, 18 (PO)
  Liver and Dumplings, 114 (BE)
  Liver Dumplings, 130 (PK)
  Liver Dumplings, Beef Soup
    with, 32 (SO)
  Noodle Soup, Chicken, 22 (PO)
  Peach Dumplings,
    Mother's, 130 (PP)
  Plump Dumplings, Chicken
    and, 21 (PO)
  Potato Dumplings, 21 (PO)
  Quenelles, 15 (SO)
  Rolled Dumplings, 13 (SO)
  Rolled Dumplings, Chicken
    and, 20 (PO)
  Slick Dumplings, Chicken
    and, 20 (PO)
  Slippery Dumplings, Chicken
    and, 19 (PO)
  Veal Pot Roast with
    Dumplings, 65 (BE)

**E**

**Eggplant**
  Baked Eggplant, 51 (VE)
  Broiled Eggplant, 51 (VE)
  Chicken Eggplant Francesca,
    Cavatoni, 95 (PO)
  Fried Eggplant, George
    Washington's, 52 (VE)
  Fritters, Eggplant, 51 (VE)
  Ham-Stuffed Eggplant, 85 (PK)
  How To Prepare Fresh
    Eggplant, 51 (VE)
  Louisiana-Style
    Eggplant, 25 (CC)
  Ratatouille,
    Italian-Style, 129 (VE)
  Scalloped Eggplant, 102 (CC)
  Smothered Eggplant with
    Shrimp, 52 (VE)
  Soup, Cream of
    Eggplant, 63 (SO)
  Stuffed Eggplant, Oaklawn
    Gardens', 52 (VE)
**Eggs**
  au Gratin, Eggs, 46 (SS)
  Baked Eggs, 118 (BB)

  Balls, Egg, 15 (SO)
  Belle Meade Specials, 24 (SP)
  Benedict, Weidmann's
    Eggs, 122 (BB)
  Braid, Swiss Egg, 47 (BR)
  Brandied Cream Sauce, Eggs
    with, 79 (FG)
  Bread, Egg, 35 (BR)
  Bread, Egg Light, 46 (BR)
  Burritos de Huevos con
    Chorizo, 119 (BB)
  Casserole, Baked Creole
    Egg, 123 (BB)
  Casserole, Cheesy Egg, 127 (BB)
  Casserole, Egg, 118 (SP)
  Casserole, Jo's Egg, 110 (CE)
  Casserole, Sausage and
    Egg, 76 (BB)
  Chausseur, Eggs, 47 (SP)
  Cheese Nest Eggs, 127 (BB)
  Cornbread, Cassie's
    Egg, 14 (BR)
  Country-Style, Eggs, 12 (BB)
  Creamed Eggs in Toast
    Cups, 78 (BB)
  Easter Eggs, Homemade
    Candy, 52 (CE)
  Easter Eggs,
    Natural-Dye, 52 (CE)
  Eggnog, 21, 136 (CE)

*As a 1915 producer, this Beltsville, Maryland, hen performed well.*

Eggs, *continued*
  Eggnog, Christmas, 50 (FG)
  Eggnog, Morning, 95 (BB)
  Florentine, Eggs, 63 (BB)
  Fried Eggs, 65 (PK)
  Fried Eggs, Country, 11 (BB)
  Ham and Eggs
    Alexandria, 50 (BB)
  Huevos Rancheros, 38 (BB)
  Noodles, Homemade
    Egg, 97 (CC)
  Omelets
    Cheese Omelet, 121 (BB)
    Chicken Liver Omelet, 129 (PO)
    Chicken Omelet, 122 (PO)
    Corn Omelet, 121 (BB)
    Ham Omelet, Fluffy, 120 (BB)
    Herb Omelet, Fresh, 120 (BB)
    Oyster Omelet, 86 (BB)
    Sour Cream Omelet, 121 (BB)
    Veal Omelet,
      Open-Face, 58 (BB)
  Onion and Eggs,
    Oklahoma, 70 (VE)
  Pastry Shells, Egg, 20 (PP)
  Pie, Egg Custard, 54 (PO)
  Pie, Egg Custard
    Meringue, 67 (PP)
  Pie, Eggnog, 106 (PP)
  Pie, Mrs. Doc's Egg
    Custard, 67 (PP)
  Poached Eggs, 118 (BB)
  Poke Greens, Arkansas, 57 (VE)
  Ramekins,
    Spinach-Egg, 103 (VE)
  Riced Eggs, 112 (FG)
  Salad, Egg, 97 (FG)
  Sandwiches, Egg Salad
    Finger, 84 (FG)

  Sandwiches,
    Olive-Mustard, 28 (FG)
  Sandwiches,
    Tomato-Egg, 11 (SS)
  Sardou, Eggs, 122 (BB)
  Sauce, Asparagus and Peas with
    Egg, 12 (VE)
  Sauce, Egg, 129 (SE)
  Sauce, Egg-Lemon, 56 (CE)
  Sauce, Irma's Eggnog, 136 (DE)

Scotch Eggs, 136 (SP)
Scrambled
  Brains Scrambled with
    Eggs, 127 (PK)
  Mushrooms and Onions,
    Scrambled Eggs
    with, 119 (BB)
  Rice, Scrambled Eggs
    and, 119 (BB)
  Rumbled Eggs, 20 (BB)
  Scrambled Eggs, 31 (BB)
Soft-Cooked Eggs, 119 (BB)
Soup, Avgolemono, 33 (SO)
Soup, Egg, 33 (SO)
Spread, Bacon and Egg
  Sandwich, 120 (PK)
Steak and Eggs, 22 (BB)
Stuffed
  Casserole, Stuffed Egg and
    Mushroom, 124 (BB)
  Deviled Eggs, 53 (CC);
    77 (PO); 75 (SP)
  Deviled Eggs, Frilly, 35 (FG)
  Deviled Eggs on
    Watercress, 120 (CC)
  Deviled Eggs with
    Anchovies, 52 (SS)
  Dressed Eggs, Turkey
    Feet, 13 (FG)
  Lobster-Stuffed Eggs,
    111 (SP) Stuffed Eggs,
    Spinach with, 105 (VE)
  Tomato Eggs, 123 (BB)

**Enchiladas**
  Green Enchiladas, 35 (CC)
  Texas Enchiladas, 48 (BE)

**Escargots**
  Escargots, 81 (CE)

**Étouffés**
  Catfish Étouffée, 112 (SE)
  Chicken Étouffée, 25 (PO)
  Crayfish Étouffée, 25 (SE);
    124 (SO)
  Shrimp Étouffée, 124 (SO)

**F**

**Figs**
  Cake, Fig Preserves, 45 (CA);
    15 (SS)
  Cake, Fresh Fig Layer, 44 (CA)
  Cobbler, Fresh Fig, 36 (PP)
  Cookies, Fig Drop, 50 (CJ)
  Filling, Fresh Fig, 44 (CA)
  Jam, Fig, 23 (GR)
  Muffins, Fresh Fig, 62 (BB)
  Pickled Figs, 36 (GR)
  Pie, Fig, 35 (PP)
  Pie, Fig Streusel, 35 (PP)
  Pie, Meeting Street Fresh
    Fig, 109 (PP)

  Preserves, Fig, 18 (BB); 17 (GR)
  Pudding, Fig, 116 (CE)
  Sauce, Fig, 88 (GR)
  Stuffed Figs, Holiday, 81 (GR)
**Filbert**
  Filbert Cream with Apricot
    Sauce, 75 (DE)
  Filbert-Graham Piecrust, 21 (PP)

**Fish.** *See also* Seafood.
  Balls, Fried Fish, 122 (SE)
  Good to Know, 134-137 (SE)
  Bouillabaisse, 136 (SO)
  Chowder, Florida Fish, 87 (SO)
  Cod Chowder, 88 (SO)
  Fried Fish, Ogeechee
    River, 96 (CE)
  Gefilte Fish, 59 (CE)
  How to Steak or Fillet a
    Fish, 134 (SE)
  Paella, 56 (SE)
  Pudding, Fish, 24 (SS)
  Sauce, Fish Basting, 131 (SE)
  Stew, Fish, 102 (SP)
  Stock, Basic Fish, 132 (SE)
  Stock, Fish, 12 (SO)
**Flounder**
  Batter-Fried Flounder, 66 (SE)
  Broiled Flounder with
    Mushroom-Wine
    Sauce, 65 (SE)
  Broiled Stuffed Flounder
    Fillets, 65 (SE)
  Court Bouillon,
    Flounder, 66 (SE)
  Crab, Flounder Stuffed
    with, 62 (SE)
  Fillet de Flounder à
    l'Orly, 66 (SE)
  Fillet of Flounder
    Marguéry, 63 (SE)
  Fillets with Shrimp Stuffing,
    Flounder, 64 (SE)
  Papillote, Flounder en, 64 (SE)
  Seafood au Gratin,
    Baked, 55 (SE)
**Frankfurters**
  Barbecue Sauce, Franks
    in, 111 (PK)

---

**BB** *Breakfast & Brunch*   **BE** *Beef, Veal & Lamb*   **BR** *Breads*   **CA** *Cakes*   **CC** *Company's Coming*   **CE** *Celebrations*
**CJ** *Cookie Jar*   **DE** *Just Desserts*   **FG** *Family Gatherings*   **GR** *Gift Receipts*   **PK** *All Pork*   **PO** *Plain & Fancy Poultry*
**PP** *Pies & Pastry*   **SE** *Sea & Stream*   **SO** *Soups & Stews*   **SP** *Sporting Scene*   **SS** *Socials & Soirees*   **VE** *Vegetables*

Frankfurters, *continued*
  Condiments, Frankfurters
    with, 95 (SP)
  Corny Dogs, 111 (PK)
  Kraut and Frankfurter
    Skillet, 112 (PK)
  Mixed Grill, 58 (PK)
  Soup, Lentil, 98 (SO)
**French Toast**
  French Toast, 112 (BB)
  Orange French Toast, 112 (BB)
  Pain Perdu, 113 (BB)
**Fritters**
  Apple Fritters, 36 (BB);
    128 (BR)
  Arlington Fritters, 127 (BR)
  Carrot Fritters, 36 (VE)
  Clam Fritters, 11 (SE)
  Conch Fritters, 13 (SE)
  Corn Fritters, 128 (BR); 46 (VE)
  Eggplant Fritters, 51 (VE)
  Fruit Fritters, 128 (BR)
  Parsnip Fritters, 74 (VE)
  Pineapple Fritters, 116 (BB)
  Potato Fritters, 92 (VE)
  Pumpkin Fritters, Smith
    House, 128 (BR)
  Rice Fritters, 129 (BR)
  Shrimp Fritters, 47 (SE)
**Frostings, Fillings, and Toppings**
  Almond-Coconut
    Filling, 117 (FG)
  Almond Frosting, 126 (DE)
  Apricot Filling, 70 (BR);
    107 (CA)
  Biscuit Topping, 41 (SE)
  Bourbon Frosting, Bluegrass
    White, 134 (CA)
  Brown Sugar Caramel
    Icing, 56 (CA)
  Brown Sugar Frosting,
    120 (CA)
  Brown Sugar Water, 20 (CJ)
  Butter Cream Frosting, 105,
    113 (CA)
  Buttercream Frosting, 117 (FG)
  Butter Frosting, 77 (FG)
  Butter Frosting,
    Browned, 135 (CA)
  Butter Frosting, Fluffy, 70 (FG)
  Butter Frosting, Rich, 67 (CA)
  Butter Frosting,
    Williamsburg, 21 (CA)
  Butter Glaze, Burnt, 22 (CJ)
  Buttermilk Candy
    Frosting, 45 (CA)
  Caramel Cream Frosting, 43,
    102 (CA)
  Caramel Frosting, 22, 49,
    84 (CA)
  Caramel Frosting,
    Heritage, 47 (CA)
  Caramel Frosting,
    Sorghum, 136 (CA)
  Caramelized Frosting, 130 (CA)
  Cherry Filling, 98 (CA)
  Cherry Frosting, 29 (CE)
  Cherry Glaze, 104 (BB)
  Chocolate-Bourbon
    Frosting, 99 (FG)

Chocolate Bourbon
  Frosting, 89 (SS)
Chocolate Butter
  Frosting, 24 (CA); 124 (DE)
Chocolate Filling,
  Creamy, 40 (CJ)
Chocolate Frosting, 74 (BB); 16,
  82, 83, 125, 137 (CA);
  82 (CC); 125 (DE); 67 (FG)
Chocolate Frosting,
  Easy, 84 (CA)
Chocolate Frosting,
  Glossy, 137 (CA)
Chocolate Frosting,
  Quick, 137 (CA)
Chocolate Frosting,
  Rich, 137 (CA)
Chocolate Frosting,
  Special, 108 (CA)
Chocolate Fudge
  Frosting, 101 (CA)
Chocolate Glaze, 29 (CJ);
  75 (SS)
Chocolate Icing, 27 (CA)
Chocolate Pastry
  Cream, 122 (DE)
Chocolate-Peanut
  Frosting, 81 (CA)

Cider Filling, 59 (CC)
Cider Frosting, Creamy, 59 (CC)
Cinnamon Frosting,
  Buttery, 50 (CA)
Cinnamon Glaze, 46 (BB)
Citrus Icing, Tangy, 135 (CA)
Cocoa Cream Frosting, 104 (CE)
Coconut Filling, 25 (CA)
Coconut-Pecan Filling, 27 (CA)
Coconut-Pineapple
  Glaze, 92 (PK)
Coconut Topping, 70 (SP)
Coconut Topping,
  Toasted, 74 (CA)
Cranberry Glaze, 90 (BE);
  92 (PK)
Cranberry-Raisin Glaze, 92 (PK)
Cream Cheese Frosting, 25,
  51 (CA); 85 (CE)
Cream Cheese Glaze, 102 (CE)
Cream Filling, 33 (CA)
Cream Frosting, 69 (CA)
Cream Frosting,
  Cooked, 33 (CA)
Crème Pâtissière, 124 (DE)
Crumb Topping, 105 (BB)
Crumb Topping, Coffee Cake
  with, 117 (BR)

*Spinning sugar from* Fancy Ices, *1894.*

Frostings, Fillings, and Toppings,
  *continued*
  Custard, Boiled, 117 (SS)
  Custard Cream
    Frosting, 124 (CE)
  Custard Filling,
    Creamy, 125 (CA)
  Decorator Frosting, 91 (CC);
    134 (CJ)
  Decorator Icing, 67 (FG)
  Divinity Frosting, 132 (CA);
    83 (FG)
  Drippy Icing, 80 (CA)
  Easter Dawn Frosting, 49 (CC)
  Egg Nog Icing, 46 (CA)
  Fig Filling, Fresh, 44 (CA)
  Fluffy Filling, 63 (CA)
  Fluffy Frosting, 103 (CA)

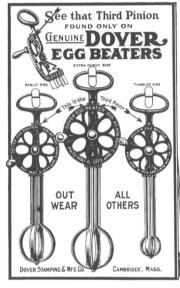

  Fruit Filling, Dried, 123 (CJ)
  Fruit Filling, Kentucky, 45 (CA)
  Fudge Frosting, Dark, 82 (CA)
  Fudge Frosting, Quick, 78 (CA)
  Grape Filling, 30 (CA)
  Grape Frosting, 30 (CA)
  Honey-Crisp Topping, 64 (CA)
  Honey Glaze, 26 (PK)
  Lemon Butter Cream Frosting,
    135 (CA); 53 (CJ); 84 (FG)
  Lemon Cream Frosting, 33 (CA);
    127 (SP)
  Lemon Filling, 33, 103 (CA)
  Lemon Filling, Tart, 127 (CA)
  Lemon Fluffy Frosting, 115 (CA)
  Lemon Frosting, 44 (CE);
    90 (CJ)
  Lemon Frosting,
    Creamy, 65 (CA)
  Lemon Glaze, 75 (CA)
  Lemon Jelly Filling, 18 (CA)
  Lemon-Orange Frosting, 18 (CA)

Lemon Seven-Minute
  Frosting, 132 (CA)
Lord Baltimore Filling, 13 (CA)
Marshmallow Frosting, 25,
  26 (CA)
Marshmallow Glaze, 93 (CA)
Meringue, Basic, 24 (PP)
Mint Frosting, 75 (SS)
Mocha Frosting, 29 (CA);
  54 (SS)
Mocha Icing, Creamy, 29 (CA)
Mushroom Pâté Filling, 12 (BE)
Orange Butter Frosting, 65 (SS)
Orange Coconut Filling, 22 (CA)
Orange Filling, 100, 126 (CA)
Orange Frosting, 102, 132 (CA);
  75 (SS)
Orange Glaze, 68 (CA); 98 (SP)
Orange Glaze, Baked, 49 (PK)
Ornamental Frosting, 107 (CA)
Ornamental Icing, 107 (CA)
Pastel Icing, 82 (SS)
Peach Filling, 117 (DE)
Peanut Butter Frosting, 51 (CA)
Peanut Butter Spice
  Frosting, 136 (CA)
Pecan Topping, Toasted, 96 (CA)
Peppermint Frosting, 133 (CA)
Peppermint Silhouette
  Frosting, 133 (CA)
Pineapple Filling, 70 (BR);
  137 (PP)
Pineapple Frosting, 123 (FG)
Pineapple Glaze, 12 (CC)
Pineapple Meringue, 25 (PP)
Pineapple Topping, 113 (CA)
Powdered Sugar
  Frosting, 133 (CJ)
Powdered Sugar Glaze, 64 (BR);
  58 (CJ)
Powdered Sugar Icing, 49 (CJ)
Powdered Sugar
  Meringue, 25 (PP)
Prune Filling, 70 (BR)
Quick 'n' Easy Frosting, 74 (CA)
Raisin Filling, 82 (CJ)
Rocky Mountain Filling, 15 (CA)
Royal Frosting, 52 (CE);
  135 (GR)
Royal Icing, 13 (SP); 71 (SS)
Rum-Butter Mixture, 80 (BB)
Rum Cream, 63 (CC)
Sea Foam Frosting, 132 (CA)
Seven-Minute Double Boiler
  Frosting, 98 (CA)
Seven-Minute Frosting, 85,
  93 (SS)
Sour Cream Chocolate
  Frosting, 28 (CA)
Spiced Whipped Cream, 57 (CA)
Stay-Soft Frosting, 136 (CA)
Streusel Topping, 137 (CC)
Sweet Bun Topping, 67 (BR)
Sweet Potato Filling, 126 (CE)
Tutti-Frutti Filling, 31 (CA)
Unbaked Meringue, 25 (PP)

Vanilla Butter Frosting, 86 (CA)
White Frosting, 22 (CA)
White Frosting, Fluffy, 55,
  95 (CA); 13 (FG)
White Frosting,
  Seven-Minute, 134 (CA)
White Icing, Fluffy, 134 (CA)
**Fruit.** *See also* specific types.
  Ambrosia, 30 (DE); 57 (FG)
  Ambrosia, Holiday, 30 (DE)
  Bars, Rum, 99 (CJ)
  Basket, Watermelon
    Fruit, 85 (CE)

  Biscuits, Fruit Drop, 96 (BR)
  Brandied Fruit, 83 (GR)
  Bread, Cornish Saffron, 62 (BR)
  Cake, Fruit Cocktail, 76 (CA)
  Cake, Groom's, 118 (FG)
  Cantaloupe Melon Cups, 32 (DE)
  Cherry Winks, 116 (CJ)
  Citrus Peel, Candied, 89 (GR);
    71 (SS)
  Citrus Peel,
    Chocolate-Covered, 89 (GR)
  Compote, Cranberry, 43 (DE)
  Compote, Hot Spiced, 32 (SP)
  Compote, Sunrise, 30 (DE)
  Conserve, Fresh Fruit, 30 (GR)
  Cookies, Aiken's Row
    Bourbon, 113 (CJ)
  Cookies, Christmas
    Fruit, 117 (CJ)
  Cookies, Fruitcake, 117 (CJ)
  Cookies, Fruit-Shaped
    Butter, 133 (CJ)
  Cookies, Greek Holiday, 122 (CJ)
  Cookies, Italian
    Christmas, 124 (CJ)
  Cookies, St. Augustine Fiesta
    Butter, 125 (CJ)
  Curried Fruit, 110 (CE)
  Dressing, Fruit, 85 (BE)
  Dried Fruit in Rum, 84 (GR)
  Filling, Dried Fruit, 123 (CJ)
  Filling, Kentucky Fruit, 45 (CA)
  Fritters, Fruit, 128 (BR)
  Fruitcake, Japanese, 57 (FG)

**BB** *Breakfast & Brunch*   **BE** *Beef, Veal & Lamb*   **BR** *Breads*   **CA** *Cakes*   **CC** *Company's Coming*   **CE** *Celebrations*
**CJ** *Cookie Jar*   **DE** *Just Desserts*   **FG** *Family Gatherings*   **GR** *Gift Receipts*   **PK** *All Pork*   **PO** *Plain & Fancy Poultry*
**PP** *Pies & Pastry*   **SE** *Sea & Stream*   **SO** *Soups & Stews*   **SP** *Sporting Scene*   **SS** *Socials & Soirees*   **VE** *Vegetables*

48

Fruit, *continued*

Glacé, Fruit, 90 (GR)
Hamantaschen, 123 (CJ)
Ice Cream,
Banana-Fruit, 82 (FG)
Ice Cream,
Tutti-Frutti, 101 (DE)
Kugel, Matzo Fruit, 61 (CE)
Lebkuchen,
Nürnberger, 128 (CJ)
Lizzies, 118 (CJ)
Logs, Brandied Fruit, 119 (CJ)
Logs, Holiday Delight, 119 (GR)
Mincemeat, Mrs. Fitzhugh
Lee's, 44 (PP)
Mold, Wine Jelly, 70 (DE)
Muffins, Spiced Fruit, 115 (BR)
Pie, Festive Cream, 101 (PP)
Pie, Nesselrode, 108 (PP)
Punch, Fruited
Champagne, 86 (FG)
Punch with Ice Ring,
Fruit, 26 (SP)
Roll, Tutti-Frutti
Icebox, 129 (DE)
Salads
Cantaloupe Lilies with Melon
Balls, 109 (FG)
Compote Amulet, 26 (CC)
Creamy Fruit Salad, 95 (SS)
Fresh Fruit Salad, 76 (BB);
76 (FG)
Fresh Fruit Salad with Celery
Seed Dressing, 100 (SS)
Fresh Fruit Salad with
Horseradish
Dressing, 34 (SS)
Frozen Fruit Salad, 55 (CE);
34 (SS)
Fruit Salad, 78 (SP)
Ginger Fruit Cups, 26 (SP)
Hot Caramel Fruit, 85 (BB)
Melon Balls in Mint-Rum
Sauce, 72 (SS)
Peppered Fruit, 64 (CE)
Stewed Mixed Fruits, 25 (BB)
Strudel, Fruit, 101 (FG)
Summer Fruit
Combination, 99 (CC)
Waldorf Salad, 40 (SS)
Waldorf Salad with
Wine, 31 (SP)
Sauce, Spicy Fruit, 129 (BE)

Sauce, Tropical Fruit, 135 (DE)
Soup, Dried Fruit, 43 (SO)
Soup, Scandinavian
Fruit, 43 (SO)
Squares,
Butterscotch-Fruit, 91 (CJ)
Starter, Brandied
Fruit, 135 (DE)
Steak Roll, Fruited, 29 (BE)
Stewed Mixed Fruits, 25 (BB)
Stuffed Dried Fruit, 23 (SS)
Sweets, Fruit, 81 (GR)
Tarts, Charleston
Fruit, 128 (CE)
Tarts, Glazed Fruit, 112 (SP)
Tea, Fruited Iced, 20 (SP)
Tutti-Frutti, 84 (GR)
Wafers, Citrus, 69 (CJ)
Watermelon Bowl, 32 (DE)
Wine, Lamb Shanks Baked in
Fruited, 97 (BE)

# G

**Ginger**

Cakes, Winkler's Ginger, 20 (CJ)
Cookies, Moravian
Ginger, 20 (CJ)
Cookies, Tyron Palace
Ginger, 18 (CJ)
Fruit Cups, Ginger, 26 (SP)
Gingerbread, Lafayette, 89 (CC)
Gingersnaps, 94 (CE); 23 (FG)
Piecrust, Gingersnap, 22 (PP)
Snaps, Old-Fashioned
Ginger, 19 (CJ)

**Goose**

Good to Know, 130 (PO)
Roast Goose with Baked
Apples, 40 (PO)
Roast Goose with Potato and
Peanut Stuffing, 41 (PO)
Roast Goose with Sausage
Stuffing, 41 (PO)

**Grapefruit**

Broiled Grapefruit, 53 (BB)
Candied Citrus Peel, 89 (GR)

Compote, Sunrise, 30 (DE)
Conserve, Citrus, 31 (GR)
Marmalade, Starlight, 55 (BB)
Parfait, Texas
Grapefruit, 81 (DE)
Salad, Florida
Grapefruit-Avocado, 135 (FG)
Salad,
Grapefruit-Avocado, 64 (CC)
Salad Supreme,
Grapefruit, 42 (SS)
Salty Dog, 93 (BB)
Sherbet, Grapefruit, 93 (DE)

**Grapes**

Butter, Grape, 26 (GR)
Cake, Mayflower Grape, 30 (CA)
Cobbler, Green Grape, 37 (PP)
Filling, Grape, 30 (CA)
Frosting, Grape, 30 (CA)
Ice, Grape, 90 (DE)
Jelly, Grape, 12 (GR)
Jelly, Muscadine Grape, 10 (GR)
Pie, Grape Juice, 96 (PP)
Pie, Muscadine, 36 (PP)
Relish, Grape, 47 (GR)
Sauce, Grape Wine, 13 (DE)
Sherbet, Grape, 93 (DE)
Spiced Grapes, 36 (GR)
Stuffed Grape Leaves, 61 (FG)
Syrup, Grape, 92 (CC)

**Gravies**

Brown Crumb Gravy, 84 (PO)
Brown Gravy, 63 (BE)
Brown Gravy, Rich, 14 (PK)
Capon Gravy, 94 (CC)
Chicken and Gravy,
Steamed, 100 (CC)
Chicken with Gravy, Old
Dominion Fried, 84 (PO)
Cream Gravy, 131 (BE); 62 (SP)
Cream Gravy, Fried Ham
with, 75 (FG)
Cream Gravy, Fried Quail
with, 134 (CC)
Cream Gravy, Maryland Fried
Chicken with, 83 (PO)
Cream Gravy, Pork Chops
with, 31 (BB)
Giblet Gravy, 114 (CE); 49,
120 (PO)
Herb Gravy, Roast Cornish Hens
with, 39 (PO)
Milk Gravy, Fried Breakfast
Bacon with, 119 (PK)
Milk Gravy, Fried Ham
with, 75 (PK)
Mushroom Gravy, 25 (SS)
Mushroom Pan Gravy, 131 (BE)
Red-Eye Gravy, Fried Country
Ham with, 10 (BB); 64 (PK)
Red Gravy Sauce, 95 (PO)
Roast Fowl Gravy, 49 (PO)
Roast Pan Gravy, 131 (BE)
Saw Mill Gravy, Fried Chicken
with, 84 (PO)
Shrimp Gravy, 48 (SE)
Spareribs with Gravy, 32 (PK)
Stock, Basic Brown, 125 (BE)
Tomatoes with Gravy,
Fried, 121 (VE)

Gravies, *continued*
  Tomato Gravy, 103 (BE)
  Wine Gravy, Meatballs in, 91 (FG)
**Greens**
  Autumn Greens, 56 (CC)
  Collard Greens, 53 (VE)
  Collard Green Soup, 101 (SO)
  Collards, Ham Hocks
    and, 125 (PK)
  Collards, Ocracoke, 53 (VE)
  Field Cress, 56 (VE)
  Gumbo z'Herbes, 114 (SO);
    126 (VE)
  How To Prepare Fresh
    Greens, 53 (VE)
  Kale Salad Greens, 56 (VE)
  Lettuce, Braised, 56 (VE)
  Mustard Greens and
    Turnips, 54 (VE)
  Mustard Greens,
    Louisiana, 54 (VE)
  Mustard Greens,
    Southern-Style, 54 (VE)
  Poke Greens, Arkansas, 57 (VE)
  Poke Sallet, 57 (VE)
  Poke Sallet with Bacon, 56 (VE)
  Swiss Chard, Creamed, 58 (VE)
  Swiss Chard, Sautéed, 58 (VE)
  Swiss Chard, Steamed, 58 (VE)
  Turnip Greens, 117 (PK)
  Turnip Greens and Cornmeal
    Dumplings, 54 (VE)
  Turnip Greens and Hog
    Jowl, 125 (PK)
  Turnip Greens, Fresh, 17 (CE)
  Turnip Greens in , 54 (VE)
**Grilled.** *See* Barbecue.
**Grits**
  Awendaw, 31 (BR)
  Baked Grits, 55 (BB); 65 (PK)
  Cheese Grits, 26 (SP)
  Cheese Grits, Southern, 50 (BB)
  Chile-Cheese Grits, 127 (BB)
  Fried Grits, 87 (BB)
  Grits, Southern, 110 (CE)
  Ovendaugh, South
    Carolina, 31 (BR)
  Sausage, Country Grits
    and, 131 (BB)
  Soufflé, Cheese Grits, 72 (BB)
  Soufflé, Grits, 112 (FG)
**Grouper**
  Baked Grouper, 67 (SE)
  Baked Grouper with Lemon
    Stuffing, 67 (SE)
  Grilled Grouper, 69 (SE)
  Italiano, Grouper, 69 (SE)
  Kabobs, Grouper, 69 (SE)
  Poached Grouper, 69 (SE)
  Spanish Sauce, Grouper
    with, 69 (SE)
**Guava**
  Cobbler, Fresh Guava, 43 (DE)
**Gumbos**
  Beef and Ham Gumbo, 114 (SO)
  Cajun Gumbo, 120 (SO)

Chicken-Andouille
  Gumbo, 113 (PK)
Chicken and Oyster
  Gumbo, 62 (PO)
Chicken Gumbo, 62 (PO)
Chicken Gumbo,
  Creole, 114 (SO)
Chicken Gumbo, Easy, 63 (PO)
Chicken Gumbo Filé, 116 (SO)
Chicken Gumbo,
  Savannah, 62 (PO)
Crab Gumbo, 118 (SO)
Duck Gumbo, 63 (PO);
  116 (SO); 59 (SP)
Filé, Gumbo, 30 (CC)
Louisiana Gumbo, 119 (SO)
Marlin Gumbo, White, 104 (SP)
Monticello Gumbo, 121 (CC)
Oyster Creole, 121 (SO)
Oyster Gumbo, 118 (SO)
Seafood Gumbo, 119 (SO)
Shrimp Gumbo, 50 (SE)
Turkey-Sausage
  Gumbo, 117 (SO)
Vegetable Gumbo, 126 (VE)
z'Herbes, Gumbo, 114 (SO);
  126 (VE)

# H

**Haddock**
  Baked Haddock, 70 (SE)
  Baked Haddock with Lemon
    Sauce, 70 (SE)
  Loaf, Haddock, 71 (SE)
  Poached Haddock, 71 (SE)
  Scalloped Haddock, 71 (SE)
**Ham**
  Appetizers, Ham and
    Cheese, 124 (SS)
  Baked Ham. *See also* Country
    Ham.
  Bourbon-Glazed
    Ham, 118 (SP)
  Champagne Baked
    Ham, 70 (PK)
  Cola Baked Ham with
    Applesauce Aspic, 70 (PK)
  Leg of Pork, Arkansas, 22 (PK)
  Orange Glaze, Baked Ham
    with, 72 (PK)
  Pastry, Baked Ham
    in, 53 (CE)
  Peanut Ham with Sherry,
    Baked, 71 (PK)
  Raisin Sauce, Baked Ham
    with, 47 (CC)
  Sauce, Baked Ham
    with, 72 (PK)
  Snow-Frosted Ham, 72 (PK)
  Whole Ham, Baked, 68 (PK)
  Canapés, Creole, 29 (CC)

Country Ham
  Baked Country-Cured
    Ham, 93 (CE)
  Baked Country Ham, 68 (PK)
  Baked Ham, Old
    Maryland, 67 (BB)
  Baked Kentucky Ham, 77 (CE)
  Baked Virginia Ham, 124 (CC)
  Baked Virginia Ham
    Madeira, 131 (SS)
  Biscuits, Smithfield
    Ham, 91 (PK)
  Chicken and Country Ham,
    Maryland, 104 (PO)
  Cooked in a Blanket, Country
    Ham, 68 (PK)
  Country Ham, 86 (BB)
  Fried Country Ham with
    Red-Eye Gravy, 10 (BB);
    64 (PK)
  Oysters with Virginia Ham,
    Creamed, 28 (PO)
  Sandwiches, Baked
    Ham, 28 (SP)
  Smithfield Ham, Sykes
    Inn, 66 (PK)
  Stew, Ham, 83 (PK)
  Stuffed Ham, Belle Meade
    Mansion, 11 (FG)
  Stuffed Ham,
    Maryland, 66 (PK)
  Stuffed Ham,
    Mississippi, 67 (PK)
  Stuffed Ham, Pecan-, 67 (PK)
  Stuffed Ham, Southern
    Maryland, 34 (FG)
Cubed Ham
  Creamed Ham, 79 (PK)
  Eggplant,
    Ham-Stuffed, 85 (PK)
  Jambalaya, Creole, 109 (PK)
  Jambalaya, Ham and
    Chicken, 69 (PO)
  Macaroni and Cheese with
    Ham, 80 (PK)
  Mousse, Ham, 132 (BB)
  Omelet, Fluffy Ham, 120 (BB)
  Pie, Picnic, 82 (PK)
  Red Beans and Rice, 110 (PK)
  Salad, Baked Ham, 80 (PK)
  Salad, Virginia Ham, 69 (CE)
  Stew, Ham, 83 (PK)
  Tetrazzini, Ham, 81 (PK)
  Timbales with Béchamel
    Sauce, Ham, 80 (PK)
  Waffles, Ham, 114 (BB)
Eggs, Scotch, 136 (SP)
Gumbo, Beef and Ham, 114 (SO)
Gumbo, Louisiana, 119 (SO)
Gumbo, Oyster, 118 (SO)
Gumbo z'Herbes, 114 (SO)
Ham Hocks
  Black-Eyed Peas with Ham
    Hock, 17 (CE)
  Collards, Ham Hocks
    and, 125 (PK)

---

**BB** *Breakfast & Brunch*  **BE** *Beef, Veal & Lamb*  **BR** *Breads*  **CA** *Cakes*  **CC** *Company's Coming*  **CE** *Celebrations*
**CJ** *Cookie Jar*  **DE** *Just Desserts*  **FG** *Family Gatherings*  **GR** *Gift Receipts*  **PK** *All Pork*  **PO** *Plain & Fancy Poultry*
**PP** *Pies & Pastry*  **SE** *Sea & Stream*  **SO** *Soups & Stews*  **SP** *Sporting Scene*  **SS** *Socials & Soirées*  **VE** *Vegetables*

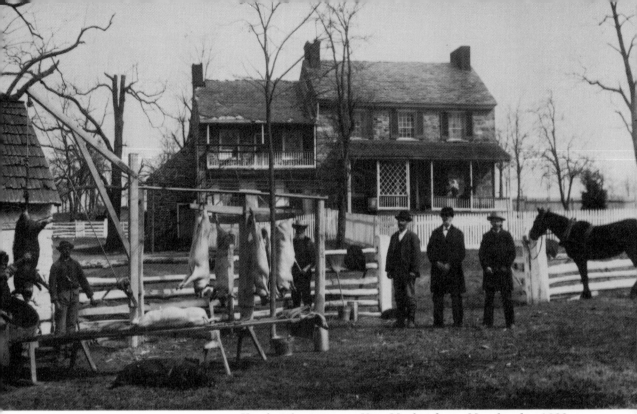

*Hog butchering on a New Market farm, Maryland, c.1890.*

Ham, Ham Hocks, *continued*
  Cornmeal Dumplings, Ham
    Hocks with, 124 (PK)
  Soup, Ham Bone, 81 (SO)
Ham Slices
  Baked Ham Slice, 75 (PK)
  Baked Ham Steak with
    Sauce, 76 (PK)
  Baked Ham, Sweet Potato
    Biscuits with, 106 (SS)
  Baked Ham with Pickled
    Peaches, 76 (PK)
  Baked Ham with Sweet
    Potatoes, 77 (PK)
  Barbecued Ham
    Steaks, 53 (PK)
  Chicken, The Homestead
    Fried, 97 (PO)
  Cranberry-Glazed Ham
    Slice, 76 (PK)
  Eggs Alexandria, Ham
    and, 50 (BB)
  Eggs Benedict,
    Weidmann's, 122 (BB)
  Fried Country Ham, 109 (CE)
  Fried Ham with Cream
    Gravy, 75 (FG)
  Fried Ham with Milk
    Gravy, 75 (PK)
  Mushrooms à la King, Ham
    and, 78 (PK)
  Mustard Sauce, Ham
    in, 75 (PK)
  Orange-Rice Stuffing, Ham
    Steak with, 78 (PK)

Rolls, Ham-Asparagus, 78 (PK)
Turkey au
  Rochambeau, 106 (PO)
Jambalaya, Pork, 121 (SO)
Pie, Chicken and Country Ham
  Deep Dish, 18 (CC)
Puffs, Deviled Ham, 18 (SS)
Salad, Normandy
  Luncheon, 56 (SS)
Sandwiches, Baked
  Ham, 60 (SS)
Sandwiches, Domino, 52 (SS)
Sandwiches, Ham, 68 (SS)
Sandwiches, Princess, 21 (SS)
Sauce, Sherried Ham, 92 (PK)
Soup, Split Pea, 65 (SO)
Soup, Vegetable
  Hambone, 124 (PK)
Stuffed Ham
  Belle Meade Mansion Stuffed
    Ham, 11 (FG)
  Maryland Stuffed
    Ham, 66 (PK)
  Maryland Stuffed Ham,
    Southern, 34 (FG)
  Mississippi Stuffed
    Ham, 67 (PK)
  Pecan-Stuffed Ham, 67 (PK)
Toast Rounds, Ham and
  Cheese, 115 (SS)
**Ham, Ground**
  au Gratin, Ham, 79 (PK)
  Balls in Sauce, Ham, 89 (PK)
  Bell Peppers with Ham,
    Stuffed, 85 (PK)

Biscuits, Smithfield
  Ham, 91 (PK)
Casserole, Ham, 85 (PK)
Croquettes, Ham, 89 (PK)
Deviled Ham, 89 (PK)
Jambalaya, Ham, 85 (PK)
Loaf, Ham, 86 (PK)
Loaf, Upside-Down
  Ham, 86 (PK)
Mousse, Ham, 86 (PK)
Ring, Savory Ham-Veal, 87 (PK)
Rolls, Ham, 91 (PK)
Soufflé, Ham, 83 (PK)
Spread, Ham Sandwich, 89 (PK)
Turnovers, Ham, 91 (PK)
**Hog Jowl**
  Black-Eyed Peas and Hog
    Jowl, 126 (PK)
  Pinto Beans, Seasoned, 126 (PK)
  Turnip Greens and Hog
    Jowl, 125 (PK)
**Hominy**
  Bacon Hominy, 47 (VE)
  Chili Hominy, 47 (VE)
  Chorizo and Hominy
    Skillet, 113 (PK)
  Posole Ortiz, 37 (PK)
  Shrimp with Hominy, 135 (BB)
  Spanish Hominy, 47 (VE)
**Honey**
  Butter, Honey, 98 (BB); 65 (PK)
  Cake, Apple Honey
    Upside-Down, 39 (CA)
  Cake, Honey-Crisp
    Coffee, 64 (CA)

**Honey,** *continued*
- Cookies, Hard Honey, 95 (CJ)
- Cookies, Honey, 71 (CJ)
- Diples, 64 (FG)
- Flummery, Honey, 75 (DE)
- Glaze, Honey, 26 (PK)
- Pear Honey, 11 (BB); 27 (GR)
- Pork Chops, Honey, 51 (PK)
- Rolls, Anna Maude's Honey Almond, 69 (BR)

**Horseradish**
- Dip,
  - Bacon-Horseradish, 125 (SP)
- Dressing, Fresh Fruit Salad with Horseradish, 34 (SS)
- Mustard, Horseradish, 73 (GR)
- Prepared Horseradish, 76 (GR)
- Relish,
  - Beet-Horseradish, 75 (GR)
- Sauce, Horseradish, 17, 21, 128 (BE); 120 (SS); 134 (VE)
- Sauce, Horseradish and Sour Cream, 128 (BE)
- Sauce, Horseradish Barbecue, 60 (PK)
- Sauce, Horseradish-Mustard, 128 (BE)
- Sauce, Kehoe Horseradish, 92 (PK)

**Huckleberries**
- Cake, Huckleberry, 43 (CA)
- Coffee Cake, Huckleberry, 105 (BB)
- Pie, Huckleberry, 47 (PP)

*Eating the rewards of turning the crank in 1922.*

# I

**Ice Creams and Sherbets**
- Apricot Ice Cream, Hannah Glasse's, 97 (DE)
- Apricot Sherbet, 91 (DE); 127 (FG)
- Banana-Fruit Ice Cream, 82 (FG)
- Blackberry Sherbet, 92 (DE)
- Buttermilk Sherbet, 95 (DE)
- Butter Pecan Ice Cream, 97 (DE)
- Cake, Ice Cream, 67 (CA); 121 (SP)
- Caramel Ice Cream, 99 (DE); 81 (FG)
- Chocolate Ice Cream, 90 (CE); 98 (DE)
- Coconut Ice Cream, 130 (CC)
- Coffee Ice Cream, 98 (DE)
- Cranberry Frappé, 114 (CE)
- Cranberry Sherbet, 92 (DE)
- Custard, Frozen, 97 (DE)
- Grapefruit Sherbet, 93 (DE)
- Grape Sherbet, 93 (DE)
- Lime Sherbet, 94 (DE)
- Mocha Ice Cream Roll, 102 (DE)
- Orange Cream Sherbet, 94 (DE)
- Peach Ice Cream, 122 (SS)
- Peach Ice Cream, Fresh, 90 (CE); 100 (DE); 17 (FG)
- Peach Sherbet, 94 (DE)
- Peppermint Ice Cream, 101 (DE)
- Peppermint Stick Ice Cream, 86 (CE)
- Pie, Mile High Ice Cream, 105 (DE)
- Pineapple Buttermilk Sherbet, 95 (DE)
- Pineapple-Lemon Sherbet, 81 (SS)
- Pineapple Sherbet, 40 (FG)
- Pistachio Ice Cream, 113 (SS)
- Plum Ice Cream, Greengage, 101 (DE)
- Sandwiches, Ice Cream, 93 (SS)
- Snowballs, 111 (PO)
- Strawberry Ice Cream, 101 (DE)
- Strawberry Surprise, 47 (SS)
- Tutti-Frutti Ice Cream, 101 (DE)
- Vanilla Ice Cream, 123 (CC); 90 (CE); 95 (DE); 81 (FG)
- Vanilla Ice Cream, Easy, 96 (DE)
- Vanilla Ice Cream, Homemade, 78 (PO)
- Vanilla Ice Cream, No-Cook, 96 (DE)
- Wafers, Ice Cream, 91 (CE)

**Ices**
- Cherry Ice, 80 (CC)
- Cranberry Ice, 90 (DE)
- Grape Ice, 90 (DE)
- Orange Ice, 118 (SS)
- Orange Ice with Minted Pineapple, 84 (SS)
- Pomegranate Ice, 91 (CC)
- Ring, Ice, 118 (SS)
- Sicilian Ice, 91 (CC)
- Strawberry Ice, 27 (SS)
- Watermelon Ice, 90 (CC)
- Wine Ice, 90 (DE)

# J

**Jambalayas**
- Chicken, Jambalaya of, 122 (SO)
- Chicken-Sausage Jambalaya, 109 (PK)
- Crayfish Jambalaya, 24 (SE)
- Creole Jambalaya, 109 (PK)
- Ham and Chicken Jambalaya, 69 (PO)
- Ham Jambalaya, 85 (PK)
- Pork Jambalaya, 121 (SO)
- Pork Rib Jambalaya, 34 (PK)
- Shrimp and Oyster Jambalaya, 124 (SO)
- Vegetable Jambalaya, 125 (VE)

**Jams and Jellies**
- Apple Jelly, 10 (GR)
- Apple-Raspberry Jelly, 10 (GR)
- Apricot-Orange Marmalade, 21 (GR)
- Basil Jelly, 16 (GR)
- Blackberry Jam Cake, "Little Nanny's," 46 (CA)
- Blackberry Jam (*Note*), 23 (GR)
- Blackberry Jelly, 10 (GR)
- Blueberry Jam, 23 (GR)

---

**BB** *Breakfast & Brunch*   **BE** *Beef, Veal & Lamb*   **BR** *Breads*   **CA** *Cakes*   **CC** *Company's Coming*   **CE** *Celebrations*
**CJ** *Cookie Jar*   **DE** *Just Desserts*   **FG** *Family Gatherings*   **GR** *Gift Receipts*   **PK** *All Pork*   **PO** *Plain & Fancy Poultry*
**PP** *Pies & Pastry*   **SE** *Sea & Stream*   **SO** *Soups & Stews*   **SP** *Sporting Scene*   **SS** *Socials & Soirees*   **VE** *Vegetables*

**Jams and Jellies,** *continued*
Cake, Brown's Church
Jam, 46 (CA)
Cake, Heritage Jam, 45 (CA)
Cake, Jam, 95 (CE)
Cake, Tennessee Jam, 17 (FG)
Champagne Jelly, Pink, 16 (GR)
Cherry Preserves, 17 (GR)
Christmas Jam, 25 (GR)
Cookies, Bird's Nest, 79 (CJ)
Cookies, Cream Cheese
Thumbprint, 63 (CJ)
Cookies, Greek Holiday, 122 (CJ)
Cookies, Linzer, 63 (CJ)
Crab Apple Jelly, 10 (GR)
Cream Cheese Horns, 63 (CJ)
Fig Jam, 23 (GR)
Fig Preserves, 18 (BB); 17 (GR)
Fig Preserves Cake, 15 (SS)
Grape Jelly, 12 (GR)
Grape Jelly, Muscadine, 10 (GR)
Green Pepper Jelly, 15 (GR)
How to Make Jelly Without
Added Pectin, 32 (GR)
Italian Pillows, 65 (CJ)
Jalapeño Jelly, 130 (BE)
Jalapeño Pepper Jelly, 15 (GR)
Jelly Sauce, 70 (PK)
Kumquat Jelly, 12 (GR)
Lemon Jelly Filling, 18 (CA)
Lemon Marmalade, 14 (SS)
London Bars, 95 (CJ)
Marmalade Nut Bread, 104 (BR)
Marmalade, Starlight, 55 (BB)
Mint Jelly, 16 (GR)
Orange-Lemon
Marmalade, 22 (GR)
Orange Marmalade, 21 (GR)
Peach Jam, Spiced, 24 (GR)
Peach Preserves, 17 (GR)
Pear Honey, 11 (BB)
Pear Marmalade
Magnolia, 22 (GR)
Pear Preserves, 18 (GR)
Pear Preserves Cake, 47 (CA)
Plum Jam, Red, 48 (BB)
Plum Jelly, Fresh, 48 (FG)
Plum Jelly, Red, 11 (BB);
13 (GR)
Raspberry Jam, 23 (GR)
Raspberry Jam Logs, 99 (CJ)
Raspberry Jelly, 32 (GR)
Raspberry Preserves, 18 (GR)
Rhubarb Marmalade, 22 (GR)
Sandwiches, Pinwheel
Jelly, 28 (CE)
Strawberry Jam, 24 (GR)
Strawberry Jelly, 13 (GR)
Strawberry-Lemon
Preserves, 19 (GR)
Strawberry-Orange
Jam, 24 (GR)
Strawberry Preserves, 16 (CC);
19 (GR)
Tomato Marmalade,
Green, 22 (GR)
Tomato Preserves,
Favorite, 20 (GR)
Watermelon Rind
Preserves, 20 (GR)

Wine Jelly, 16 (GR)
Wine Jelly Mold, 70 (DE)
Wine Jelly with Sabayon
Sauce, 40 (SS)

### Kabobs

Grouper Kabobs, 69 (SE)
Pork Kabobs, 58 (PK)
Shish Kabobs, 98 (BE)
Southern Tender
Kabobs, 58 (PK)
Steak on a Stick, 102 (CE)

### Kidney

Pie, Kidney, 110 (BE)
Pudding, Steak and
Kidney, 109 (BE)
Red Wine, Bahama Kidneys
in, 108 (BE)
Stew, Son-of-a-Gun, 120 (BE)

### Kumquats

Jelly, Kumquat, 12 (GR)

### Lamb

Burgoo, 135 (SO)
Chops
Baked Lamb Chops, 96 (BE)
Breaded Lamb Chops, 95 (BE)
Broiled Lamb Riblets, 94 (BE)
Grilled Lamb Chops, 94 (BE)
Pineapple, Lena's Lamb Chops
and, 96 (BE)
Planked Lamb Chops, 95 (BE)
Sautéed Lamb Chops, 95 (BE)
Crown Roast of Lamb with Fruit
Dressing, 85 (BE)
Curry, Lamb, 105 (BE)
Cuts of Lamb, 136 (BE)

Good to Know, 133-137 (BE)
Greek Lamb with
Zucchini, 98 (BE)
Hash, Lamb, 104 (BE)
Leg of Lamb
à la Béarnaise, Lamb
Roast, 90 (BE)
Anchovies, Roast Lamb
with, 88 (BE)
Braised Leg of Lamb, Troth's
Fortune, 89 (BE)
Glazed Leg of Lamb, 90 (BE)
Glazed Stuffed Lamb, 92 (BE)
Grilled Lamb, 86 (BE)
Herbed Roast Lamb, 88 (BE)
Lemon Garlic Leg of
Lamb, 86 (BE)
Oven-Barbecued
Lamb, 87 (BE)
Pineapple-Mint Glazed
Lamb, 115 (SP)
Plum Sauce, Leg of Lamb
with, 90 (BE)
Potatoes, Roast Leg of Lamb
with, 56 (CE)
Roasted Leg of Lamb with
Oven-Browned
Potatoes, 10 (CC)
Scottish Brew, 132 (SO)
Stuffed Leg of Lamb, 92 (BE)
Pastitsio, 104 (BE)
Patties with Tomato Gravy,
Lamb, 103 (BE)
Pie, A Savory Lamb, 103 (BE)
Pie, 1944 Crustless
Lamb, 101 (BE)
Pie, Kidney, 110 (BE)
Pie, Shepherd's, 103 (BE)
Pie, Wartime Lamb, 102 (BE)
Pilaf, Lamb, 99 (BE)
Pot Roast, Lamb, 93 (BE)
Pudding, Steak and
Kidney, 109 (BE)
Rack of Lamb, 84 (BE)

Lamb, *continued*
Rack of Lamb de
Simone, 110 (CC)
Ragout of Lamb, 101 (BE)
Ring, Pineapple-Mint
Lamb, 105 (BE)
Ring, Springtime
Lamb, 104 (BE)
Saddle of Lamb, 84 (BE)
Shanks Baked in Fruited Wine,
Lamb, 97 (BE)
Shanks, Barbecued
Lamb, 97 (BE)
Shanks, Braised Lamb, 97 (BE)
Shish Kabobs, 98 (BE)
Shoulder, Roasted
Lamb, 93 (BE)
Soup, Lamb and
Vegetable, 80 (SO)
Soup with Egg-Lemon Sauce,
Easter, 56 (CE)
Stew, Caesar, 131 (SO)
Stew, Creole Lamb, 99 (BE)
Stew, Indian, 100 (BE)
Stew, Ireland Lamb, 46 (CE)
Stew, Irish, 131 (SO)
Stew, Lamb, 99 (BE)
Stew, Navajo, 100 (BE)

**Leeks**
Braised Leeks, 60 (VE)
Creamed Leeks, 60 (VE)
How To Prepare Fresh
Leeks, 59 (VE)
New Potatoes, Leeks
and, 60 (VE)
Soup, Creamy Herb
Potato, 67 (SO)
Tomatoes, Leeks with, 60 (VE)
Vichyssoise, 67 (SO)

**Lemon**
Beverages
Apple Lemonade, 86 (CE)
Lemonade, 17 (FG)
Lemonade, Claret, 94 (BB)
Lemonade, Fresh, 123 (SP)
Lemonade,
Refreshing, 113 (SS)
Biscuits, Lemon Tea, 63 (BB)
Bread, Lemon, 104 (BR)
Broccoli, Lemon, 26 (VE)
Butter, Asparagus with
Lemon, 110 (FG)
Candied Citrus Peel, 89 (GR)
Candied Orange and Lemon
Peel, 25 (CE)
Carrots, Shaker
Lemon-Glazed, 35 (VE)
Chicken Breasts, Lemon, 18 (SP)
Chicken,
Lemon-Roasted, 44 (CC)
Desserts
Bars, Lemon, 98 (FG)
Bars, Lemon-Glazed
Chess, 90 (SP)
Cake, General Robert E.
Lee, 18 (CA)

Cake, Lemon Angel
Food, 112 (CA)
Cake, Lemon Gold, 115 (CA);
84 (FG)
Cake, Lemon Pecan, 49 (CA)
Cake, Lemon Pound, 123 (SP)
Cake, Lemon Sheet, 127 (SP).
Charlotte Russe,
Lemon, 15 (PK)
Coconut Crunch,
Lemon-, 127 (DE)
Cookies, Lemon, 59 (CJ);
45 (FG)

Cookies, Lemon Drop
Sugar, 33 (CJ)
Cookies, Lemon
Praline, 76 (CJ)
Curd, Lemon, 61 (CE)
Curd, Meringue Shells with
Lemon, 74 (SS)
Custard, Frozen
Lemon, 112 (DE)
Filling, Lemon, 33, 103 (CA)
Filling, Lemon Jelly, 18 (CA)
Filling, Tart Lemon, 127 (CA)
Frosting, Creamy
Lemon, 65 (CA)
Frosting, Lemon, 44 (CE);
90 (CJ)
Frosting, Lemon Butter
Cream, 135 (CA); 53 (CJ);
84 (FG)
Frosting, Lemon
Cream, 33 (CA); 127 (SP)

Frosting, Lemon
Fluffy, 115 (CA)
Frosting,
Lemon-Orange, 18 (CA)
Frosting, Lemon
Seven-Minute, 132 (CA)
Frozen Lemon
Dessert, 112 (DE)
Glaze, Lemon, 75 (CA)
Icing, Tangy Citrus, 135 (CA)
Meringue, Lemon
Cream, 23 (CC); 119 (DE)
Parfait, Lemon, 116 (SP)
Pudding, Lemon
Sponge, 23 (DE)
Roll, Lemon, 127 (CA)
Roll, Tender Lemon
Sponge, 126 (CA)
Sherbet,
Pineapple-Lemon, 81 (SS)
Soufflé, Hot Lemon, 67 (DE)
Soup,
Champagne-Lemon, 38 (SO)
Squares, Lemon, 96 (CJ);
26 (FG)
Triangles, Lemon, 11 (SS)
Trifle, Lemon Curd, 61 (CE)
Wafers, Citrus, 69 (CJ)
Wafers, Thin Lemon, 136 (CE)
Leg of Lamb, Lemon
Garlic, 86 (BE)
Marmalade, Lemon, 14 (SS)
Marmalade,
Orange-Lemon, 22 (GR)
Pies and Tarts
Chess Pie, Tennessee
Lemon, 74 (PP)
Chiffon Pie, Tart
Lemon, 107 (PP)
Heavenly Lemon Pie, 96 (PP)
Icebox Pie, Old Southern Tea
Room Lemon, 113 (PP)
Lemon Pie, 17 (CC); 64 (CE)
Meringue Pie, Lemon, 98 (PP)
Meringue Pie, Tart
Lemon, 108 (CC)
Nashville Lemon Pie, 76 (PP)
Silver Pie, High Hampton Inn
Sunny, 106 (PP)
Slice Pie, Lemon, 37 (PP)
Tarts, Citron, 19 (CC)
Tarts, Dainty Lemon, 125 (PP)
Tarts, Lemon, 118 (PP)
Tarts, Lemon Chess, 15 (PK)
Tarts, Lemon
Chiffon, 118 (PP)
Tarts, Lemon
Meringue, 117 (PP)
Tarts, Tiny Lemon, 87 (CC)
Preserves,
Strawberry-Lemon, 19 (GR)
Quail, Lemon-Baked, 50 (SP)
Sauce, Baked Haddock with
Lemon, 70 (SE)
Sauce, Broiled Sweetbreads with
Lemon, 115 (BB)

---

**BB** *Breakfast & Brunch*   **BE** *Beef, Veal & Lamb*   **BR** *Breads*   **CA** *Cakes*   **CC** *Company's Coming*   **CE** *Celebrations*
**CJ** *Cookie Jar*   **DE** *Just Desserts*   **FG** *Family Gatherings*   **GR** *Gift Receipts*   **PK** *All Pork*   **PO** *Plain & Fancy Poultry*
**PP** *Pies & Pastry*   **SE** *Sea & Stream*   **SO** *Soups & Stews*   **SP** *Sporting Scene*   **SS** *Socials & Soirees*   **VE** *Vegetables*

**Lemon,** *continued*
Sauce, Creamy Lemon, 136 (DE)
Sauce, Egg-Lemon, 56 (CE)
Sauce, Lemon, 13, 18, 41 (DE);
  128 (SE); 54 (SS)
Sauce, Lemon-Butter, 132 (VE)
Sauce, Lemon Hard, 36 (DE)
Sauce, Mary Randolph's Lemon
  Cream, 86 (GR)
Sauce, Oil and Lemon, 134 (VE)
Sauce, Old-Fashioned Golden
  Lemon, 137 (DE)
Sauce, Tart Lemon, 137 (DE)
Sauce, Trout with
  Almond-Lemon, 121 (SE)
Stuffing, Baked Grouper with
  Lemon, 67 (SE)
Sugar, Lemon-Mint, 62 (GR)
Sweet Potatoes with Lemon
  Slices, Candied, 95 (VE)
Turkey,
  Lemon-Barbecued, 88 (PO)
**Lettuce.** *See also* Salads.
Braised Lettuce, 56 (VE)
Salad, Wilted Lettuce, 48 (CC)
Soup, Lettuce, 35 (SO)
Wedges with Onion Salad
  Dressing, Lettuce, 47 (SS)

**Lime**
Pie, Florida Key Lime, 112 (PP)
Pie, Florida Lime, 98 (PP)
Pie, Florida Lime
  Custard, 70 (PP)
Pie, Luscious Lime, 107 (PP)
Sherbet, Lime, 94 (DE)
Tarts, Lime Chiffon, 118 (PP)
**Linguine**
Clam Sauce, Linguine with
  White, 11 (SE)
**Liver**
Baked Liver in Creole
  Sauce, 113 (BE)
Baked Liver, Maryland, 112 (BE)
Dumplings, Liver and, 114 (BE)
Grilled Calves' Liver, 112 (BE)
Nips, Liver, 114 (BE)
Pâté, Cajun Liver, 130 (PK)
Sautéed Liver with
  Avocado, 110 (BE)
Smothered Liver and
  Onions, 110 (BE)

Sour Cream, Calves' Liver
  in, 112 (BE)
Stew, Son-of-a-Gun, 120 (BE)
**Lobster**
Boiled Lobster with Dill
  Sauce, 29 (SE)

Bouillabaisse, New
  Orleans, 55 (SE)
Broiled Lobster Tails, 31 (SE)
Cocktail, Lobster, 33 (SE)
Creamed Lobster, 33 (SE)
Cucumber Sauce, Lobster Tails
  with, 31 (SE)
Curried Lobster, 33 (SE)
Eggs, Lobster-Stuffed, 111 (SP)
Grilled Lobster Tails, 31 (SE)
How to Boil Lobster, 29 (SE)
How to Remove Meat from a
  Lobster, 28 (SE)
How to Steam Lobster, 29 (SE)
Newburg in Patty Shells,
  Lobster, 111 (SP)
Newburg, Lobster, 33 (SE)
Salad with Mustard Mayonnaise,
  Lobster, 124 (SS)
Sherry Sauce, Lobster
  in, 32 (SE)
Soup, Cream of Lobster, 54 (SO)
Tenderloin of Beef,
  Lobster-Stuffed, 129 (CC)
Thermidor, Arnaud's
  Lobster, 27 (SE)
Thermidor, Lobster, 29 (SE)
**Loquat**
Cobbler, Loquat, 38 (PP)

# M

**Macaroni**
au Gratin, Macaroni, 40 (FG)
Beef Porcupines, 39 (BE)
Casserole, Pork and
  Macaroni, 38 (PK)
Cheese with Ham, Macaroni
  and, 80 (PK)

German-Style Meatballs, 39 (BE)
Pastichio, 58 (CE)
Pastitsio, 104 (BE)
Pie, Tony's Italian
  Pasta-Meat, 43 (BE)
Pudding, Macaroni, 122 (CC)
Soup, Macaroni-Beef, 80 (SO)
**Mackerel**
Broiled Salt Mackerel, 136 (BB)
King Mackerel, Grilled, 73 (SE)
King Mackerel Steaks,
  Marinated, 73 (SE)
King Mackerel Steaks with
  Tomato-Wine Sauce, 73 (SE)
Spanish Mackerel,
  Baked, 72 (SE)
Spanish Mackerel,
  Broiled, 72 (SE)
**Mangos**
Chutney, Mango, 56 (GR)
Custard, Mango, 132 (FG)
Flameador, Mango, 44 (DE)
Pie, Mango, 38 (PP)
Salad, Mango, 38 (BB)
Spiced Mangos, 37 (GR)
**Marinades**
Dill Marinade, 114 (SP)
Sauce, Seafood
  Marinade, 132 (SE)
Sauce, Tangy
  Marinade, 127 (BE)
Seafood Marinade,
  Spicy, 132 (SE)
**Marlin**
Barbecued Marlin, 106 (SP)
Chowder, Marlin, 104 (SP)
Gumbo, White Marlin, 104 (SP)
Nuggets, Fried Marlin, 106 (SP)
**Marshmallows**
Candy, Cathedral, 103 (GR)
Dessert, Chocolate Marshmallow
  Icebox, 85 (DE)
Frosting, Marshmallow, 25,
  26 (CA)
Fudge, Angel, 122 (GR)
Fudge, Festive, 122 (GR)
Glaze, Marshmallow, 93 (CA)
Marshmallows, 103 (GR)
Mint Marshmallows, 73 (CE)
Pie, Weidmann's
  Bourbon, 113 (PP)
S'Mores, 95 (SP)
**Mayonnaise**
Blender Mayonnaise, 134 (VE)
Dip, Garlic-Mayonnaise, 95 (FG)
Dressing, Mayonnaise, 134 (VE)
Homemade Mayonnaise,
  127 (SE); 134 (VE)
Lobster Salad with Mustard
  Mayonnaise, 124 (SS)
**Meatballs**
Danish Meatballs, 11 (CE)
Scandinavian Meatballs, 18 (FG)
Wine Gravy, Meatballs
  in, 91 (FG)
**Melons**
Balls in Mint-Rum Sauce,
  Melon, 72 (SS)
Cantaloupe Lilies with Melon
  Balls, 109 (FG)

*Pies aplenty in the preparation stage, c.1910.*

Brown Brothers

Melons, *continued*
Cantaloupe Melon
  Cups, 32 (DE)
Cantaloupe Soup, Cold, 38 (SO)
Salad, Fruit, 78 (SP)
Watermelon Bowl, 32 (DE)
Watermelon Fruit
  Basket, 85 (CE)
Watermelon Ice, 90 (CC)
Watermelon Rind,
  Pickled, 39 (GR)
Watermelon Rind
  Pickles, 54 (SS)
Watermelon Rind
  Preserves, 20 (GR)
**Meringues**
Almond Meringue
  Cookies, 23 (SS)
Asparagus Meringue, 13 (VE)
Bars, Meringue, 72 (CC)
Breadcrumb Meringue
  Cookies, 11 (CJ)
Brown Sugar
  Meringues, 128 (CE)
Butterscotch Meringue Pie,
  Smith and Welton's Tea
  Room, 90 (PP)

Chess Meringue Pie, 73 (PP)
Chocolate Meringue Pie, 91 (PP)
Chocolate Torte, 119 (DE)
Coconut Meringue Pie, 95 (PP)
How-To, Basic
  Meringue, 24 (PP)
Lemon Cream
  Meringue, 23 (CC); 119 (DE)
Pale Green Meringue Hearts with
  Pastel Sherbets, 110 (FG)
Peach Meringues,
  Fresh, 117 (DE)
Pecan Meringues, 116 (DE)
Pineapple Meringue, 25 (PP)
Plum Meringue Pie, 42 (PP)
Powdered Sugar
  Meringue, 25 (PP)
Pumpkin Meringue Pie, 61 (PP)
Schaum Torte, 118 (DE)
Shell, Cinnamon
  Meringue, 119 (DE)
Shells with Lemon Curd,
  Meringue, 74 (SS)
Spiced Meringues, 116 (DE)
Strawberry Meringues, 79 (CC)
Strawberry Meringue
  Torte, 118 (DE)

Sweet Potatoes with
  Meringue, 96 (VE)
Unbaked Meringue, 25 (PP)
**Mincemeat**
Cake, Thanksgiving
  Mincemeat, 102 (CA)
Cookies, Orange-Mincemeat
  Filled, 119 (CJ)
Drops, Mincemeat, 118 (CJ)
Mrs. Fitzhugh Lee's
  Mincemeat, 44 (PP)
Pear Mincemeat, 49 (GR)
Pie, Bourbon
  Christmas, 133 (CE)
Pie, Homemade
  Mincemeat, 120 (CE)
Pie, Pear Mincemeat, 41 (PP)
Pie with Bourbon Sauce,
  Mincemeat, 44 (PP)
Tarts Flambé,
  Mincemeat, 120 (PP)
Tomato Mincemeat,
  Green, 52 (GR)
**Mousses**
Amaretto Mousse, 13 (SP)
Avocado Mousse, 105 (CC)
Blue Cheese Mousse, 97 (SS)

Mousses, *continued*
  Chicken Mousse, 112 (PO)
  Chocolate Mousse, 78, 108 (DE)
  Coffee Mousse, 79 (DE)
  Ham Mousse, 132 (BB); 86 (PK)
  Orange Mousse, 108 (DE)
  Peach Mousse, 109 (DE)
  Raspberry Mousse, 109 (DE)
  Rum Mousse, Snowden
    House, 79 (DE)
  Salmon Mousse, 85 (SE)
  Shrimp and Crabmeat
    Mousse, 103 (FG)
  Shrimp Mousse, 51 (SE)
  Strawberry Mousse, 109 (DE)

**Muffins**
  Apple Butter Muffins, 31 (SS)
  Applesauce Muffins, 111 (BR)
  Blueberry Muffins, 101 (BB);
    112 (BR)
  Blueberry Muffins,
    Petite, 80 (BB)
  Bran Muffins, 50 (BB); 127 (FG)
  Bran Muffins, Grove Park
    Inn, 110 (BR)
  Cheese Puffs, 118 (SP)
  Cornbread Muffins, 56 (CC)
  Cornmeal Muffins, 29 (BB);
    103 (SP)
  Cornmeal Muffins,
    Tennessee, 18 (BR)
  Corn Muffins,
    Richmond, 113 (BR)
  Crackling Cornbread
    Muffins, 18 (BR)
  Cranberry Muffins, Robert
    Morris Inn, 101 (BB)
  Date-Bacon Muffins, 113 (BR)
  Dinner Muffins, 108 (BR)
  English Muffins, 106 (BB)
  English Muffins Toasted with
    Cheese Butter, 123 (SP)
  Fig Muffins, Fresh, 62 (BB)
  Fruit Muffins, Spiced, 115 (BR)
  Gem Muffins, 18 (BB)
  Luncheon Muffins,
    Miniature, 108 (BR)
  Maids of Honor, 119 (CC)
  Molasses Muffins, 113 (BR)
  Oatmeal Muffins, 99 (BB)
  Orange Blossom Muffins,
    Excelsior House, 113 (BR)
  Peanut Butter Muffins, 99 (BB)
  Pecan Muffins, Georgia, 79 (FG)
  Popovers, 99 (BB); 110 (BR)
  Popovers, Our
    Famous, 105 (CC)
  Puffs, Breakfast, 61 (BB)
  Puffs, French
    Breakfast, 112 (BR)
  Pumpkin Muffins, 57 (SS)
  Pumpkin Muffins,
    Greenbrier, 116 (BR)
  Pumpkin Muffins, Old
    Salem, 115 (BR)
  Raisin Bran Muffins, 115 (BR)

  Rice Muffins,
    Charleston, 111 (BR)
  Sally Lunn Muffins, 61 (BR);
    11 (CC)
  Sausage Corn Muffins, 18 (BR)
  Shirley Graham
    Muffins, 110 (BR)
  Sour Cream Gems, 26 (SP)
  Sour Cream Muffins, 108 (BR)
  Spice Muffins,
    Mississippi, 102 (BB)
  Squash Muffins, 116 (BR)
  Strawberry Muffins, 26 (SP)
  Sweet Potato Muffins, 116 (CE)
  Tea Muffins, 112 (FG)
  Vanilla Muffins, The Peabody's
    Famous, 109 (BR)

**Mullet**
  Amandine, Mullet, 75 (SE)
  Baked Mullet, 74 (SE)
  Fillets with Shrimp Stuffing,
    Mullet, 75 (SE)
  Fried Mullet, Peck
    Smith's, 74 (SE)
  Grilled Mullet, 76 (SE)
  Poached Mullet, 76 (SE)
  Smoked Mullet, 76 (SE)
  Stew, Florida's Mullet, 76 (SE)

**Mushrooms**
  Asparagus with Mushrooms and
    Cream Sauce, 11 (VE)
  Bouchées à la Reine, 133 (SO)
  Broiled Mushrooms, 62 (VE)
  Broth, Mushroom, 35 (SO)

  Casserole, Stuffed Egg and
    Mushroom, 124 (BB)
  Celery with Mushrooms, 40 (VE)
  Chicken with Wine and
    Mushrooms, Baked, 109 (FG)
  Chowder, Mushroom and
    Barley, 102 (SO)
  Crabmeat-Stuffed Mushroom
    Caps, 78 (BB)
  Creamed Mushrooms, 62 (VE)
  Custard,
    Mushroom-Onion, 49 (FG)

  Dressing, Mushroom
    Cornbread, 64 (SP)
  Eggs with Mushrooms and
    Onions, Scrambled, 119 (BB)
  Filling, Mushroom Pâté, 12 (BE)
  Gravy, Mushroom, 25 (SS)
  Gravy, Mushroom Pan, 131 (BE)
  Ham and Mushrooms à la
    King, 78 (PK)
  Herbed Mushrooms, 11 (SP)
  How To Prepare Fresh
    Mushrooms, 61 (VE)
  Marinated Mushrooms, 11 (CE)
  Paprika, Mushroom, 64 (VE)
  Pie, Mushroom, 64 (VE)
  Salmon and Mushrooms,
    Creamed, 135 (BB)
  Sauce,
    Almond-Mushroom, 134 (BB)
  Sauce, Broiled Flounder with
    Mushroom-Wine, 65 (SE)
  Sauce, Broiled Steak with
    Mushroom-Wine, 27 (BE)
  Sauce, Mushroom, 126 (BE);
    59, 117 (PO); 66, 93 (SE);
    48 (SS)
  Sauce, Mushroom
    Cream, 113 (SE)
  Sauce, Sherry-Mushroom,
    11 (BE)
  Sauce, Tuna Steaks with
    Mushroom, 100 (SE)
  Sautéed Fresh Mushrooms,
    Churchill Downs, 63 (VE)
  Sherried Mushrooms, 63 (VE)
  Soup, Cream of
    Mushroom, 64 (SO)
  Soup, Seafood-Mushroom,
    64 (SO)
  Stroganoff, Mushroom, 64 (VE)
  Stuffed Mushrooms, 103 (SS)
  Stuffed Mushrooms,
    Baked, 63 (VE)
  Stuffed Mushrooms,
    Broiled, 62 (VE)
  Tenderloin of Beef with
    Mushrooms, Roast, 73 (FG)
  Tomatoes Stuffed with
    Mushrooms, 111 (SP)
  Veal Chops with
    Mushrooms, 69 (BE)

**Mustard**
  Apricot Mustard, 73 (GR)
  Beer Mustard, 73 (GR)
  Cole Slaw, Mustard, 47 (PK)
  Dill Mustard, 73 (GR)
  English Mustard, 74 (GR)
  Horseradish Mustard, 73 (GR)
  Hot Sweet Mustard, 92 (PK)
  Mayonnaise, Lobster Salad with
    Mustard, 124 (SS)
  Potato Salad, Mustard, 77 (PO)
  Potato Salad, Sour
    Cream-Mustard, 89 (FG)
  Salt Pork with Mustard,
    Fried, 117 (PK)

**BB** *Breakfast & Brunch*  **BE** *Beef, Veal & Lamb*  **BR** *Breads*  **CA** *Cakes*  **CC** *Company's Coming*  **CE** *Celebrations*
**CJ** *Cookie Jar*  **DE** *Just Desserts*  **FG** *Family Gatherings*  **GR** *Gift Receipts*  **PK** *All Pork*  **PO** *Plain & Fancy Poultry*
**PP** *Pies & Pastry*  **SE** *Sea & Stream*  **SO** *Soups & Stews*  **SP** *Sporting Scene*  **SS** *Socials & Soirees*  **VE** *Vegetables*

Mustard, *continued*
Sandwiches,
  Olive-Mustard, 28 (FG)
Sauce, Cooked Mustard, 87 (PK)
Sauce, Dill and
  Mustard, 129 (SE)
Sauce, Ham in Mustard, 75 (PK)
Sauce, Horseradish-Mustard,
  128 (BE)
Sauce, Mustard, 21, 58 (PK)
Sauce, Mustard Dip, 134 (VE)
Sauce, Tangy Mustard, 97 (SE)
Spread, Mustard, 74 (GR);
  104 (SS)
Sweet Hot Mustard, 74 (GR)

**Nectarines**
Brandied Nectarines, 47 (DE);
  83 (GR)
**Noodles**
Egg Noodles,
  Homemade, 97 (CC)
Homemade Noodles, 13 (SO)
Johnnie Marzetti, 43 (BE)
Kugel, Noodle, 97 (FG)
Soup, Chicken Noodle, 22 (PO);
  83 (SO)
Soup, Filled Noodle, 79 (SO)
Soup, German
  Beef-Noodle, 79 (SO)
Soup, Turkey-Noodle, 86 (SO)
Stew, Veal and Noodle,
  78 (BE)
Veal with Noodles,
  Baked, 77 (BE)
**Nuts.** *See* individual types.

**Oatmeal**
Cake with Coconut Topping,
  Oatmeal, 70 (SP)
Coffee Cake,
  Oatmeal-Coconut, 103 (BB)
Cookies, Chewy
  Oatmeal, 44 (CJ)
Cookies, Crunchy
  Oatmeal, 44 (CJ)
Cookies, Early American
  Peanut, 81 (CJ)
Cookies, Guess-Again, 76 (CJ)
Cookies, No-Bake
  Chocolate-Oatmeal, 44 (CJ)
Cookies, Oatmeal, 136 (SP)
Cookies, Oatmeal-Chocolate
  Chip, 45 (CJ)

Cookies, Oatmeal Lace, 42 (CJ)
Cookies, Oatmeal-Pecan
  Lace, 42 (CJ)
Cookies, Oatmeal-Raisin,
  44 (CJ)
Cookies, Raleigh Tavern
  Oatmeal, 42 (CJ)
Cookies, To-My-Valentine,
  133 (CJ)
Crinkles, Oatmeal, 76 (CJ)
Gorp, 78 (SP)
Macaroons, Oatmeal-
  Coconut, 15 (CJ)
Muffins, Oatmeal, 99 (BB)
Surprises, Date, 82 (CJ)
**Okra**
Baked Okra, 66 (VE)
Batter-Fried Okra, 66 (VE)
Croquettes, Okra, 66 (VE)
Fried Okra, 102 (CC); 16 (FG)
Gumbo, Beef and
  Ham, 114 (SO)
Gumbo, Crab, 118 (SO)
Gumbo, Creole
  Chicken, 114 (SO)
Gumbo, Duck, 116 (SO)
Gumbo, Louisiana, 119 (SO)
Gumbo, Monticello, 121 (CC)
Gumbo, Seafood, 119 (SO)
Gumbo, Turkey-Sausage,
  117 (SO)
Gumbo, Vegetable, 126 (VE)
How To Prepare Fresh
  Okra, 65 (VE)
Jambalaya, Vegetable, 125 (VE)
Pan-Fried Okra, 65 (VE)
Pilau, Okra, 66 (VE)
Soup, Savannah Okra, 101 (SO)
Tomatoes, Okra and, 66 (VE)
**Olives**
Dilled Green Olives, 56 (SS)
Sandwiches, Olive-Cheese,
  21 (SS)
Sandwiches, Olive-Mustard,
  28 (FG)
Spread, Toasted Biscuits with
  Olive, 64 (CE)
**Omelets**
Cheese Omelet, 121 (BB)
Corn Omelet, 121 (BB)
Ham Omelet, Fluffy, 120 (BB)
Herb Omelet, Fresh, 120 (BB)
Oyster Omelet, 86 (BB)
Sour Cream Omelet, 121 (BB)
Veal Omelet, Open-Face, 58 (BB)

**Onions**
au Gratin, Onions, 69 (VE)
Baked Curried Onions, 69 (VE)
Black-Eyed Peas with
  Onion, 80 (VE)
Brussels Sprouts and Onions in
  Acorn Squash,
  Creamed, 118 (CC)
Creamed Onions, 136 (CC);
  114 (CE); 29 (PO)
Custard, Mushroom-
  Onion, 49 (FG)
Dressing, Onion-Bread, 13 (PK)
Eggs, Oklahoma Onion
  and, 70 (VE)
Eggs with Mushrooms and
  Onions, Scrambled, 119 (BB)
Fried Onions, Louis Smith's
  Southern, 69 (VE)
Glazed Onions, George
  Washington's, 68 (VE)
Green Peas with Onion,
  Minted, 77 (VE)
How To Prepare Fresh
  Onions, 67 (VE)
Lima Beans with Onion, 20 (VE)
Liver and Onions,
  Smothered, 110 (BE)
Patties, Onion Dressing, 48 (PO)
Peas with Spring Onions,
  Green, 65 (CE)
Pickled Onions, Tiny, 44 (GR)
Pickles, French, 44 (GR)
Pickles, Mixed
  Vegetable, 46 (GR)
Pie, Green Onion, 70 (VE)
Rings, French Fried
  Onion, 69 (VE)
Salad, Fire and Ice, 65 (SP)
Slaw, Onion, 54 (PO)
Soup, French Onion, 35 (SO)
Soup, Green Onion, 66 (SO)
Soup, Huguenot Onion, 35 (SO)
Squash and Onions,
  Summer, 13 (PO)
Steak with Onion,
  Cubed, 31 (BE)
Vidalia Onions, Baked, 72 (VE)
Vidalia Onions, Crunchy
  Asparagus with, 72 (VE)
Vidalia Onions in Sherried
  Cream Sauce, Baked, 72 (VE)
Vidalia Onions,
  Stuffed, 70 (VE)
Wine, Onions Baked in, 43 (SP)
**Oranges**
Ambrosia, 30 (DE); 57 (FG)
Ambrosia, Holiday, 30 (DE)
Ambrosial Oranges, 31 (DE)
Ambrosia, Orange-
  Pineapple, 136 (SS)
Bars, Orange Slice, 97 (CJ)
Bass, Orange Steamed
  Black, 108 (SE)
Bigarade, Roast
  Ducklings, 44 (PO)

**BB** *Breakfast & Brunch*   **BE** *Beef, Veal & Lamb*   **BR** *Breads*   **CA** *Cakes*   **CC** *Company's Coming*   **CE** *Celebrations*
**CJ** *Cookie Jar*   **DE** *Just Desserts*   **FG** *Family Gatherings*   **GR** *Gift Receipts*   **PK** *All Pork*   **PO** *Plain & Fancy Poultry*
**PP** *Pies & Pastry*   **SE** *Sea & Stream*   **SO** *Soups & Stews*   **SP** *Sporting Scene*   **SS** *Socials & Soirees*   **VE** *Vegetables*

American Grown · Prizetaker Onion ·

Copyrighted 1891 by W. Atlee Burpee & Co.

Oranges, *continued*

Biscuits, Florida
  Orange, 97 (BR)
Biscuits, Orange, 55 (BB)
Blossom, Orange, 93 (BB)
Blush, Orange, 50 (BB)
Bonbons, Orange, 134 (GR)
Bread, Florida Orange, 105 (BR)
Bread, Marmalade Nut, 104 (BR)
Butter, Orange, 20 (BB)
Cake, Easter Orange
  Coconut, 100 (CA)
Cake, Moss Rose, 23 (CA)
Cake, Orange-Date, 68 (CA)
Cake, Orange-Glazed Pecan
  Pound, 98 (SP)
Cake, Orange Icebox, 86 (DE)
Cake, Orange-Walnut, 50 (CA)
Cake, Williamsburg
  Orange, 21 (CA)
Candied Citrus Peel, 89 (GR)
Candied Orange and Lemon
  Peel, 25 (CE)
Charlotte, Orange, 84 (DE);
  92 (SS)
Cheesecake, Blue Ribbon
  Orange, 82 (PP)
Cider, Berkeley Spiced, 116 (CE)
Coconut Vanities, 93 (CJ)
Compote Amulet, 26 (CC)
Compote, Cranberry, 43 (DE)
Compote, Sunrise, 30 (DE)
Conserve, Citrus, 31 (GR)
Cookies, Carrot-Orange, 51 (CJ)
Cookies, Frosted
  Orange, 34 (CJ)
Cookies, Gumdrop, 120 (CJ)
Cookies, Orange-Mincemeat
  Filled, 119 (CJ)

Cream, Orange
  Custard, 73 (DE)
Crêpes Suzette, 120 (DE)
Cupcakes, Orange, 86 (CA)
Custard, Orange, 55 (DE)
Doughnuts, Fredericksburg
  Orange, 117 (BB)
Doughnuts, Orange, 124 (BR)
Dressing, Orange, 51 (CC)
Filling, Orange, 100, 126 (CA)
Filling, Orange Coconut, 22 (CA)
Frosting,
  Lemon-Orange, 18 (CA)
Frosting, Orange, 102,
  132 (CA); 75 (SS)
Frosting, Orange Butter, 65 (SS)
Frosting, Williamsburg
  Butter, 21 (CA)
Fudge, Orange, 124 (GR)
Glaze, Baked Ham with
  Orange, 72 (PK)
Glaze, Baked Orange, 49 (PK)
Glaze, Orange, 68 (CA); 98 (SP)
Ice, Orange, 118 (SS)
Ice with Minted Pineapple,
  Orange, 84 (SS)
Icing, Tangy Citrus, 135 (CA)
Italian Pillows, 65 (CJ)
Jam, Strawberry-
  Orange, 24 (GR)
Jellyroll, Orange, 126 (CA)
Juice, Spiced Orange, 77 (SP)
Marlow, Orange, 107 (DE)
Marmalade, Apricot-
  Orange, 21 (GR)
Marmalade, Orange, 21 (GR)
Marmalade, Orange-
  Lemon, 22 (GR)
Marmalade, Starlight, 55 (BB)

Meat Loaf with Walnuts and
  Oranges, Rolled, 38 (BE)
Mimosa, 93 (BB)
Mousse, Orange, 108 (DE)
Muffins, Excelsior House Orange
  Blossom, 113 (BR)
Orangeade, Pineapple, 68 (FG)
Pecans, Orange-Candied,
  93 (GR)
Pie, Lee Family Orange, 76 (PP)
Pie, Old Talbott Tavern Orange
  Meringue, 99 (PP)
Pie, Orange Meringue, 100 (PP)
Pork Roast,
  Orange-Basted, 49 (PK)
Relish, Cranberry-
  Orange, 56 (FG); 75 (GR);
  43 (SP)
Rings, Candied Carrots in
  Orange, 35 (VE)
Rolls, Orange, 108 (BB);
  71 (BR)
Roll-Ups, Sweet Orange, 97 (BR)
Sauce, Beets in Orange, 25 (VE)
Sauce, Orange, 132 (CC);
  137 (DE); 88 (GR)
Sauce, Orange
  Basting, 131 (SE)
Sauce, Orange-
  Pineapple, 134 (DE)
Sauce, Roast Duckling with
  Orange, 43 (PO)
Sauce, Savory Orange, 31 (SP)
Shells, Fluffy Sweet Potatoes in
  Orange, 95 (VE)
Sherbet, Orange Cream, 94 (DE)
Shortcakes, Fresh
  Orange, 53 (CA)
Soup, Cold
  Peach-Orange, 41 (SO)
Squares, Coconut-
  Orange, 93 (CJ)
Squares, Swedish
  Orange-Nut, 96 (CJ)
Squash, Orange-Glazed
  Acorn, 114 (VE)
Stuffing, Ham Steak with
  Orange-Rice, 78 (PK)
Sugar, Orange-Spice, 62 (GR)
Syrup, Orange, 86 (CA)
Tarts, Orange, 131 (SP)

Tarts, Orange-Cheese, 118 (PP)
Tea Cakes, Orange, 65 (SS)
Toast, Orange-
  Cinnamon, 112 (BB)
Toast, Orange French, 112 (BB)
Wafers, Citrus, 69 (CJ)
Waffles with Orange Butter,
  Orange Pecan, 20 (BB)
Wine Sauce, Oranges in, 20 (SP)

**Oysters**

Angels on Horseback, 24 (FG); 37 (SE)

Baked Oysters, Savannah, 114 (CE)

Baked Stuffed Redfish, Mississippi Sound, 81 (SE)

Bienville, Oysters, 39 (SE)

Bisque, Oyster, 54 (SO)

Brochette of Shrimp and Oysters, Hotel Ponce de Leon, 56 (SE)

Broiled Oysters, 29 (CC); 34 (SE); 110 (SP)

Carpetbag Steak, 29 (BE)

Casino, Oysters, 39 (SE)

Casserole, Sausage, 131 (BB)

Chicken, Oyster-Stuffed Breast of, 98 (PO)

Chowder, Statehouse Oyster, 91 (SO)

Cocktail Sauce, Oysters with, 34 (SE)

Corn Oysters, 50 (CC)

Corn Oysters, Fresh, 46 (VE)

Creamed Oysters, 36 (SE)

Creamed Oysters with Virginia Ham, 28 (PO)

Creole, Oyster, 121 (SO)

Croquettes, Chicken, 120 (SS)

Deviled Oysters, 25 (FG); 133 (SS)

Dressing, Oyster, 117 (CC)

Forcemeat, Hannah Glasse's Veal Collops with Oyster, 76 (BE)

Fried Oysters, 61 (BB); 25 (FG)

Fried Oysters, Buttery, 67 (BB)

Fried Oysters, Southern, 36 (SE)

Gumbo, Chicken and Oyster, 62 (PO)

Gumbo Filé, 30 (CC)

Gumbo Filé, Chicken, 116 (SO)

Gumbo, Oyster, 118 (SO)

How to Shuck an Oyster, 36 (SE)

Jambalaya, Shrimp and Oyster, 124 (SO)

Loaf, New Orleans Oyster, 41 (SE)

Omelet, Oyster, 86 (BB)

Pan-Fried Oysters, Maryland, 34 (SE)

Pickled Oysters, 42 (SE)

Pie, A Savory Lamb, 103 (BE)

Pie Rappahannock, Oyster, 41 (SE)

Pie, Sweetbread and Oyster, 118 (BE)

Po-Boys, Oyster, 40 (SE)

Roasted Oysters, 97 (SP)

Rockefeller, Oysters, 39 (SE)

Rolled Oysters, Louisville, 38 (SE)

Salad, Sager's Oyster, 133 (CE)

Sauce, Baked Snapper with Oyster, 90 (SE)

Sauce, Chicken with Oyster, 98 (PO)

Sauce, Oyster, 49 (PO); 130 (SE)

Sautéed Oysters on Toast, 34 (SE)

Scalloped Oysters, 24 (CE); 39 (SE)

Scalloped Oysters, Eastern Shore, 130 (CE)

Slang Jang, 44 (SP)

Smokehouse Oysters, 37 (SE)

Soufflé, Oyster, 40 (SE)

Soup à la New Orleans, Oyster, 93 (PO)

Soup, Baked Oyster, 55 (SO)

Soup, Charleston Oyster, 60 (CC)

Soup, Jefferson Davis' Oyster, 55 (SO)

Steamed Oysters, 34 (SE)

Stew, Oyster, 53 (FG); 42 (SE)

Stuffing, Baked Snapper with Oyster, 92 (SE)

Stuffing, Roast Capon with Virginia Oyster, 37 (PO)

Stuffing, Roast Turkey with Oyster, 38 (FG)

Stuffing, Rock Cornish Hens with Oyster Cornbread, 39 (PO)

Veal Oysters, 78 (BE)

# P

**Paella**

Paella, 56 (SE)

Valenciana, Paella, 68 (PO)

**Pancakes**

Alsatian Pancake, 114 (BB)

Apple-Rice Griddle Cakes, 114 (BB)

Basic Pancakes, 34 (BB)

Blueberry Pancakes, 35 (BB)

Breadcrumb Pancakes, 35 (BB)

Buckwheat Cakes, 23 (BB)

Buttermilk Pancakes, 113 (BB)

Corn Griddle Cakes, Alabama, 26 (BR)

Cornmeal Batty Cakes, 25 (BR)

Cornmeal Cakes, Mrs. Paul's, 25 (BR)

Cornmeal Flapjacks, Arkansas, 26 (BR)

Cornmeal Pancakes, 35 (BB)

Cornmeal Patty Cakes, 16 (BB)

Corn Pancakes, 46 (VE)

Cottage Cheese Pancakes, 113 (BB)

Griddle Cakes, Indian, 56 (BE)

Hoecakes, Indian, 27 (BR)

Lace Cakes, Kentucky, 26 (BR)

Potato Griddle Cakes, 35 (BB)

Potato Pancakes, 92 (VE)

Scotch Pancakes, 112 (SS)

**Papayas**

Chutney, Papaya, 56 (GR)

Soup, Cold Papaya, 40 (SO)

Library of Congress

**BB** Breakfast & Brunch   **BE** Beef, Veal & Lamb   **BR** Breads   **CA** Cakes   **CC** Company's Coming   **CE** Celebrations
**CJ** Cookie Jar   **DE** Just Desserts   **FG** Family Gatherings   **GR** Gift Receipts   **PK** All Pork   **PO** Plain & Fancy Poultry
**PP** Pies & Pastry   **SE** Sea & Stream   **SO** Soups & Stews   **SP** Sporting Scene   **SS** Socials & Soirees   **VE** Vegetables

**Parsnips**
Baked Parsnips, 75 (VE)
Buttered Parsnips with
Parsley, 75 (VE)
Cakes, Parsnip, 75 (VE)
Creamed Parsnips, 75 (VE)
Fritters, Parsnip, 74 (VE)
How To Prepare Fresh
Parsnips, 73 (VE)
Puree, Parsnip, 74 (VE)
**Pasta.** *See also* individual types.
Pie, Tony's Italian
Pasta-Meat, 43 (BE)
Vermicelli Soufflé,
Tomato, 134 (FG)
**Pâtés**
Black-Eyed Pea Pâté, 106 (SS)
Chicken Liver Pâté, 126 (PO)
Country Pâté, 87 (SS)
Liver Pâté, Cajun, 130 (PK)
Liver Pâté on Toast Points,
Individual, 73 (FG)
Mushroom Pâté Filling, 12 (BE)
**Peaches**
Bacon Grill, 132 (BB)
Baked Peaches, 44 (DE)
Bourbon-Blazed Peaches over
Frozen Custard, 93 (SP)
Bourbon Peaches, 131 (SP)
Brandied Peaches, 123 (CC)
Butter, Old-Fashioned
Peach, 27 (GR)
Cake, Fresh Peach, 81 (SP)
Cake, South Carolina Fresh
Peach, 44 (CA)
Chutney, Texas Peach, 57 (GR)
Cobbler, Easy Peach, 40 (PP)
Cobbler, Peach, 78 (PO)
Cobbler Supreme,
Peach, 40 (PP)
Conserve, Fresh Fruit, 30 (GR)
Conserve, Peach, 29 (GR)
Crisp, Peach, 44 (DE)
Custard, Peach, 55 (DE)
Daiquiri, Peach, 78 (FG)
Dumplings, Mother's
Peach, 130 (PP)
Filling, Peach, 117 (DE)
Ice Cream, Fresh Peach,
90 (CE); 100 (DE); 17 (FG)
Ice Cream, Peach, 122 (SS)
Ice, Sicilian, 91 (CC)
Jam, Spiced Peach, 24 (GR)
Leather, Peach, 82 (GR)
Meringues, Fresh
Peach, 117 (DE)
Mousse, Peach, 109 (DE)
Pickled Peaches, 84 (CE);
38 (GR)
Pickled Peaches, Baked Ham
with, 76 (PK)
Pie, Fresh Peach, 99 (CE)
Pie, Fresh Peach
Meringue, 39 (PP)
Pie, Georgia Peach, 39 (PP)
Pie, Glazed Peach, 40 (PP)
Pies, Fried Peach, 134 (PP)
Preserves, Peach, 17 (GR)
Raspberries, Fresh Peaches
with, 33 (DE)

Relish, Peach, 48 (GR)
Sauce, Peach, 133 (DE)
Scarlett O'Hara, 94 (BB)
Sherbet, Peach, 94 (DE)
Shortcakes, Individual
Peach, 53 (CA)
Soup, Cold Peach, 41 (SO)
Soup, Cold
Peach-Orange, 41 (SO)
Spiced Peaches, 126 (CC)

Tartlets, Peach, 122 (PP)
Tart, Peach, 45 (DE)
**Peanut Butter**
Bars, No-Bake Peanut
Butter, 98 (CJ)
Bread, Peanut Butter, 105 (BR)
Clusters, Double
Peanut, 136 (GR)
Cookies, No-Bake
Chocolate-Oatmeal, 44 (CJ)
Cookies, Peanut Butter
Refrigerator, 71 (CJ)
Crunchies, Peanut
Butter, 98 (CJ)
Cups, Peanut Butter, 136 (GR)
Frosting, Peanut Butter, 51 (CA)
Frosting, Peanut Butter
Spice, 136 (CA)
Fudge, Peanut Butter, 125 (GR)
Muffins, Peanut Butter, 99 (BB)
Peanut Blossoms, 81 (CJ)
Pie, Crunchy Peanut
Cream, 96 (PP)
Salad, Banana-Peanut, 73 (CE)
Sandwiches, Pinwheel
Jelly, 28 (CE)
Sauce, Peanut Butter, 82 (FG)
Soup, Cream of Peanut, 49 (SO)
Squares, Peanut-Apple, 85 (CA)
Squares, Peanut
Butter, 107 (CJ)
**Peanuts**
Biscuits, Peanut, 89 (BR)
Blossoms, Peanut, 81 (CJ)
Brittle, Peanut, 73 (CE)
Brittle Wreath, Peanut, 112 (GR)
Brownies, Peanut, 106 (CJ)
Cake, Harvest Peanut, 51 (CA)
Chowder,
Corn-Peanut, 101 (SO)
Clusters, Double
Peanut, 136 (GR)
Cookies, Crunchy Peanut
Bar, 97 (CJ)
Cookies, Early American
Peanut, 81 (CJ)

Cracker Jacks, 114 (GR)
Dressing, Peanut, 48 (PO)
French-Fried Peanuts, 17 (SO)
Frosting, Chocolate-Peanut,
81 (CA)
Patties, Peanut, 130 (GR)
Pie, Peanut, 52 (PP)
Pie, Peanut Brittle, 113 (PP)
Pralines, Peanut, 92 (FG)
Salad, Banana-Peanut, 73 (CE)
Soup, Cream of Peanut, 49 (SO)
Stuffing, Roast Goose with
Potato and Peanut, 41 (PO)
**Pears**
Cake, Pear Preserves, 47 (CA)
Chutney, Pear, 57 (GR)
Conserve, Pear, 29 (GR)
Crumble, Pear, 46 (DE)
Fritters, Fruit, 128 (BR)
Gorgonzola Pears, 134 (FG)
Honey, Pear, 11 (BB); 27 (GR)
Marmalade Magnolia,
Pear, 22 (GR)
Mincemeat, Pear, 49 (GR)
Pickled Pears, 38 (GR)
Pie, Old-Fashioned Pear, 41 (PP)
Pie, Pear Crumble, 41 (PP)
Pie, Pear Mincemeat, 41 (PP)
Poached Pears, 46 (DE)
Poached Pears Julianne, 93 (PO)
Preserves, Pear, 18 (GR)
Relish, Pear, 48 (GR)
Salad, Pear, 127 (FG)
**Peas**
Black-Eyed
Black-Eyed Peas, 102 (CC)
Creole Black-Eyed
Peas, 80 (VE)
Ham Hock, Black-Eyed Peas
with, 17 (CE)
Hog Jowl, Black-Eyed Peas
and, 126 (PK)
Hopping John, 17 (CE)
Hoppin' John, 79 (VE)
How To Prepare Fresh
Black-Eyed or Field
Peas, 79 (VE)
Onion, Black-Eyed Peas
with, 80 (VE)
Passion Peas, 80 (VE)
Pâté, Black-Eyed Pea, 106 (SS)
"Pot Likker," Black-Eyed Peas
in, 80 (VE)
Salad, Black-Eyed
Pea, 62 (FG)
Southern-Cooked Black-Eyed
Peas, 79 (VE)
Crowder Peas, Aunt Sivie's
Green, 80 (VE)
Green
Asparagus and Peas with Egg
Sauce, 12 (VE)
Baked Green Peas, 78 (VE)
Buttered Green Peas, 77 (VE)
Confetti Rice, 109 (FG)
Creamed Green Peas, 126 (FG)
Creamed Green Peas and
Potatoes, 77 (VE)
Dumplings, Green Peas and
Drop, 78 (VE)

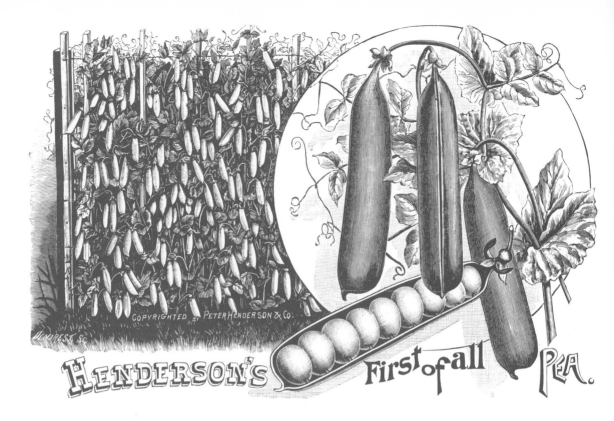

*COPYRIGHTED BY PETER HENDERSON & CO.*

**HENDERSON'S** First of all **PEA.**

Peas, Green, *continued*
Fresh Green Peas, 51 (CC)
Green Peas, 22 (CC); 48 (FG);
  46 (SS)
How To Prepare Fresh Green
  Peas, 76 (VE)
Minted Green Peas, 122 (CC)
Minted Green Peas with
  Onion, 77 (VE)
Onions, Green Peas with
  Spring, 65 (CE)
Soup, Cream of Pea, 129 (CE)
Soup, Green Pea, 65 (SO)
Soup, Split Pea, 65 (SO)
Southern-Cooked Green
  Peas, 77 (VE)
Sweetbreads with Green
  Peas, 60 (BB)
Tomato Cups, Green Peas
  in, 25 (SS)
Lady Peas, 102 (CC)

**Pecans**
Ball, Pecan Cheese, 92 (SP)
Balls with Fudge Sauce,
  Neiman-Marcus Toasted
  Pecan, 105 (DE)
Bars, Pecan, 136 (CE)
Bread, Praline, 40 (CE)
Brittle, Chocolate-Pecan,
  113 (GR)
Brittle, Pecan, 112 (GR)
Brittles, German Pecan, 55 (CJ)
Brownies, 100 (CJ)

Butter Toasted Pecans, 19 (SS)
Cake, Bringhurst Pecan, 48 (CA)
Cake, Lemon Pecan, 49 (CA)
Cake, Orange-Glazed Pecan
  Pound, 98 (SP)
Cake, Pecan-Topped Chocolate
  Pound, 118 (CA)
Cake, Pecan
  Upside-Down, 49 (CA)
Cake, Pineapple Pecan, 124 (CE)
Cake, Praline, 78 (CA)
Cake, Praline Chiffon, 115 (CA)
Cakes, Pecan Kiss, 10 (CJ)
Cake, Texas Pecan, 48 (CA)
Caramels, Creamy
  Pecan, 117 (GR)
Casserole, Celery and
  Pecan, 40 (VE)
Cheesecake, Praline, 84 (PP)
Chicken, Pecan
  Oven-Fried, 86 (PO)
Citrus-Candied Pecans, 92 (GR)
Coffee Pecans, 92 (GR)
Cookies, Cocoa-Nut, 78 (CJ)
Cookies, Crisp Molasses, 36 (CJ)
Cookies, German Pecan, 71 (CJ)
Cookies, Lemon Praline, 76 (CJ)
Cookies, Nut Drop, 32 (CJ)
Cookies, Oatmeal-Pecan
  Lace, 42 (CJ)
Cookies, Pecan Icebox, 23 (SP)
Cookies, Pecan Lace, 38 (CE);
  54 (CJ)

Cookies, Shortbread
  Surprise, 18 (CJ)
Cookies, Spicy
  Raisin-Nut, 37 (CJ)
Cookies, Vanilla Nut
  Icebox, 66 (CJ)
Crispies, Pecan, 54 (CJ)
Crunch, Pecan, 112 (GR)
Delights, Pecan, 77 (CJ)
Delight, Wyatt's Pecan, 128 (DE)
Filling, Coconut-Pecan, 27 (CA)
Fingers, Double-Dip
  Nut, 86 (CJ)
Frosted Pecans, 93 (GR)
Fudge, Blond Pecan, 125 (GR)
Fudge, Chocolate-Pecan,
  122 (GR)
Ham, Pecan-Stuffed, 67 (PK)
Hermits, Pecan, 34 (CJ)
Holiday Nuts, 96 (GR)
Hot Pepper Pecans, 103 (SS)
Hunky Dories, 136 (GR)
Ice Cream, Butter
  Pecan, 97 (DE)
Ice Cream Cups, 104 (DE)
Kisses, Chocolate-Nut, 10 (CJ)
Kisses, Praline, 10 (CJ)
Loaf, Old-Fashioned
  Nut, 105 (DE)
Loaf, Pecan, 25 (BB)
Logs, Chocolate Pecan, 134 (GR)
Logs, Holiday Delight, 119 (GR)
Macaroons, Date-Nut, 15 (CJ)

---

**BB** *Breakfast & Brunch*   **BE** *Beef, Veal & Lamb*   **BR** *Breads*   **CA** *Cakes*   **CC** *Company's Coming*   **CE** *Celebrations*
**CJ** *Cookie Jar*   **DE** *Just Desserts*   **FG** *Family Gatherings*   **GR** *Gift Receipts*   **PK** *All Pork*   **PO** *Plain & Fancy Poultry*
**PP** *Pies & Pastry*   **SE** *Sea & Stream*   **SO** *Soups & Stews*   **SP** *Sporting Scene*   **SS** *Socials & Soirees*   **VE** *Vegetables*

Pecans, *continued*
Meringues, Pecan, 116 (DE)
Millionaires, Texas, 136 (GR)
Minted Nuts, 31 (CE)
Minted Pecans, 92 (GR)
Muffins, Georgia Pecan, 79 (FG)
Nuggets, Georgia, 128 (GR)
Orange-Candied Pecans, 93 (GR)
Pastry Shell, Pecan, 20 (PP)
Peppery Spiced Nuts, 83 (CC)
Pie, Alabama Pecan, 52 (PP)
Pie, Apple-Pecan, 29 (PP)
Pie, Bourbon Chocolate
Pecan, 54 (PP)
Pie, Chocolate Pecan, 53 (PP)
Pie, Georgia Pecan, 23 (FG)
Pie, Ma Ferguson's Pecan
Cream, 100 (PP)
Pie, Pecan-Butterscotch,
101 (PP)
Pie, Pecan Chess, 74 (PP)
Pie, Pecan-Raisin, 54 (PP)
Pie, Pumpkin Pecan, 123 (CE)
Pie, Pumpkin-Pecan, 61 (PP)
Pie, Texas Pecan, 52 (PP)
Pie, Texas Poor Boy, 55 (PP)
Pie, Tupelo Honey
Pecan, 52 (PP)
Pie, Virginia Sweet
Potato-Pecan, 58 (PP)
Pie, Wayside Inn Pecan, 53 (PP)
Porcupines, 79 (CJ)
Praline Drops, 95 (GR)
Pralines, Buttermilk, 128 (GR)
Pralines, Creole, 127 (GR)
Pralines, Plantation, 128 (GR)
Rolls, Boca Raton
Pecan, 73 (BR)
Salted Nuts, 21 (CE)
Salted Pecans, 136 (CE);
86 (FG)
Sandies, Pecan, 77 (CJ)
Sandwiches, Celery-Nut, 62 (SS)
Sandwiches, Open-Face
Date-Nut, 81 (SS)
Sherried Pecans, 88 (SS)

Shortbreads, Pecan, 84 (CC)
Squares, Date-Nut, 48 (SP)
Squares, Swedish
Orange-Nut, 96 (CJ)
Strips, Kathleen Danielson's
Pecan, 98 (CJ)
Stuffing, Roast Turkey with
Rice-Pecan, 54 (FG)
Stuffing, Spit-Roasted Cornish
Hens with Raisin
Pecan, 38 (PO)
Sugar and Spice Nuts, 97 (GR)
Sugared Nuts, 25 (CE)
Sugared Pecans, 31 (CC)
Tart, Pumpkin-Praline, 129 (DE)

Tarts, Miniature
Date-Pecan, 124 (PP)
Tarts, Pecan, 28 (FG); 36 (SS)
Tassies, Pecan, 124 (PP);
126 (SS)
Toffee, Pecan, 116 (GR)
Topping, Toasted Pecan, 96 (CA)
Torte, Pecan, 98 (SS)
Twists, Pecan, 73 (BR)
Waffles with Orange Butter,
Orange Pecan, 20 (BB)

**Peppermint**
Bavarian, Peppermint, 71 (DE)
Chocolate-Covered
Mints, 132 (GR)
Dainties, Chocolate
Peppermint, 73 (CC)
Drops, Peppermint, 71 (SS)
Frosting, Mint, 75 (SS)
Frosting, Peppermint, 133 (CA)
Frosting, Peppermint
Silhouette, 133 (CA)
Ice Cream,
Peppermint, 101 (DE)
Ice Cream, Peppermint
Stick, 86 (CE)
Marshmallows, Mint, 73 (CE)
Nuts, Minted, 31 (CE)
Pastel Mints, 12 (SS)
Pecans, Minted, 92 (GR)
Pudding, Peppermint
Tapioca, 16 (DE)
Pulled Sugar Mints, 109 (SS)
Ring, Pineapple-Mint
Lamb, 105 (BE)
Twists, Mint, 115 (FG)
**Peppers**
Banana Peppers,
Stuffed, 84 (VE)
Chicago Hot, 76 (GR)
Chile
Cheese, Chiles Rellenos
with, 82 (VE)
Grits, Chile-Cheese, 127 (BB)
Pico de Gallo, 75 (GR)
Rice, Chile-Cheese, 38 (BB)
Salsa, Chile, 75 (GR)
Sauce, Mexican, 38 (BB)
Vinegar, Chile Pepper, 69 (GR)
Datil Pepper Vinegar, 69 (GR)
Green
Beef-Stuffed Green
Peppers, 50 (BE)
How To Prepare Green
Peppers, 81 (VE)
Jelly, Green Pepper, 15 (GR)
Pie, Green Pepper, 84 (VE)
Pot, Pepper, 76 (SO)
Stuffed Bell Peppers with
Ham, 85 (PK)
Stuffed Green Peppers, 82 (VE)
Stuffed with Fresh Vegetables,
Green Peppers, 82 (VE)
Hash, Pepper, 50 (GR)
Jalapeño
Cornbread, Jalapeño, 16 (BR)
Jelly, Jalapeño
Pepper, 15 (GR)
Pickled Jalapeño
Peppers, 76 (GR)

Soup, Jalapeño
Cheese, 47 (SO)
Piccalilli, 53 (GR)
Pickles, French, 44 (GR)
Relish, Red Pepper, 50 (GR)
Roasted Peppers,
Italian, 134 (FG)
Sauce, Green, 35 (CC)
Sauce, Hot Pepper, 135 (VE)
**Perch**
Boiled Perch, Spicy, 117 (SE)
Fried Perch, 117 (SE)
**Persimmons**
Bread, Persimmon
Nut, 105 (BR)
Cake, Persimmon, 44 (CA)
Cookies, Persimmon, 51 (CJ)
Pie, Persimmon, 42 (PP)
Pudding, Persimmon, 56 (CC);
22 (DE); 49 (FG)

**Pheasants**
aux Fines Herbes,
Pheasant, 42 (SP)
**Pickles and Relishes**
Artichoke Pickles,
Jerusalem, 40 (GR)
Artichokes, Pickled
Jerusalem, 78 (CE)
Beans, Dilly, 40 (GR)
Beans, Pickled Green, 77 (PO)
Beet-Horseradish
Relish, 75 (GR)
Beet Pickles, 40 (GR)
Bowl, Relish, 14 (CC)
Bread and Butter
Pickles, 20 (FG); 43 (GR)
Carrot Pickles, 16 (CC)
Carrot Relish, 50 (GR)
Carrots, Pickled, 41 (GR)
Cauliflower Pickles, 41 (GR)
Celery Relish, Tart, 136 (VE)
Chicago Hot, 76 (GR)
Chile Salsa, 75 (GR)
Chutney
Apple Chutney, 55 (GR)
Cranberry Chutney,
Hot, 55 (GR)
Mango Chutney, 56 (GR)
Papaya Chutney, 56 (GR)

*Preserved wealth by two farm women in Pulaski County, Arkansas, c.1942.*

Pickles and Relishes, Chutney,
  *continued*
    Peach Chutney,
      Texas, 57 (GR)
    Pear Chutney, 57 (GR)
    Sandwiches, Chutney, 62 (SS)
    Tomato Chutney, 48 (SP)
  Corn Relish, 49 (GR)
  Corn Relish Salad, 69 (SP)
  Crab Apples, Spiced, 36 (GR)
  Cranberry-Orange
    Relish, 56 (FG); 75 (GR); 43 (SP)
  Cucumber Pickles,
    Sweet, 43 (GR)
  Cucumber Relish, 50 (GR)
  Cucumber Rings,
    Sweet, 43 (GR)
  Dill Chips, 44 (GR)
  Dill Pickles, 43 (GR)
  Figs, Pickled, 36 (GR)
  French Pickles, 44 (GR)
  Good to Know About
    Pickling, 58-59 (GR)
  Grape Relish, 47 (GR)
  Grapes, Spiced, 36 (GR)
  Hayden Salad, 12 (FG)
  Horseradish, Prepared, 76 (GR)
  Jalapeño Peppers,
    Pickled, 76 (GR)
  Mangos, Spiced, 37 (GR)
  Mason County Relish, 136 (VE)
  Onions, Tiny Pickled, 44 (GR)

Oysters, Pickled, 42 (SE)
Peaches, Pickled, 84 (CE); 38 (GR)
Peach Relish, 48 (GR)
Pear Mincemeat, 49 (GR)
Pear Relish, 48 (GR)
Pears, Pickled, 38 (GR)
Pepper Hash, 50 (GR)
Piccalilli, 53 (GR)
Pico de Gallo, 75 (GR)
Pineapple Sticks, Spicy, 39 (GR)
Piquant Relish, 129 (BE)
Red Pepper Relish, 50 (GR)
Salsify, Pickled, 100 (VE)
Sauerkraut Relish, 136 (CC);
  76 (GR)
Shrimp, Chilled Pickled, 22 (SP)
Shrimp, Pickled, 23 (CE);
  51 (SE)
Squash Pickles, 45 (GR)
Squash Relish, 52 (GR)
Sweet-and-Sour Pickles, 48 (SS)
Tomato Chow Chow,
  Green, 52 (GR)
Tomato Mincemeat,
  Green, 52 (GR)
Tomato Pickles, Green, 45 (GR)
Tomato Relish, 52 (GR)
Tongue, Pickled, 119 (BE)
Vegetable Pickles,
  Mixed, 46 (GR)
Vegetable Relish,
  Summer, 54 (GR)

Watermelon Rind,
  Pickled, 39 (GR)
Watermelon Rind Pickles, 54 (SS)
Zucchini Pickles, 45 (GR)

**Pies and Pastries**
Apple Brown Betty, 39 (DE)
Apple-Cranberry Pie with Cheese
  Pastry, 32 (PP)
Apple Crisp, 36 (DE)
Apple Crumble, 36 (DE)
Apple Custard Pie, Marion
  Flexner's, 69 (PP)
Apple Pandowdy, 39 (DE)
Apple-Pecan Pie, 29 (PP)
Apple Pie, 23 (BB)
Apple Pie, Carolina, 30 (PO)
Apple Pie, Cheese-, 137 (CC)
Apple Pie, Country, 29 (PP)
Apple Pie, Crumb-Topped,
  31 (PP)
Apple Pie, Duncan
  Hines, 28 (PP)
Apple Pie Goody, 32 (PP)
Apple Pie, Old-Time, 96 (CC)
Apple Pie, Praline-Topped,
  30 (PP)
Apple Pie, Travellers' Rest
  Skillet, 31 (PP)
Apple Pot Pie, 33 (PP)
Apricot Chiffon Pie, 109 (PP)
Banana Cream Pie,
  Kentucky, 93 (PP)

**BB** *Breakfast & Brunch*   **BE** *Beef, Veal & Lamb*   **BR** *Breads*   **CA** *Cakes*   **CC** *Company's Coming*   **CE** *Celebrations*
**CJ** *Cookie Jar*   **DE** *Just Desserts*   **FG** *Family Gatherings*   **GR** *Gift Receipts*   **PK** *All Pork*   **PO** *Plain & Fancy Poultry*
**PP** *Pies & Pastry*   **SE** *Sea & Stream*   **SO** *Soups & Stews*   **SP** *Sporting Scene*   **SS** *Socials & Soirees*   **VE** *Vegetables*

Pies and Pastries, *continued*

Bavarian Pie, 104 (PP)
Beef Pot Pie, 56 (BE)
Berry Pie, 47 (PP)
Black Bun, 15 (CE)
Bourbon Christmas
  Pie, 133 (CE)
Bourbon Pie,
  Weidmann's, 113 (PP)
Buttermilk Cream Pie, 88 (PP)
Buttermilk Custard Pie, 95 (CE)
Buttermilk Pie, German, 67 (PP)
Buttermilk Pie, Mary's, 66 (PP)
Butterscotch Meringue Pie,
  Smith and Welton's Tea
  Room, 90 (PP)
Caramel Cream Pie,
  Old-Fashioned, 91 (PP)
Caramel Pie, Damson, 75 (PP)
Cheese-Apple Pie, 137 (CC)
Cherry Pie, 114 (CC)
Cherry Pie, Mount Vernon
  Red, 34 (PP)
Cherry Pie, Royal Anne, 35 (PP)
Chess Meringue Pie, 73 (PP)
Chess Pie, 54 (PO)
Chess Pie, Brown Sugar, 73 (PP)
Chess Pie, Chocolate, 73 (PP)
Chess Pie, Hermitage, 72 (PP)
Chess Pie, Pecan, 74 (PP)
Chess Pie, Rebecca
  Boone's, 72 (PP)
Chess Pie, Tennessee
  Lemon, 74 (PP)
Chicken Salad Pies, 114 (PO)
Chocolate
  Angel Pie, Chocolate, 92 (PP)
  Black Bottom Pie,
    Delta, 105 (PP)
  Bourbon Chocolate Pecan
    Pie, 54 (PP)
  Chess Pie, Chocolate, 73 (PP)
  Chip Pie, Chocolate, 70 (SP)
  Chocolate Morsel Pie, Pleasant
    Hill, 68 (PP)
  Chocolate Pie, 110 (CE)
  Cream Pie, Chocolate, 92 (PP)
  French Huguenot Chocolate
    Pie, 68 (PP)
  French Silk Chocolate
    Pie, 112 (PP)
  Fudge Pie, 127 (SP)
  Fudge Pie, Chocolate
    Lover's, 67 (PP)
  Fudge Pie, No-Crust, 68 (PP)
  Icebox Pie, Chocolate, 112 (PP)
  Jockey's Reward Pie, 78 (CE)
  Meringue Pie,
    Chocolate, 51 (CC); 91 (PP)
  Pecan Pie, Chocolate, 53 (PP)
  Refrigerator Pie,
    Chocolate, 43 (SP)
  Rum Cream Pie,
    Chocolate, 104 (PP)
Cobblers
  Apple Cobbler,
    Kentucky, 33 (PP)
  Berry Cobbler, 47 (PP)
  Blackberry Cobbler,
    Deep-Dish, 48 (PP)

Blackberry Cobbler,
  Easy, 123 (FG)
Blackberry Cobbler,
  Quick, 103 (SP)
Blueberry Cobbler
  Roll, 47 (PP)
Dewberry Cobbler, 37 (SP)
Fig Cobbler, Fresh, 36 (PP)
Grape Cobbler, Green, 37 (PP)
Guava Cobbler, Fresh, 43 (DE)
Loquat Cobbler, 38 (PP)
Peach Cobbler, 78 (PO)
Peach Cobbler, Easy, 40 (PP)
Peach Cobbler
  Supreme, 40 (PP)
Rhubarb-Strawberry
  Cobbler, 43 (PP)
Sweet Potato Cobbler,
  Grandmother's, 58 (PP)
Coconut-Cherry Cream
  Pie, 94 (PP)
Coconut Cream Pie, Allison's
  Little Tea House, 94 (PP)
Coconut Cream Pie,
  Fresh, 96 (PP)

Coconut Custard Pie,
  Old-Fashioned, 71 (PP)
Coconut Meringue Pie, 95 (PP)
Coconut-Pineapple Cream
  Pie, 95 (PP)
Coffee-Almond Cream
  Pie, 93 (PP)
Cottage Cheese Pie,
  Kleeman's, 78 (PP)
Cranberry Pie, 48 (PP)
Cranberry Pie with Cheese
  Pastry, Apple-, 32 (PP)
Cream Pie, Festive, 101 (PP)
Cream Pie, Virginia
  Holiday, 89 (PP)
Cream Puffs, Miniature, 40 (CE)
Dewberry Custard Pie, 70 (PP)
Egg Custard Meringue
  Pie, 67 (PP)
Egg Custard Pie, 54 (PO)
Egg Custard Pie, Mrs.
  Doc's, 67 (PP)
Eggnog Pie, 106 (PP)
Fig Pie, 35 (PP)
Fig Pie, Meeting Street
  Fresh, 109 (PP)
Fig Streusel Pie, 35 (PP)
Fruit Strudel, 101 (FG)
Grape Juice Pie, 96 (PP)
Huckleberry Pie, 47 (PP)
Ice Cream Pie, Mile
  High, 105 (DE)
Jeff Davis Pie, 89 (PP)

Lemon Chess Pie,
  Tennessee, 74 (PP)
Lemon Chiffon Pie,
  Tart, 107 (PP)
Lemon Cream
  Meringue, 23 (CC)
Lemon Icebox Pie, Old Southern
  Tea Room, 113 (PP)
Lemon Meringue Pie, 98 (PP)
Lemon Meringue Pie,
  Tart, 108 (CC)
Lemon Pie, 17 (CC); 64 (CE)
Lemon Pie, Heavenly, 96 (PP)
Lemon Pie, Nashville, 76 (PP)
Lemon Slice Pie, 37 (PP)
Lime Custard Pie,
  Florida, 70 (PP)
Lime Pie, Florida, 98 (PP)
Lime Pie, Florida Key, 112 (PP)
Lime Pie, Luscious, 107 (PP)
Main Dish
  Beef Pie —a Special Way with
    Leftovers, 56 (BE)
  Beef Pie, Deep-Dish, 55 (BE)
  Chicken and Country Ham
    Deep Dish Pie, 18 (CC)
  Chicken in Patty Shells,
    Creamed, 104 (FG)
  Chicken Pie,
    Grandmother's, 53 (PO)
  Chicken Pie, Real, 55 (PO)
  Chicken Pie with Sweet Potato
    Crust, 56 (PO)
  Chicken Pot Pie,
    Golden, 56 (PO)
  Crayfish Pie, 25 (SE)
  Hot Tamale Pie, 46 (BE)
  Kidney Pie, 110 (BE)
  Lamb Pie, A Savory, 103 (BE)
  Lamb Pie, 1944
    Crustless, 101 (BE)
  Lamb Pie, Wartime, 102 (BE)
  Meat Pie, Louisiana, 45 (BE)
  Montezuma Pie, 40 (PK)
  Oyster Pie
    Rappahannock, 41 (SE)
  Pasta-Meat Pie, Tony's
    Italian, 43 (BE)
  Picnic Pie, 82 (PK)
  Pigeon Pie, 57 (PO)
  Pork and Apple Pie, 38 (PK)
  Pork Pie, Cajun, 40 (PK)
  Sausage Pie, 105 (PK)
  Shepherd's Pie, 103 (BE)
  Shrimp Pie, 48 (SE)
  Steak and Kidney
    Pudding, 109 (BE)

Pies and Pastries, Main Dish,
  *continued*
    Tuna Pot Pie, 101 (SE)
  Mango Pie, 38 (PP)
  Meringue, Basic, 24 (PP)
  Meringue, Pineapple, 25 (PP)
  Meringue, Powdered
    Sugar, 25 (PP)
  Meringue, Unbaked, 25 (PP)
  Mincemeat, Mrs. Fitzhugh
    Lee's, 44 (PP)
  Mincemeat Pie,
    Homemade, 120 (CE)
  Mincemeat Pie with Bourbon
    Sauce, 44 (PP)
  Moonshine Pie, 90 (PP)
  Muscadine Pie, 36 (PP)
  Nesselrode Pie, 108 (PP)
  Orange Meringue Pie, 100 (PP)
  Orange Meringue Pie, Old
    Talbott Tavern, 99 (PP)
  Orange Pie, Lee Family, 76 (PP)
  Osgood Pie, 13 (FG); 77 (PP)
Pastries and Crusts
  Basic Pastry, 14 (PP)
  Butter Pastry, Basic, 12 (PP)
  Cheese Pastry, 137 (CC)
  Cheese Pastry, Cheddar, 16 (PP)
  Cheese Pastry,
    Double-Crust, 32 (PP)
  Cheese Pastry Shells, 114 (PO)
  Chocolate Crumb
    Piecrust, 104 (PP)
  Chocolate Wafer
    Piecrust, 22 (PP)
  Coconut-Graham
    Piecrust, 21 (PP)
  Coconut Piecrust, 23 (PP)
  Corn Flake Piecrust, 23 (PP)
  Cream Cheese
    Pastry, 123 (PP); 126 (SS)
  Cream Cheese Pastry
    Shell, 20 (PP)
  Croquette Dough, 21 (SE)
  Deep-Dish Pastry, 16 (PP)
  Double-Crust Pastry, 17 (CC);
    25, 120 (CE); 30 (PO)
  Double-Crust Pastry,
    Basic, 12 (PP)
  Egg Pastry Shells, 20 (PP)
  Filbert-Graham
    Piecrust, 21 (PP)
  Gingersnap Piecrust, 22 (PP)
  Graham Cracker
    Piecrust, 21 (PP)
  How-To, Basic Pastry, 14 (PP)
  How-To, Puff Pastry, 18 (PP)
  Lard Pastry, Best, 12 (PP)
  Lattice-Crust Pastry, 96,
    114 (CC); 64 (VE)
  Lattice-Top Pastry, 12, 43 (PP)
  Meringue Pie Shell, 92 (PP)
  Mint Pastry Shell, 102 (BE)
  Mix, Pastry, 12 (PP)
  Pâte Brisée Sucrée, 78 (SS)
  Pâte Sucrée, 16 (PP)

Pecan Pastry Shell, 20 (PP)
Phyllo-Pastry Basket, 99 (SS)
Pie Strip Pastry, 78 (PO)
Puff Paste, 18 (PP)
Quantity Pastry, 12 (PP)
Shortcake Pastry, 53 (CA)
Single-Crust Pastry
  Shell, 12 (PP)
Stir 'n' Roll Pastry Shell, Dr.
  David Wesson's, 17 (PP)
Suet Crust, 109 (BE)
Sweet Potato Crust, 56 (PO)
Sweet Potato Pastry, 47 (BE)
Tart Pastry, 128 (CE)
Tart Shells, 122 (PP);
  112 (SP); 131 (SP)
Tart Shells,
  All-Purpose, 20 (PP)
Tart Shells, Hot
  Water, 50 (SS)
Vanilla Wafer Piecrust, 22 (PP)
Zwieback Piecrust, 23 (PP)
Peach Meringue Pie,
  Fresh, 39 (PP)
Peach Pie, Fresh, 99 (CE)
Peach Pie, Georgia, 39 (PP)
Peach Pie, Glazed, 40 (PP)
Peanut Brittle Pie, 113 (PP)
Peanut Cream Pie,
  Crunchy, 96 (PP)
Peanut Pie, 52 (PP)
Pear Crumble Pie, 41 (PP)
Pear Mincemeat Pie, 41 (PP)

Pear Pie, Old-Fashioned, 41 (PP)
Pecan
  Alabama Pecan Pie, 52 (PP)
  Apple-Pecan Pie, 29 (PP)
  Bourbon Chocolate Pecan
    Pie, 54 (PP)
  Butterscotch Pie,
    Pecan-, 101 (PP)
  Chess Pie, Pecan, 74 (PP)
  Chocolate Pecan Pie, 53 (PP)
  Cream Pie, Ma Ferguson's
    Pecan, 100 (PP)

Georgia Pecan Pie, 23 (FG)
Honey Pecan Pie,
  Tupelo, 52 (PP)
Pumpkin Pecan Pie, 123 (CE)
Pumpkin-Pecan Pie, 61 (PP)
Raisin Pie, Pecan-, 54 (PP)
Sweet Potato-Pecan Pie,
  Virginia, 58 (PP)
Tassies, Pecan, 124 (PP);
  126 (SS)
Texas Pecan Pie, 52 (PP)
Texas Poor Boy Pie, 55 (PP)
Wayside Inn Pecan Pie, 53 (PP)
Persimmon Pie, 42 (PP)
Pineapple Chiffon Pies,
  Individual, 37 (CE)
Pineapple-Cottage Cheese
  Pie, 82 (PP)
Pineapple Meringue
  Pie, 117 (PK)
Pineapple Pie, 17 (FG)
Plum Meringue Pie, 42 (PP)
Pudding Pie, Tyler, 75 (PP)
Raisin Pie, 44 (PP)
Raspberry Pie, 49 (PP)
Rhubarb Pie, 43 (PP)
Rum Pie, Savannah
  Christmas, 108 (PP)
Sherry Chiffon Pie,
  Weidmann's, 109 (PP)
Silver Pie, High Hampton Inn
  Sunny, 106 (PP)
Sorghum-Molasses Pie,
  Ozark, 77 (PP)
Sour Cream-Raisin Pie, 70 (PP)
Strawberry Pie, Plant
  City, 49 (PP)
Sweetbread and Oyster
  Pie, 118 (BE)
Sweetbreads in Pastry Shells,
  Sherried, 118 (BE)
Tarts
  Apricot Cream Tarts, 29 (FG)
  Apricot Tarts, 116 (PP)
  Blueberry Tarts, 116 (PP)
  Brown Sugar Tarts, 119 (PP)
  Caramel Cream
    Tarts, 119 (PP)
  Cheese Tartlets, 122 (PP)
  Cherry Tarts, 78 (SS)
  Cherry Tarts, Petite, 121 (PP)
  Chess Tarts, 119 (PP)
  Chicken Salad in Tart
    Shells, 80 (SS)
  Chocolate Tarts, Swiss, 50 (SS)
  Citron Tarts, 19 (CC)
  Coconut Tarts,
    Miniature, 37 (CE)
  Date-Pecan Tarts,
    Miniature, 124 (PP)
  Fruit Tarts,
    Charleston, 128 (CE)
  Fruit Tarts, Glazed, 112 (SP)
  Gazpacho Tarts, 106 (SS)
  Lemon Chess Tarts, 15 (PK)
  Lemon Chiffon Tarts, 118 (PP)

---

**BB** *Breakfast & Brunch*   **BE** *Beef, Veal & Lamb*   **BR** *Breads*   **CA** *Cakes*   **CC** *Company's Coming*   **CE** *Celebrations*
**CJ** *Cookie Jar*   **DE** *Just Desserts*   **FG** *Family Gatherings*   **GR** *Gift Receipts*   **PK** *All Pork*   **PO** *Plain & Fancy Poultry*
**PP** *Pies & Pastry*   **SE** *Sea & Stream*   **SO** *Soups & Stews*   **SP** *Sporting Scene*   **SS** *Socials & Soirees*   **VE** *Vegetables*

*In 1910 the mincemeat had to be prepared before the pies were made.*

Pies and Pastries, Tarts, *continued*
Lemon Meringue
  Tarts, 117 (PP)
Lemon Tarts, 118 (PP)
Lemon Tarts, Dainty, 125 (PP)
Lemon Tarts, Tiny, 87 (CC)
Lime Chiffon Tarts, 118 (PP)
Maids of Honor, 120 (PP)
Mincemeat Tarts
  Flambé, 120 (PP)
Orange-Cheese Tarts, 118 (PP)
Orange Tarts, 131 (SP)
Peach Tart, 45 (DE)
Peach Tartlets, 122 (PP)
Pecan Tarts, 28 (FG); 36 (SS)
Pecan Tassies, 124 (PP);
  126 (SS)
Pineapple Chiffon Pies,
  Individual, 37 (CE)
Pumpkin Chiffon
  Tarts, 118 (PP)
Pumpkin-Praline
  Tart, 129 (DE)
Shells, All-Purpose
  Tart, 20 (PP)
Shells, Hot Water
  Tart, 50 (SS)
Shells, Tart, 122 (PP); 112,
  131 (SP)
Sherry Tarts, 120 (PP)

Strawberry Tarts,
  Glazed, 67 (CE); 117 (PP)
Tassies, Martha White's
  Teatime, 123 (PP)
Vienna Tarts, 81 (CC)
Telfair Transparent Pie, 75 (PP)
Torte, Huguenot, 123 (CE)
Turnovers and Fried Pies
  Apple Pies, Fried, 42 (CC);
    132 (PP)
  Applesauce
    Turnovers, 135 (PP)
  Apricot Pies, Fried, 132 (PP)
  Apricot Turnovers, 65 (CJ)
  Banbury Tarts, 25 (CE);
    137 (PP)
  Beef and Pork Pasties, 45 (BE)
  Beef Empanadas, 47 (BE)
  Buñuelos, 59 (FG)
  Cheese Fingers, 19 (SO)
  Cranberry Pies, Southern
    Fried, 134 (PP)
  Cream Cheese
    Pastries, 135 (PP)
  Date Triangles, 136 (PP)
  Diples (Rolled Honey
    Pastry), 64 (FG)
  Empanades Dulces (Sweet
    Potato Pies), 37 (CC);
    136 (PP)

Forfar Bridies, 13 (CE)
Ham Turnovers, 91 (PK)
Meat Pies, Polish, 46 (BE)
Meat Pies, Scottish, 134 (SP)
Meat Turnovers, 73 (CE)
Oreilles de Cochon (Pigs'
  Ears), 40 (CE)
Peach Pies, Fried, 134 (PP)
Pineapple
  Pocketbooks, 137 (PP)
Sausage Rolls, 13 (CE);
  107 (PK)
Spinach Puffs, 124 (SS)
Sugar Pies, 135 (PP)
Sweet Potato
  Empanadas, 126 (CE)
Tea Turnovers, 136 (PP)
Tyler Pudding, 127 (CC)
Vanilla Chiffon Pie, 104 (PP)
Vanilla Cream Pie, 88 (PP)
Vegetable
  Bean Pie, Oklahoma, 57 (PP)
  Green Pepper Pie, 84 (VE)
  Mushroom Pie, 64 (VE)
  Onion Pie, Green, 70 (VE)
  Potato Pie, Maryland
    White, 116 (CE); 57 (PP)
  Pumpkin Chiffon
    Pie, 111 (PP); 65 (SP)
  Pumpkin Meringue Pie, 61 (PP)

Pies and Pastries, Vegetable,
  *continued*
    Pumpkin Pecan Pie, 123 (CE)
    Pumpkin-Pecan Pie, 61 (PP)
    Pumpkin Pie,
      Bourbon-, 62 (PP)
    Pumpkin Pie,
      Virginia, 61 (PP)
    Spinach Pie, 62 (FG)
    Squash Pie,
      Butternut, 63 (PP)
    Squash Pie, Yellow, 63 (PP)
    Sweet Potato Chiffon
      Pie, 111 (PP)
    Sweet Potato Cobbler,
      Grandmother's, 58 (PP)
    Sweet Potato-Coconut
      Pie, 58 (PP)
    Sweet Potato Custard
      Pie, 103 (CC); 23 (FG)
    Sweet Potato-Pecan Pie,
      Virginia, 58 (PP)
    Sweet Potato Pie,
      1894, 57 (PP)
    Sweet Potato Pie, Mary
      Randolph's, 57 (PP)
    Sweet Potato-Pumpkin Pie,
      Hermitage, 59 (PP)
    Tomato Pie, 68 (BB)
    Tomato Pie, Green, 63 (PP);
      68 (SP)
    Vinegar Pie, James K.
      Polk's, 77 (PP)
    Walnut Pie, Black, 55 (PP)
**Pineapple**
    Ambrosia, Holiday, 30 (DE)
    Ambrosia,
      Orange-Pineapple, 136 (SS)
    Cake, Pineapple, 123 (FG)
    Cake, Pineapple-Ambrosia
      Upside-Down, 71 (CA)
    Cake, Pineapple Angel
      Food, 112 (CA)
    Cake, Pineapple Icebox, 86 (DE)
    Cake, Pineapple
      Meringue, 77 (CA)
    Cake, Pineapple Pecan, 124 (CE)
    Cake, Pineapple Pound, 12 (CC)
    Cake, Pineapple
      Upside-Down, 70 (CA)
    Candied Pineapple and
      Cherries, 90 (GR)
    Cheesecake, Pineapple, 83 (PP)
    Compote, Sunrise, 30 (DE)
    Conserve, Rhubarb-
      Pineapple, 29 (GR)
    Conserve, Strawberry-
      Pineapple, 30 (GR)
    Cookies, Pineapple, 53 (CJ)
    Empanadas Dulces, (Sweet
      Potato Pies), 37 (CC); 136 (PP)
    Filling, Pineapple, 70 (BR);
      137 (PP)
    Filling, Tutti-Frutti, 31 (CA)
    Fritters, Pineapple, 116 (BB)
    Frosting, Pineapple, 123 (FG)

Frozen Pineapple
  Delight, 112 (DE)
Glaze,
  Coconut-Pineapple, 92 (PK)
Glaze, Pineapple, 12 (CC)
Jam, Christmas, 25 (GR)
Lamb Chops and Pineapple,
  Lena's, 96 (BE)

Lamb, Pineapple-Mint
  Glazed, 115 (SP)
Lamb Ring,
  Pineapple-Mint, 105 (BE)
Meringue, Pineapple, 25 (PP)
Minted Pineapple, 84 (SS)
Mold, Raspberry-
  Pineapple, 76 (CC)
Orangeade, Pineapple, 68 (FG)
Pie, Coconut-Pineapple
  Cream, 95 (PP)
Pie, Pineapple, 17 (FG)
Pie, Pineapple-Cottage
  Cheese, 82 (PP)
Pie, Pineapple
  Meringue, 117 (PK)
Pies, Individual Pineapple
  Chiffon, 37 (CE)
Pocketbooks, Pineapple,
  137 (PP)
Pork Chops, Pineapple, 29 (PK)
Rum Bits, Pineapple-, 124 (SS)
Salad, Pineapple
  Cheddar, 96 (CC)
Sandwiches, Cream Cheese and
  Pineapple, 52 (SS)
Sauce, Orange-
  Pineapple, 134 (DE)
Sherbet, Pineapple, 40 (FG)
Sherbet, Pineapple
  Buttermilk, 95 (DE)
Sherbet, Pineapple-
  Lemon, 81 (SS)
Snowy Nests with Pineapple and
  Spun Sugar, 133 (SS)
Sticks, Spicy Pineapple, 39 (GR)
Topping, Pineapple, 113 (CA)
**Pizza**
Mini Pizzas, 80 (CE)

**Plum Puddings**
  Hard Sauce, Plum Pudding with
    Sherried, 12 (CC)
  Plum Pudding, 26 (DE); 40 (FG)
  Sauce, Plum Pudding, 26 (DE)
  Steamed English Plum
    Pudding, 26 (DE)
**Plums**
  Butter, Spiced Plum, 27 (GR)
  Conserve, Plum, 29 (GR)
  Ice Cream, Greengage
    Plum, 101 (DE)
  Jam, Red Plum, 48 (BB)
  Jelly, Fresh Plum, 48 (FG)
  Jelly, Red Plum, 11 (BB);
    13 (GR)
  Pie, Plum Meringue, 42 (PP)
  Sauce, Leg of Lamb with
    Plum, 90 (BE)
  Sauce, Sweet-and-Sour
    Plum, 126 (PO)
**Pomegranates**
  Ice, Pomegranate, 91 (CC)
**Pompano**
  à la Gherardi, Henry's
    Restaurant Pompano, 78 (SE)
  Amandine, Pompano, 80 (SE)
  Broiled Pompano, 80 (SE)
  Jacques Latour,
    Pompano, 79 (SE)
  Papillote, Pompano en, 77 (SE)
  Wine-Baked Pompano in
    Sauce, 79 (SE)
**Popcorn**
  Balls, Popcorn, 134 (CE);
    114 (GR)
  Cracker Jacks, 114 (GR)
  Hunky Dories, 136 (GR)
**Pork.** *See also* Bacon, Ham,
Sausage.
  Barbecue
    Chops, Barbecued
      Pork, 52 (PK)
    Chops, Country-Pride
      Pork, 52 (PK)
    Chops, Grilled Pork,
      51 (PK)
    Chops, Hickory-Smoked
      Stuffed Pork, 51 (PK)
    Chops, Honey Pork, 51 (PK)
    Chops, Oven-Barbecued
      Pork, 27 (PK)
    Cubes, Oven-Barbecued
      Pork, 35 (PK)
    Kabobs, Pork, 58 (PK)
    Kabobs, Southern
      Tender, 58 (PK)
    Leg of Pork,
      Barbecued, 49 (PK)
    Mixed Grill, 58 (PK)
    Ribs, Barbecued Pork, 88 (CE)
    Ribs, Country-Style, 54 (PK)
    Ribs, Florida Barbecued
      Country-Style, 57 (PK)
    Ribs, Hickory-Smoked
      Pork, 54 (PK)

**BB** *Breakfast & Brunch*   **BE** *Beef, Veal & Lamb*   **BR** *Breads*   **CA** *Cakes*   **CC** *Company's Coming*   **CE** *Celebrations*
**CJ** *Cookie Jar*   **DE** *Just Desserts*   **FG** *Family Gatherings*   **GR** *Gift Receipts*   **PK** *All Pork*   **PO** *Plain & Fancy Poultry*
**PP** *Pies & Pastry*   **SE** *Sea & Stream*   **SO** *Soups & Stews*   **SP** *Sporting Scene*   **SS** *Socials & Soirees*   **VE** *Vegetables*

68

Pork, Barbecue, *continued*
  Ribs, Oven-Barbecued Country
    Pork, 16 (CE)
  Roast, Louisiana-
    Style, 48 (PK)
  Roast, Orange-Basted
    Pork, 49 (PK)
  Roast, Spit-Roasted Pork
    Loin, 48 (PK)
  Sausage and Cabbage, Grilled
    Polish, 59 (PK)
  Shoulder, Barbecued
    Pork, 15 (FG)
  Shoulder, Smoked
    Pork, 50 (PK)
  Sliced Barbecued
    Pork, 50 (PK)
  Spareribs, Barbecued, 68 (SP)
  Spareribs, Grilled
    Sweet-and-Sour, 56 (PK)
  Spareribs, Marinated
    Smoked, 56 (PK)
  Spareribs, Southern
    Barbecued, 53 (PK)
  Spareribs, Texas, 54 (PK)
  Steaks, Marinated
    Pork, 52 (PK)
  Stove-Top Pork
    Barbecue, 22 (PK)
Burgoo, 135 (SO)
Chops and Steaks
  Apples, Pork Chops with
    Fried, 29 (PK)
  Baked Chops with
    Vegetables, 30 (PK)
  Baked Pork Chops,
    Autumn, 29 (PK)
  Baked Pork Steaks, 24 (PK)
  Baked Stuffed Pork
    Chops, 26 (PK)
  Barbecued Pork
    Chops, 52 (PK)
  Braised Pork Chops, 25 (PK)
  Broiled Pork Chops with
    Robert Sauce, 25 (PK)
  Broiled Pork Steaks, 23 (PK)
  Broiled Pork
    Tenderloin, 23 (PK)
  Country-Pride Pork
    Chops, 52 (PK)
  Cranberry-Glazed Pork
    Chops, 27 (PK)
  Creole Pork Chops, 31 (PK)
  Fricassee, Pork Steak, 24 (PK)

Fried Pork Chops, 25 (PK)
Gravy, Pork Chops
  and, 26 (PK)
Gravy, Pork Chops with
  Cream, 31 (BB)
Grilled Pork Chops, 51 (PK)
Hickory-Smoked Stuffed Pork
  Chops, 51 (PK)
Honey Pork Chops, 51 (PK)
Marinated Pork
  Steaks, 52 (PK)
One-Dish Pork Chops, 30 (PK)
Oven-Barbecued Pork
  Chops, 27 (PK)
Pineapple Pork Chops, 29 (PK)
Prunes, Pork Tenderloin
  with, 23 (PK)
Raisin Dressing, Pork Steaks
  with, 23 (PK)
Sauerkraut Dinner, Pork
  and, 31 (PK)
Vermouth, Pork Chops
  in, 26 (PK)
Cubed Pork
  Barbecued Pork Cubes,
    Oven-, 35 (PK)
  Casserole, Pork and
    Corn, 37 (PK)
  Casserole, Pork and
    Macaroni, 38 (PK)

Chop Suey, Pork, 37 (PK)
Fried Rice, Savannah's
  Famous, 40 (PK)
Hash, Pork, 40 (PK)
Jambalaya, Creole, 109 (PK)
Jambalaya, Pork, 121 (SO)
Kabobs, Pork, 58 (PK)
Kabobs, Southern
  Tender, 58 (PK)
Paella Valenciana, 68 (PO)
Paprika Pork, 35 (PK)
Pie, Montezuma, 40 (PK)
Pie, Pork and Apple, 38 (PK)
Posole Ortiz, 37 (PK)
Scrapple, 128 (PK)
Sweet-and-Sour Pork, 37 (PK)
Turnips over Rice, Pork
  and, 35 (PK)
Cuts of Pork, 132 (PK)
Good to Know, 132-137 (PK)
Hog Jowl, Black-Eyed Peas
  and, 126 (PK)
Hog Jowl, Turnip Greens
  and, 125 (PK)
Pig, Barbecued Whole, 45 (PK)
Pig, Roast Suckling, 12 (PK)
Pig, Stuffed Roast
  Suckling, 16 (PK)
Ribs
  Barbecued Country-Style Ribs,
    Florida, 57 (PK)
  Barbecued Pork Ribs, 88 (CE)
  Barbecued Spareribs, 68 (SP)
  Barbecued Spareribs,
    Southern, 53 (PK)
  Broiled Ribs, 32 (PK)
  Country-Style Ribs, 54 (PK)
  Gravy, Spareribs with, 32 (PK)
  Grilled Sweet-and-Sour
    Spareribs, 56 (PK)
  Hickory-Smoked Pork
    Ribs, 54 (PK)
  Jambalaya, Pork Rib, 34 (PK)
  Marinated Smoked
    Spareribs, 56 (PK)
  Oven-Barbecued Country Pork
    Ribs, 16 (CE)
  Oven-Barbecued Ribs, Deep
    South, 33 (PK)
  Roasted Spareribs, 32 (PK)
  Sauerkraut, Old Dominion
    Pork and, 34 (PK)
  Sauerkraut, Spareribs
    and, 34 (PK)

*This Crown sausage stuffer was patented in 1899.*

Pork, Ribs, *continued*
    Sherried Spareribs, 33 (PK)
    Stuffed Baked
      Spareribs, 33 (PK)
    Sweet-and-Sour
      Spareribs, 32 (PK)
    Texas Spareribs, 54 (PK)
  Roasts
    Barbecued Pork,
      Sliced, 50 (PK)
    Barbecue, Stove-Top
      Pork, 22 (PK)
    Crown Roast of Pork with
      Sausage Stuffing, 20 (PK)
    Grecian-Style Roast Pork with
      Potatoes, 62 (FG)
    Louisiana-Style Pork
      Roast, 48 (PK)
    Marinated Pork Roast, 17 (PK)
    Orange-Basted Pork
      Roast, 49 (PK)
    Ozark Pork Roast, 18 (PK)
    Pork Loin Roast, 54 (CC)
    Pork Royal, 21 (PK)
    Roast Loin of Pork, 18 (PK)
    Sandwiches, Razorback
      Roast, 30 (FG)
    Smoked Pork
      Shoulder, 50 (PK)
    Spit-Roasted Pork Loin
      Roast, 48 (PK)
    Sweet Potatoes, Roast Pork
      and, 20 (PK)
    Vegetables, Roast Loin of Pork
      with, 18 (PK)
  Salt Pork
    Apples, Salt Pork
      and, 124 (PK)
    Cake, Williamsburg
      Pork, 62 (CA)
    Creamed Salt Pork over Toast
      Points, 123 (PK)
    Fried Salt Pork with
      Mustard, 117 (PK)
    Green Beans with Salt
      Pork, 21 (VE)
    Pork and Beans, 122 (PK)
    Red Beans and Rice, 29 (CC)
    Stew, Salt Pork and
      Potato, 123 (PK)
  Stew, Brunswick, 135 (SO)
  Stew, Camp, 134 (SO)
  Tenderloin
    Apple Rings, Pork Tenderloin
      with Sherried, 21 (PK)
    Broiled Pork
      Tenderloin, 23 (PK)
    Casserole, Pork and
      Macaroni, 38 (PK)
    Cutlets, Pan-Fried
      Pork, 130 (BB)
    Marinated Pork
      Tenderloin, 21 (PK)
    Pork Tenderloins, 89 (SP)
    Prunes, Pork Tenderloin
      with, 23 (PK)

  Stuffed Pork
    Tenderloins, 115 (SS)
  Variety Meat
    Brains Scrambled with
      Eggs, 127 (PK)
    German Pannas, 130 (PK)
    Head Cheese, 129 (PK)
    Liver Dumplings, 130 (PK)
    Liver Pâté, Cajun, 130 (PK)
    Pig's Feet, Fried, 127 (PK)
    Pig's Feet, Pickled, 127 (PK)
    Scrapple, 128 (PK)

**Pork, Ground**
  Cabbage Rolls, Greek, 39 (PK)
  Cakes, Pork, 39 (PK)
  Chili, Cold Weather, 113 (SO)
  Loaf, Ham, 86 (PK)
  Loaf, Upside-Down
    Ham, 86 (PK)
  Loaf, Veal, 79 (BE)
  Meatballs, German-Style,
    39 (BE)
  Meatballs, Scandinavian,
    18 (FG)
  Pasties, Beef and Pork, 45 (BE)
  Pâté, Cajun Liver, 130 (PK)
  Patties, Dixie Pork, 38 (PK)
  Pie, Cajun Pork, 40 (PK)
  Stew, Easy Southern, 39 (PK)

**Potatoes**
  Bacon Grill, 132 (BB)
  Baked
    Baked Potatoes, 112 (CC)
    Charcoal-Baked
      Potatoes, 97 (SP)
    Puffs, Baked Potato, 110 (CC)
    Quick-Baked Potatoes, 86 (VE)
    Stuffed Baked
      Potatoes, 86 (VE)
  Boiled Potatoes with
    Jackets, 86 (VE)
  Boiled Potatoes without
    Jackets, 87 (VE)

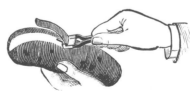

  Bread, Dunleith
    Potato, 133 (CC)
  Bread, Pumpernickel, 53 (BR)
  Bubble and Squeak, 31 (VE)
  Cake, Mashed Potato, 57 (CA)
  Cakes, Greek Mashed
    Potato, 91 (VE)
  Camp-Style Potatoes, 36 (SP)
  Casserole, Creamy
    Potato, 57 (CC)
  Cheese Potatoes, 55 (SP)
  Creamed Potatoes, 87 (VE)
  Creamed Red Potatoes, 34 (FG)
  Dauphine Potatoes, 64 (BE)

  Doughnuts, Potato, 126 (BR)
  Dumplings, Potato, 21 (PO)
  Eggs Florentine, 63 (BB)
  Escalloped Potatoes, 88 (VE)
  French-Fried Potatoes, 61 (SP)
  Fried Boiled Potatoes, 58 (BB)
  Fritters, Potato, 92 (VE)
  Green Beans with
    Potatoes, 48 (CC)
  Green Peas and Potatoes,
    Creamed, 77 (VE)
  Griddle Cakes, Potato, 35 (BB)
  Hash Brown Potatoes, 91 (VE)
  Hash Browns,
    Riverboat, 21 (BB)
  How To Prepare
    Potatoes, 85 (VE)
  Kugel, Potato, 60 (CE)
  Lamb with Potatoes, Roast Leg
    of, 56 (CE)
  Lefse, 20 (FG)
  Lyonnaise Potatoes, 23 (BB)
  Marraine, Potato (Potato
    Puffs), 24 (CC)
  Mashed Potatoes, 64 (SP);
    89 (VE)
  Medley, Parsley Potato, 94 (CC)
  Medley, Potato, 127 (VE)
  New Potatoes, Boiled, 87 (VE)
  New Potatoes, Browned, 91 (VE)
  New Potatoes, Fried, 91 (VE)
  New Potatoes, Green Beans
    and, 23 (VE)
  New Potatoes, Green Beans
    with, 121 (SS)
  New Potatoes, Leeks
    and, 60 (VE)
  New Potatoes, Oven-Roasted Veal
    with, 60 (BE)
  New Potatoes, Parsley
    Buttered, 93 (CE)
  New Potatoes with Parsley
    Butter, 46 (CC)
  Ocracoke Collards, 53 (VE)
  Oven-Browned Potatoes, Roasted
    Leg of Lamb with, 10 (CC)
  Oven-Fried Potatoes, 91 (VE)
  Pancakes, Potato, 92 (VE)
  Pan-Fried Potatoes, 91 (VE)
  Patties, Dixie Pork, 38 (PK)
  Pepper Pot, 76 (SO)
  Pie, Maryland White
    Potato, 116 (CE); 57 (PP)
  Planked Shad, 89 (SE)
  Pork with Potatoes, Grecian-Style
    Roast, 62 (FG)
  Puffs, Mashed Potato, 89 (VE)
  Ranch-Style Potatoes, 97 (PK)
  Roasted Potatoes,
    Campfire, 102 (CE)
  Rolls, Icebox Potato, 77 (BB)
  Rolls, Potato, 50 (SS)
  Rolls, Potato Ice Box, 61 (BR)
  Rosettes, Potato, 42 (SS)
  Salads
    German Potato Salad, 15 (CC)

---

**BB** *Breakfast & Brunch*   **BE** *Beef, Veal & Lamb*   **BR** *Breads*   **CA** *Cakes*   **CC** *Company's Coming*   **CE** *Celebrations*
**CJ** *Cookie Jar*   **DE** *Just Desserts*   **FG** *Family Gatherings*   **GR** *Gift Receipts*   **PK** *All Pork*   **PO** *Plain & Fancy Poultry*
**PP** *Pies & Pastry*   **SE** *Sea & Stream*   **SO** *Soups & Stews*   **SP** *Sporting Scene*   **SS** *Socials & Soirees*   **VE** *Vegetables*

*Potato peeling was serious business in this 1900s cooking class.*

Potatoes, Salads, *continued*
Hot German Potato
Salad, 22 (FG)
Hot Potato Salad, 40 (CC)
Molded Potato Salad, 88 (CE)
Mustard Potato Salad, 77 (PO)
Scottish Potato
Salad, 136 (SP)
Sour Cream-Mustard Potato
Salad, 89 (FG)
Sour Cream Potato
Salad, 107 (SP)
Saratoga Potatoes, 92 (VE)
Sausage Dish,
German, 108 (PK)
Shoe-String Potatoes, 40 (BB)
Soup, Creamy Herb
Potato, 67 (SO)
Soup, Jalapeño Cheese, 47 (SO)
Soup, Potato, 67 (SO)
Soup, Southern
Jugged, 106 (SO)
Starter, Potato-Yeast, 40 (BR)
Stew, Pine Bark, 136 (SO)
Stew, Salt Pork and
Potato, 123 (PK)
Stuffing, Potato, 48 (PO)
Stuffing, Roast Goose with
Potato and Peanut, 41 (PO)
Vichyssoise, 67 (SO)

**Potatoes, Sweet**
Apple-Sausage Loaf, 105 (PK)
Biscuits, Sweet Potato, 97 (BB);
89 (BR)
Biscuits with Baked Ham, Sweet
Potato, 106 (SS)

Bread, Sweet Potato, 106 (BR);
30 (CC)
Buns, Sweet Potato, 130 (SP)
Cake, Sweet Potato, 56 (CA)
Cake, Sweet Potato
Pound, 56 (CA)
Candied Sweet Potatoes,
126 (CC); 53 (PO); 95 (VE)
Candied Sweet Potatoes with
Lemon Slices, 95 (VE)
Candy, Mexican Sweet
Potato, 127 (GR)
Casserole, Sweet Potato, 96 (VE)
Casserole, Virginia Sweet
Potato, 96 (VE)
Cobbler, Grandmother's Sweet
Potato, 58 (PP)
Company Sweet
Potatoes, 119 (CE)
Corn Pones, Sweet
Potato, 24 (BR)
Croquettes, Sweet
Potato, 96 (VE)
Crust, Sweet Potato, 56 (PO)
Empanadas Dulces (Sweet Potato
Pies), 37 (CC); 136 (PP)
Empanadas, Sweet
Potato, 126 (CE)
Filling, Sweet Potato, 126 (CE)
Fried Sweet Potatoes, 95 (VE)
Glazed Sweet Potatoes, 117 (PK)
Ham with Sweet Potatoes,
Baked, 77 (PK)
Holiday Sweet Potatoes, 96 (VE)
How To Prepare Sweet
Potatoes, 93 (VE)

Meringue, Sweet Potatoes
with, 96 (VE)
Muffins, Sweet Potato, 116 (CE)
Orange Shells, Fluffy Sweet
Potatoes in, 95 (VE)
Pastry, Sweet Potato, 47 (BE)
Pie, Hermitage Sweet
Potato-Pumpkin, 59 (PP)
Pie, Mary Randolph's Sweet
Potato, 57 (PP)
Pie, 1894 Sweet Potato, 57 (PP)
Pie, Sweet Potato
Chiffon, 111 (PP)
Pie, Sweet
Potato-Coconut, 58 (PP)
Pie, Sweet Potato
Custard, 103 (CC); 23 (FG)
Pie, Virginia Sweet
Potato-Pecan, 58 (PP)
Pone, Sweet Potato, 22 (DE)
Pudding, Sweet Potato, 96 (VE)
Roast Pork and Sweet
Potatoes, 20 (PK)
Soufflé, Sweet Potato, 54 (CC)
Waffles, Sweet Potato, 116 (BB)
Yam Variation, 126 (CC)
**Pralines**
Bread, Praline, 40 (CE)
Buttermilk Pralines, 128 (GR)
Cake, Praline, 78 (CA)
Cake, Praline Chiffon, 115 (CA)
Cheesecake, Praline, 84 (PP)
Coconut Pralines, 130 (GR)
Cookies, Lemon Praline, 76 (CJ)
Creole Pralines, 127 (GR)
Georgia Nuggets, 128 (GR)

**Pralines,** *continued*
  Kisses, Praline, 10 (CJ)
  Maple Pralines, 130 (GR)
  Peanut Patties, 130 (GR)
  Peanut Pralines, 92 (FG)
  Pie, Praline-Topped
    Apple, 30 (PP)
  Plantation Pralines, 128 (GR)
  Tart, Pumpkin-Praline, 129 (DE)
**Prunes**
  Bread, Prune, 106 (BR)
  Cake, Prune, 69 (CA)
  Cake, Prunella, 69 (CA)
  Filling, Prune, 70 (BR)
  Pork Tenderloin with
    Prunes, 23 (PK)
  Stewed Prunes, 31 (BB)
  Stuffed Prunes, 127 (FG)
  Whip, Prune, 47 (DE)
**Puddings**
  Apple Pudding, 18 (DE)
  Banana Cream Pudding, 55 (DE)
  Banana Custard
    Pudding, 54 (DE)
  Banana Pudding, 103 (CC)
  Bird's Nest Pudding, 53 (DE)
  Bishop Whipple
    Pudding, 20 (DE)
  Blueberry Pudding, 42 (DE)
  Bread and Butter Pudding with
    Bourbon Sauce, 15 (SP)
  Bread Pudding, Bon
    Ton's, 12 (DE)
  Bread Pudding,
    Caramel, 13 (DE)
  Bread Pudding with Lemon
    Sauce, 13 (DE)
  Bread Pudding with Wine
    Sauce, 13 (DE)
  Caramel Sponge
    Pudding, 23 (DE)
  Cardinal Pudding, 36 (FG)
  Cheese Pudding, 74 (CC)
  Chicken Pudding,
    Maryland, 58 (PO)
  Chicken Pudding, Mary
    Randolph's, 59 (PO)
  Chicken Pudding,
    Virginia, 58 (PO)
  Chocolate Pudding,
    Steamed, 24 (DE)
  Chocolate Sponge
    Pudding, 24 (DE)
  Christmas Pudding, 27 (DE)
  Corn Pudding, 133 (CE)
  Corn Pudding,
    Plantation, 46 (VE)
  Corn Pudding,
    Southern, 114 (CE)
  Cottage Pudding with Lemon
    Sauce, 18 (DE)
  Cranberry-Molasses
    Pudding, 25 (DE)
  Cushaw Pudding, 116 (VE)
  Cushaw Pudding,
    Spiced, 116 (VE)

  Date Pudding, 127 (FG)
  Date Pudding with Cherry
    Sauce, 21 (DE)
  Date Tapioca Pudding, 17 (DE)
  Fig Pudding, 116 (CE)
  Fish Pudding, 24 (SS)
  Flan, Spanish, 136 (FG)
  Ginger-Apple Pudding, 18 (DE)
  Ginger Pudding, 20 (DE)
  Hasty Pudding, 10 (DE)
  Indian Pudding, 11 (DE)
  Kiss Pudding, 53 (DE)
  Lemon Sponge
    Pudding, 23 (DE)
  Macaroni Pudding, 122 (CC)
  Macaroon Pudding, 76 (DE)
  Mango Custard, 132 (FG)
  Melrose Pudding, 26 (CC)
  Mush Pudding, 11 (DE)
  Nesselrode Pudding, 77 (DE)
  Ozark Pudding, 40 (DE)
  Peppermint Tapioca
    Pudding, 16 (DE)
  Persimmon Pudding, 56 (CC);
    22 (DE); 49 (FG)
  Pie, Tyler Pudding, 75 (PP)
  Pistachio Tapioca
    Pudding, 17 (DE)
  Plum Pudding, 26 (DE); 40 (FG)
  Plum Pudding, Steamed
    English, 26 (DE)

  Plum Pudding with Sherried
    Hard Sauce, 12 (CC)
  Porridge, Scandinavian
    Creamy, 10 (DE)
  Queen of Puddings, 14 (DE)
  Rice Pudding,
    Arkansas, 14 (DE)
  Rice Pudding, Baked, 15 (DE)
  Rice Pudding,
    Norwegian, 15 (DE)
  Rice Pudding with
    Currants, 15 (DE)
  Rum Pudding with Blackberry
    Sauce, 104 (FG)
  Rutabaga Pudding, 99 (VE)
  Snow Pudding, 76 (DE)
  Squash Pudding,
    Winter, 114 (VE)
  Steak and Kidney
    Pudding, 109 (BE)
  Sweet Potato Pone, 22 (DE)
  Sweet Potato Pudding, 96 (VE)
  Tyler Pudding, 127 (CC)
  Vanilla Pudding, 31 (SS)
  Woodford Pudding, 21 (DE)
  Yorkshire Puddings,
    Individual, 14 (BE)
**Pumpkin**
  Bread, Pumpkin, 106 (BR)
  Cake, Pumpkin, 57 (CA);
    102 (CE)

*To become a jack o'lantern is every pumpkin's dream, c.1905.*

Brown Brothers

---

**BB** *Breakfast & Brunch*   **BE** *Beef, Veal & Lamb*   **BR** *Breads*   **CA** *Cakes*   **CC** *Company's Coming*   **CE** *Celebrations*
**CJ** *Cookie Jar*   **DE** *Just Desserts*   **FG** *Family Gatherings*   **GR** *Gift Receipts*   **PK** *All Pork*   **PO** *Plain & Fancy Poultry*
**PP** *Pies & Pastry*   **SE** *Sea & Stream*   **SO** *Soups & Stews*   **SP** *Sporting Scene*   **SS** *Socials & Soirees*   **VE** *Vegetables*

Pumpkin, *continued*
Charlotte, Pumpkin-
Almond, 63 (CC)
Cheesecake, Pumpkin, 85 (PP)
Cookies, Pumpkin
Spice, 53 (CJ)
Corn Pones, Ozark
Pumpkin, 24 (BR)
Fritters, Smith House
Pumpkin, 128 (BR)
Muffins, Greenbrier
Pumpkin, 116 (BR)
Muffins, Old Salem
Pumpkin, 115 (BR)
Muffins, Pumpkin, 57 (SS)
Pie, Bourbon-Pumpkin, 62 (PP)
Pie, Hermitage Sweet
Potato-Pumpkin, 59 (PP)
Pie, Pumpkin Chiffon, 111 (PP);
65 (SP)
Pie, Pumpkin Meringue, 61 (PP)
Pie, Pumpkin Pecan, 123 (CE)
Pie, Pumpkin-Pecan, 61 (PP)
Pie, Virginia Pumpkin, 61 (PP)
Soup, Baked-in-a-Pumpkin,
68 (SO)
Tart, Pumpkin-Praline, 129 (DE)
Tarts, Pumpkin
Chiffon, 118 (PP)

## Q

**Quail**
Baked Quail, Holiday, 48 (FG)
Baked Quail, Lemon-, 50 (SP)
Breakfast Quail, 46 (SP)
Broiled Quail on Toast, 53 (BB)
Fried Quail with Cream
Gravy, 134 (CC)
Roast Quail with Savory Orange
Sauce, Cold, 31 (SP)
**Quiches**
Artichoke Quiche, 125 (BB)
Party Quiches, 80 (CE)
Spinach Quiche, 125 (BB)

## R

**Rabbit**
Fried Rabbit, 50 (SP)
**Raisins**
Bars, Gottlieb's Bakery
Fruit, 94 (CJ)
Biscuits, Raisin, 91 (BR);
14 (SS)
Bread, Raisin, 110 (BB);
22 (FG)
Bread, Salzburger
Raisin, 63 (BR)
Cake, John Garner, 76 (CA)
Cake, Dolly Varden, 20 (CA)
Cake, Raisin-
Applesauce, 69 (CA)

Cakes, Mary Telfair's
Derby, 28 (CJ)
Cake, Welcome, 62 (CA)
Coffee Cake, 1860
Raisin, 64 (BR)
Cookies, Alsatian
Plum, 128 (CJ)
Cookies, Applesauce, 48 (CJ)
Cookies, Guess-Again, 76 (CJ)
Cookies, Maryland Black
Pepper, 37 (CJ)
Cookies, Mother Kearney's
Sugar-Raisin, 82 (CJ)
Cookies, Oatmeal-Raisin,
44 (CJ)
Cookies, Rock, 36 (CJ)
Cookies, Spicy
Raisin-Nut, 37 (CJ)
Cookies, Susan G. Cooke's
Exposition, 61 (CJ)
Crinkles, Oatmeal, 76 (CJ)
Custard, Baked Raisin, 58 (DE)
Dressing, Pork Steaks with
Raisin, 23 (PK)
Ducklings with Apples and
Raisins, 60 (CC)
Fat Rascals, 134 (BR)
Filling, Raisin, 82 (CJ)
Glaze, Cranberry-Raisin, 92 (PK)
Hermits, 34 (CJ)
Hermits, Pecan, 34 (CJ)
Lizzies, 118 (CJ)
Logs, Brandied Fruit, 119 (CJ)
Muffins, Raisin Bran, 115 (BR)
Penuche, Raisin, 126 (GR)
Pie, Osgood, 13 (FG); 77 (PP)
Pie, Pecan-Raisin, 54 (PP)
Pie, Raisin, 44 (PP)
Pie, Sour Cream-Raisin, 70 (PP)
Pudding, Christmas, 27 (DE)
Pudding with Currants,
Rice, 15 (DE)
Rocks, Chocolate, 40 (CJ)
Rocks, Maryland, 69 (BB);
34 (CJ)
Rocks, Sour Cream, 36 (CJ)
Sauce, German Tongue with
Raisin, 120 (BE)
Sauce, Raisin, 47 (CC)
Sauce, Raisin-
Chocolate, 86 (GR)
Sauce, Spiced Raisin, 92 (PK)
Soup, Sweet, 18 (FG)
Stuffing, Raisin, 32 (PO)
Stuffing, Spit-Roasted Cornish
Hens with Raisin
Pecan, 38 (PO)
Tarts, Banbury, 25 (CE);
137 (PP)
Waffles, Raisin, 61 (BB)
**Raspberries**
Berry Roly-Poly, 53 (CC)
Cobbler, Berry, 47 (PP)
Custard Sauce over Strawberries
and Raspberries,
Chilled, 84 (SP)
Fool, Raspberry, 46 (CC)
Jam, Raspberry, 23 (GR)
Jelly, Apple-Raspberry, 10 (GR)
Logs, Raspberry Jam, 99 (CJ)

Mold, Raspberry-
Pineapple, 76 (CC)
Mousse, Raspberry, 109 (DE)
Peaches with Raspberries,
Fresh, 33 (DE)
Pie, Berry, 47 (PP)
Pie, Raspberry, 49 (PP)
Preserves, Raspberry, 18 (GR)
Sauce, Raspberry, 111 (DE)
Shrub, 26 (CE)
Soup, Chilled
Raspberry, 42 (SO)
Torte, Opa's, 125 (DE)
Truffles, Raspberry, 132 (GR)
**Redfish**
Aspic, Redfish, 83 (SE)
Baked Stuffed Redfish,
Mississippi Sound, 81 (SE)
Bouillabaisse, New
Orleans, 55 (SE)
Court Bouillon of
Redfish, 83 (SE)
Fried Redfish, Gulf City, 83 (SE)
Poached Redfish, 62 (BB)
**Relishes.** *See* Pickles and Relishes.
**Rhubarb**
Cobbler, Rhubarb-
Strawberry, 43 (PP)
Conserve, Rhubarb-
Pineapple, 29 (GR)
Crumble, Rhubarb, 47 (DE)
Marmalade, Rhubarb, 22 (GR)
Pie, Rhubarb, 43 (PP)
**Rice**
Arroz con Pollo, Hearty, 67 (PO)
Baked Rice, 102 (CC)
Balls, Rice, 15 (SO)
Beef Porcupines, 39 (BE)
Beef-Stuffed Green
Peppers, 50 (BE)
Bread, Brown Rice, 31 (FG)
Bread, Mrs. Yohe's Original
Brown Rice, 55 (BR)
Brown Rice, 60 (CC)
Calas, 68 (CJ)
Calas "Tout" Chaud, 127 (BR)
Carne Guisada on
Rice, 131 (FG)
Casserole, Black Beans and
Rice, 136 (FG)
Casserole, Ham, 85 (PK)
Casserole, Sausage, 131 (BB)

Chicken Loaf,
Symphony, 59 (PO)
Chicken and Yellow
Rice, 67 (PO)
Chicken Scallop,
Georgia, 117 (PO)
Chicken Wiggle, 69 (PO)
Chile-Cheese Rice, 38 (BB)
Confetti Rice, 109 (FG); 51 (SP)
Curried Rice, 22 (SE)

Rice, *continued*
 Curry, Shrimp, 49 (SE)
 Dirty Rice, 129 (PO)
 Eggs and Rice,
   Scrambled, 119 (BB)
 Eggs, Riced, 112 (FG)
 Fried Rice, Savannah's
   Famous, 40 (PK)
 Fritters, Rice, 129 (BR)
 Griddle Cakes,
   Apple-Rice, 114 (BB)
 Hopping John, 17 (CE)
 Hoppin' John, 79 (VE)
 Jambalaya, Chicken-Sausage,
   109 (PK)
 Jambalaya, Crayfish, 24 (SE)
 Jambalaya, Creole, 109 (PK)
 Jambalaya, Ham, 85 (PK)
 Jambalaya, Ham and
   Chicken, 69 (PO)
 Jambalaya of Chicken, 122 (SO)
 Jambalaya, Pork, 121 (SO)
 Jambalaya, Pork Rib, 34 (PK)
 Jambalaya, Shrimp and
   Oyster, 124 (SO)
 Jambalaya, Vegetable, 125 (VE)
 Mold, Curried Shrimp in
   Rice, 97 (SS)
 Mold, Rice, 49 (SE)
 Muffins, Charleston
   Rice, 111 (BR)
 Paella, 56 (SE)
 Paella Valenciana, 68 (PO)
 Persian Rice, 130 (CC)
 Philpy, 101 (BR)
 Pilaf, Charleston
   Chicken, 69 (PO)
 Pilaf, Lamb, 99 (BE)
 Pilaf, Rice, 57 (CE)
 Pilau, Low Country Roast Squab
   with Rice, 46 (PO)
 Pilau, Okra, 66 (VE)
 Pilau, Pirates' House
   Shrimp, 48 (SE)
 Pilau, Plantation
   Shrimp, 21 (CC)
 Pilau, Roast Squab, 46 (PO)
 Pilau, Turn-of-the-Century
   Chicken, 69 (PO)
 Pinto Beans, Seasoned, 126 (PK)
 Pork and Turnips over
   Rice, 35 (PK)
 Pudding, Arkansas Rice, 14 (DE)
 Pudding, Baked Rice, 15 (DE)
 Pudding, Norwegian
   Rice, 15 (DE)
 Pudding with Currants,
   Rice, 15 (DE)
 Red Beans and Rice, 29 (CC);
   110 (PK)
 Red Beans and Rice,
   Buster's, 133 (SP)
 Red Beans and Rice,
   Louisiana, 19 (VE)
 Riz Isle Brevelle (Rice
   Croquettes), 25 (CC)

Salad, Tuna-Rice, 12 (SP)
Sautéed Rice and
  Tomatoes, 119 (VE)
Sopa de Arroz (Mexican
  Rice), 37 (CC)
Soup, Avgolemono, 33 (SO)
Soup, Cauliflower, 62 (SO)
Soup, Cream of
  Chicken, 59 (SO)
Soup, Cream of Rice, 50 (SO)
Soup, Southern
  Jugged, 106 (SO)
Stuffed Grape Leaves, 61 (FG)
Stuffed Green Peppers, 84 (VE)
Stuffing, Ham Steak with
  Orange-Rice, 78 (PK)
Stuffing, Rice, 62 (BE)
Stuffing, Roast Turkey with
  Rice-Pecan, 54 (FG)
Wild Rice
  Baked Wild Rice, 127 (FG)
  Casserole, Wild Rice and
    Cheese, 42 (SP)
  Dressing, Wild Rice, 49 (PO)
  Soup, Cream of Wild
    Rice, 50 (SO)
  Wild Rice, 133 (CC); 48 (FG)
**Rolls and Buns**
 All-Occasion Rolls, 57 (BR)
 Banana Puffs, 117 (BB)
 Black Bun, 15 (CE)

Butterhorns, 127 (CC)
Buttermilk Rolls, 57 (BR)
Butter Rolls, 123 (CC)
Cabbage Rolls, Greek, 39 (PK)
Caraway Rolls, 99 (CE)
Cheese Rolls,
  Quick-Fried, 19 (SO)
Cinnamon Biscuit Rolls, 94 (BR)
Cinnamon Rolls, 48 (BB)
Cinnamon Rolls, Southern
  Kitchen, 68 (BR)
Cinnamon Rolls, S&S, 79 (CC)
Cloverleaf Rolls, 65 (SP)
Cornmeal Rolls,
  Oklahoma, 23 (BR)
Crescent Rolls, 107 (FG)
Crescent Rolls, Rich, 58 (BR)
Croissants, 44 (BB)
Generals, 57 (BR)
Ham-Asparagus Rolls, 78 (PK)
Ham Rolls, 91 (PK)
Harvest Rolls, 58 (CC)
Hearty Rolls, 126 (SP)
Homemade Rolls, 54 (PO)
Honey Almond Rolls, Anna
  Maude's, 69 (BR)
Hot Cross Buns, 108 (BB);
  66 (BR)
Icebox Rolls, 60 (BR)
Icebox Rolls, Luncheon, 27 (SS)
Jubilee Rolls, 67 (CE)

**BB** *Breakfast & Brunch*   **BE** *Beef, Veal & Lamb*   **BR** *Breads*   **CA** *Cakes*   **CC** *Company's Coming*   **CE** *Celebrations*
**CJ** *Cookie Jar*   **DE** *Just Desserts*   **FG** *Family Gatherings*   **GR** *Gift Receipts*   **PK** *All Pork*   **PO** *Plain & Fancy Poultry*
**PP** *Pies & Pastry*   **SE** *Sea & Stream*   **SO** *Soups & Stews*   **SP** *Sporting Scene*   **SS** *Socials & Soirees*   **VE** *Vegetables*

**Rolls and Buns,** *continued*
Kolaches, 70 (BR)
Louisiana Bullfrogs, 60 (BR)
Lovefeast Buns, 49 (CE)
Miniature Rolls, 24 (CE)
Orange Rolls, 108 (BB); 71 (BR)
Pan Dulce, 67 (BR)
Parkerhouse Rolls, 119 (CE)
Pecan Rolls, Boca
   Raton, 73 (BR)
Philadelphia Buns, Nellie Custis
   Lewis's, 68 (BR)
Picnic Rolls, 84 (CE)
Popovers, 99 (BB); 110 (BR);
   48 (CC)
Popovers, Our
   Famous, 105 (CC)
Poppy Seed Rolls,
   Party, 115 (FG)
Potato Ice Box Rolls, 61 (BR)
Potato Rolls, 50 (SS)
Potato Rolls, Icebox, 77 (BB)
Quick Rolls, 58 (BR)
Refrigerator Rolls, 107 (BB)
Rusk, Mr. Paca's, 131 (BR)
Sausage Rolls, 13 (CE);
   107 (PK)
Sixty-Minute Rolls, 62 (CC)
Southern Rolls, 59 (BR)
Spoon Rolls, 114 (CC)
Sweet Potato Buns, 130 (SP)
Sweet Rolls, Herren's, 72 (BR)
Sweet Rolls in New
   Dress, 71 (BR)
Sweet Rolls, Miniature, 73 (BB)
Sweet Rolls, Tiny, 25 (CE)
Tea Rolls, Miniature, 24 (CE)
Twists, Pecan, 73 (BR)
Whole Wheat Rolls, 107 (BB);
   16 (CC); 47 (SS)
Yeast Rolls, Quick, 106 (BB)
Yeast Rolls, Tiny, 121 (SS)

**Rutabagas**
How To Prepare
   Rutabagas, 98 (VE)
Pot o' Gold, 98 (VE)
Pudding, Rutabaga, 99 (VE)
Southern-Cooked
   Rutabagas, 99 (VE)

# S

**Salad Dressings**
Blue Cheese Dressing,
   Creamy, 114 (CC)
Celery Seed Dressing, 100 (SS)
Country Club Salad
   Dressing, 136 (SS)
Dill Marinade, 114 (SP)
French Dressing, 58, 64 (CC);
   20, 55 (SP); 132 (VE)
French Dressing,
   Century-Old, 72 (BB)
French Dressing,
   Golden, 42 (SS)

Gargogle Sauce, 131 (CC)
Garlic Dressing, 36 (SP)
Horseradish Dressing, 34 (SS)
Martinique Dressing, 130 (CE)
Mary Randolph's Salad
   Dressing, 125 (SS)
Mayonnaise, Blender, 134 (VE)
Mayonnaise Dressing, 134 (VE)
Mustard Mayonnaise, Lobster
   Salad with, 124 (SS)
Onion Salad Dressing, Lettuce
   Wedges with, 47 (SS)
Orange Dressing, 51 (CC)
Paprika Dressing, 97 (CE)
Savannah Dressing, 83 (SP)
Sour Cream Dressing, 98 (SS);
   135 (VE)
Stilton Dressing, 128 (SS)
Sweet-and-Sour
   Dressing, 135 (VE)
Thousand Island
   Dressing, 44 (SS)
Vinaigrette Dressing, 122 (CC)

**Salads**
Apple Salads,
   Individual, 75 (CC)
Artichoke Salad,
   Marinated, 110 (CC)
Aspics
   Apple Aspic, 55 (CE)
   Applesauce Aspic, 70 (PK)
   Cucumber Aspic, 107 (CC)
   Redfish Aspic, 83 (SE)
   Red Snapper in Aspic,
      Poached, 94 (SE)
   Shrimp Aspic, 87 (SS)
   Tomato Aspic, 44 (CC)
   Tomato Aspics,
      Individual, 107 (FG)
   Tomato Aspic, Spicy, 49 (SS)
Avocado Salad, Florida
   Grapefruit, 135 (FG)
Avocado Salad,
   Grapefruit-, 64 (CC)
Banana-Peanut Salad, 73 (CE)
Bean Salad, Cold, 89 (SP)
Bean Salad, Kidney, 69 (SP)
Bean Salad, Piquant
   Green, 32 (FG)
Bean Salad, Winter
   Green, 98 (CC)
Beet Salad with Pickled
   Herring, 19 (FG)
Black-Eyed Pea Salad, 62 (FG)
Broccoli Salad in Lettuce Cups,
   Fresh, 68 (BB)
Cabbage Salad, 19 (CC)
Chicken
   Amandine, Chicken
      Salad, 113 (PO)
   Baked Chicken
      Salad, 114 (PO)
   Cheese Puffs, Chicken Salad
      in, 74 (SS)
   Chicken Salad, 105 (CC);
      36 (CE)
   Curried Chicken
      Salad, 112 (PO)
   Luncheon Salad,
      Normandy, 56 (SS)

Maryland Chicken
   Salad, 113 (PO)
Mousse, Chicken, 112 (PO)
Patty Shells, Chicken Salad
   in, 114 (PO)
Pies, Chicken Salad, 114 (PO)
Sandwiches, Chicken
   Salad, 29 (CE)
Sandwiches, Highland Park
   Chicken Salad, 111 (PO)
Tart Shells, Chicken Salad
   in, 80 (SS)
Confetti Rice, 109 (FG)
Corn Relish Salad, 69 (SP)
Crab Louis, 23 (SE)
Crab Salad Sandwiches, 16 (SS)
Cranberry Salad, 136 (CC)
Cucumbers in Sour
   Cream, 52 (CC)
Cucumbers with Tomatoes,
   Dressed, 116 (SS)
Egg Salad, 97 (FG)
Egg Salad Finger
   Sandwiches, 84 (FG)
Emerald Salad, 120 (SP)
Fire and Ice Salad, 65 (SP)
Fruit
   Cantaloupe Lilies with Melon
      Balls, 109 (FG)
   Compote Amulet, 26 (CC)
   Creamy Fruit Salad, 95 (SS)
   Fresh Fruit Salad, 76 (BB);
      76 (FG)
   Fresh Fruit Salad with Celery
      Seed Dressing, 100 (SS)

Salads, Fruit, *continued*
  Fresh Fruit Salad with
    Horseradish
    Dressing, 34 (SS)
  Frozen Fruit Salad, 55 (CE);
    34 (SS)
  Fruit Salad, 78 (SP)
  Ginger Fruit Cups, 26 (SP)
  Hot Caramel Fruit, 85 (BB)
  Melon Balls in Mint-Rum
    Sauce, 72 (SS)
  Peppered Fruit, 64 (CE)
  Stewed Mixed Fruits, 25 (BB)
  Strudel, Fruit, 101 (FG)
  Summer Fruit
    Combination, 99 (CC)
  Waldorf Salad, 40 (SS)
  Waldorf Salad with
    Wine, 31 (SP)
Grapefruit-Avocado
  Salad, 64 (CC)
Grapefruit-Avocado Salad,
  Florida, 135 (FG)
Grapefruit Salad
  Supreme, 42 (SS)

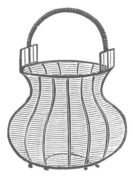

Green
  Endive Salad with Stilton
    Dressing, 128 (SS)
  Garden Salad, 122 (CC)
  Garden Salad with French
    Dressing, 103 (SP)
  Greek Salad, 57 (CE)
  Green Salad with French
    Dressing, 55 (SP)
  Lettuce Wedges with Onion
    Salad Dressing, 47 (SS)
  Ports of Call Salad, 130 (CC)
  Savannah Salad, 83 (SP)
  Tossed Green Salad, 114 (CC)
  Tossed Salad with Garlic
    Dressing, 36 (SP)
  Watercress Salad,
    Wilted, 33 (CC)
  Wilted Lettuce Salad, 48 (CC)
Green Peas in Tomato
  Cups, 25 (SS)
Ham Mousse, 86 (PK)
Ham Salad, Baked, 80 (PK)
Ham Salad, Virginia, 69 (CE)
Hayden Salad, 12 (FG)

Layered Salad,
  Pensacola, 100 (SP)
Lobster Salad with Mustard
  Mayonnaise, 124 (SS)
Luncheon Salad,
  Normandy, 56 (SS)
Mango Salad, 38 (BB)
Oyster Salad, Sager's, 133 (CE)
Pear Salad, 127 (FG)
Perfection Salad, 76 (FG)
Pineapple Cheddar
  Salad, 96 (CC)
Pineapple-Mint Lamb
  Ring, 105 (BE)
Pineapple Mold,
  Raspberry-, 76 (CC)
Poinsettia Salad, 130 (CE)
Potato
  German Potato Salad, 15 (CC)
  Hot German Potato
    Salad, 22 (FG)
  Hot Potato Salad, 40 (CC)
  Molded Potato Salad, 88 (CE)
  Mustard Potato Salad, 77 (PO)
  Scottish Potato
    Salad, 136 (SP)
  Sour Cream-Mustard Potato
    Salad, 89 (FG)
  Sour Cream Potato
    Salad, 107 (SP)
Prunes, Stuffed, 127 (FG)
Roast Beef Salad, Cold, 92 (SP)
Salmagundi, 125 (SS)
Seafood Salad, Hot, 136 (BB)
Seafood Salad, Old St.
  Augustine, 136 (SE)
Shrimp Remoulade, 53 (SE)
Shrimp, St. Augustine, 53 (SE)
Slang Jang, 44 (SP)
Slaws
  Almond Coleslaw, 74 (SP)
  Cabbage Slaw, 16 (FG)
  Cold Slaw, 65 (CE)
  Cole Slaw, 44 (CE)
  Coleslaw, 61, 89 (SP)
  German Slaw, 97 (PK)
  Marinated Cole Slaw, 77 (PO)
  Mustard Cole Slaw, 47 (PK)
  Onion Slaw, 54 (PO)
  Summer Slaw, 106 (SP)
  Sweet-and-Sour
    Slaw, 119 (CE)
  Texas Coleslaw, 40 (CC)
Tomato Caviar Salad, 131 (CC)

Tomato Salad, Cold, 13 (PO)
Tuna-Rice Salad, 12 (SP)
Tuna Salad, 101 (SE)
Tuna Salad, Congealed
  Tomato-, 32 (SS)
Turkey Salad, 49 (SS)
Vegetable
  Fresh Vegetable Salad, 73 (SP)
  Marinated Vegetable Salad,
    78 (CE); 89 (FG); 20 (SP)
  Mold, Vegetable
    Salad, 111 (SP)
  Riverboat Salad, 72 (BB)
  Seven-Layer Congealed
    Vegetable Salad, 98 (FG)
  Spinach Mold, 114 (SP)
  Summer Salad, 52 (CC)
  Tomato Juice Salad, 82 (BB)
  Tomato Salad,
    Marinated, 81 (SP)
  Vinaigrette,
    Vegetables, 125 (SP)
West Indies Salad, Bayley's
  Original, 23 (SE)

**Salmon**
Creamed Salmon, 84 (SE)
Creamed Salmon and
  Mushrooms, 135 (BB)
Croquettes, Salmon, 85 (SE);
  46 (SS)
Grilled Salmon Steaks, 84 (SE)
Mold, Salmon, 19 (FG)
Mold with Bagels, Smoked
  Salmon, 97 (FG)
Mousse, Salmon, 85 (SE)
Smoked Salmon, 84 (SE)
Spread, Smoky
  Salmon, 129 (SP)

**Salsify**
Bisque, Salsify, 69 (SO);
  100 (VE)
How To Prepare Fresh
  Salsify, 100 (VE)
Pickled Salsify, 100 (VE)
Scalloped Salsify, 100 (VE)

**Sandwiches**
Asparagus Sandwiches,
  Rolled, 51 (SS)
Bacon and Egg Sandwich
  Spread, 120 (PK)
Burgers, Bonfire, 101 (CE)
Calla Lily Sandwiches, 68 (SS)
Carrot Sandwiches, 77 (SS)
Catfish Sandwiches,
  Fried, 111 (SE)
Celery-Nut Sandwiches, 62 (SS)
Chicken-Almond
  Sandwiches, 51 (SS)
Chicken Salad
  Sandwiches, 29 (CE)
Chicken Salad Sandwiches,
  Highland Park, 111 (PO)
Chicken Sandwiches, 71 (CC);
  27 (FG)
Chicken Sandwiches,
  Amandine, 87 (CC); 11 (SS)

**BB** *Breakfast & Brunch*  **BE** *Beef, Veal & Lamb*  **BR** *Breads*  **CA** *Cakes*  **CC** *Company's Coming*  **CE** *Celebrations*
**CJ** *Cookie Jar*  **DE** *Just Desserts*  **FG** *Family Gatherings*  **GR** *Gift Receipts*  **PK** *All Pork*  **PO** *Plain & Fancy Poultry*
**PP** *Pies & Pastry*  **SE** *Sea & Stream*  **SO** *Soups & Stews*  **SP** *Sporting Scene*  **SS** *Socials & Soirees*  **VE** *Vegetables*

*Sandwiches, a Model T, and a warm summer day make for a family picnic, c.1915.*

Sandwiches, *continued*
  Chicken Sandwiches,
    Hot, 114 (PO)
  Chutney Sandwiches, 62 (SS)
  Corned Beef
    Sandwiches, 17 (SP)
  Crab Cake Sandwiches,
    Chesapeake Bay, 28 (SP)
  Crabmeat Sandwiches, 77 (SS)
  Crab Salad Sandwiches, 16 (SS)
  Cream Cheese and Pineapple
    Sandwiches, 52 (SS)
  Cucumber and Watercress
    Sandwiches, 52 (SS)
  Cucumber-Cheese
    Sandwiches, 87 (CC)
  Cucumber-Cream Cheese
    Sandwiches, 28 (FG)
  Cucumber Sandwiches, 81 (SS)
  Date-Nut Sandwiches,
    Open-Face, 81 (SS)
  Date Roll Sandwiches, 61 (SS)
  Domino Sandwiches, 52 (SS)
  Duke of Windsor Sandwich,
    The, 115 (PO)
  Egg Salad Finger
    Sandwiches, 84 (FG)
  Ginger Cream
    Triangles, 69 (CE)
  Ham Sandwiches, 68 (SS)
  Ham Sandwiches,
    Baked, 28 (SP); 60 (SS)
  Ham Sandwich Spread, 89 (PK)

  Heart and Diamond
    Sandwiches, 72 (CC)
  Herbed Party Triangles, 68 (SS)
  Hero Sandwiches, 69 (FG)
  Hot Brown Sandwiches,
    Louisville, 115 (PO)
  Ice Cream Sandwiches, 93 (SS)
  Jelly Sandwiches,
    Pinwheel, 28 (CE)
  Meal-in-a-Sandwich, 74 (SP)
  Noisette Sandwiches, 42 (FG)
  Olive-Cheese
    Sandwiches, 21 (SS)
  Olive-Mustard
    Sandwiches, 28 (FG)
  Oyster Po-Boys, 40 (SE)
  Pimiento Cheese
    Sandwiches, 29 (CE);
    100 (SP)
  Pimiento Cheese Sandwiches,
    Anne's, 16 (SS)
  Princess Sandwiches, 21 (SS)
  Ribbon Sandwiches, 88 (SS)
  Ribbon Sandwich Loaf, 71 (CC)
  Roast Sandwiches,
    Razorback, 30 (FG)
  Shrimp and Cream Cheese
    Triangles, 81 (SS)
  Shrimp Paste
    Sandwiches, 72 (SS)
  Shrimp Rolls, 81 (SP)
  Tomato-Egg
    Sandwiches, 11 (SS)

  Vegetable Sandwiches, 21 (SS)
**Sardines**
  Toast, Sardines on, 60 (BB)
**Sauces**
  Almond-Lemon Sauce, Trout
    with, 121 (SE)
  Almond-Mushroom
    Sauce, 134 (BB)
  Asparagus Sauce, Grandmother
    Flexner's, 132 (VE)
  au Beurre Noir, Sauce, 124 (BE)
  Barbecue
    Barbecue Sauce, 16, 126 (BE);
      38 (CC); 71 (GR); 45,
      54 (PK); 34 (PO); 72 (SP);
      104 (SS)
    Basting Sauce, 34 (SP)
    Basting Sauce,
      Carolina, 60 (PK)
    Basting Sauce,
      Tennessee, 60 (PK)
    Basting Sauce, Texas, 60 (PK)
    Beer Sauce for
      Barbecue, 60 (PK)
    Bonaventure Barbecue
      Sauce, 22 (PK)
    Creole Barbecue
      Sauce, 127 (BE)
    Deep South Barbecue
      Sauce, 33 (PK)
    Easy Barbecue Sauce, 52 (SP)
    Franks in Barbecue
      Sauce, 111 (PK)

Sauces, Barbecue, *continued*
  Horseradish Barbecue
    Sauce, 60 (PK)
  Hot Barbecue Sauce, 49 (PK)
  LBJ's Barbecue
    Sauce, 127 (BE)
  Low Country Barbecue
    Sauce, 60 (PK)
  Molasses Barbecue
    Sauce, 60 (PK)
  1948 Original Barbecue
    Sauce, 87 (PO)
  Panhandle Barbecue
    Sauce, 16 (BE)
  Western Kentucky-Style
    Barbecue Sauce, 88 (CE)
Basil Vinegar, 136 (VE)
Basting Sauce, 14 (BE);
  65 (SE); 34 (SP)
Basting Sauce,
  Carolina, 60 (PK)
Basting Sauce, Fish, 131 (SE)
Basting Sauce,
  Orange, 131 (SE)
Basting Sauce,
  Tennessee, 60 (PK)
Basting Sauce, Texas, 60 (PK)
Basting Sauce,
  Tropical, 131 (SE)
Béarnaise, Sauce, 124 (BE)
Béarnaise Sauce, 15, 128 (SE);
  24 (SP); 131 (SS)
Béchamel, Sauce, 124 (BE)
Béchamel Sauce, 80 (PK)

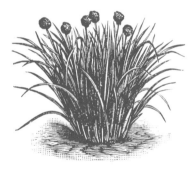

Bordelaise Sauce, 10, 125 (BE)
Brown Sauce, 128 (PO)
Brown Sauce, Basic, 125 (BE)
Butter Sauce, Boiled Chicken
  with, 17 (PO)
Butter Sauce, Clarified, 12 (PO)
Butter Sauce, Tangy, 132 (VE)
Caper Sauce, 129 (SE)
Cardinal Sauce, Shrimp
  in, 105 (FG)
Celery Sauce, Creole, 15 (BR)
Cheese Sauce, 114 (PO);
  133 (VE)
Cheese Sauce, Asparagus with
  Chicken-, 132 (BB)
Cheese Sauce, Broccoli Baked
  with, 26 (VE)

Cheese Sauce, Creamy, 115 (PO)
Chili Sauce, 71 (GR)
Chive Blossom
  Vinegar, 135 (VE)
Chive Vinegar, 136 (VE)
Clam Sauce, Linguine with
  White, 11 (SE)
Cocktail Sauce, Oysters
  with, 34 (SE)
Crab Sauce Lorenzo, 22 (SE)
Cranberry-Cumberland
  Sauce, 38 (FG)
Cream Sauce, 103 (VE)
Cream Sauce, Asparagus with
  Mushrooms and, 11 (VE)
Cream Sauce, Baked Vidalia
  Onions in Sherried, 72 (VE)
Cream Sauce, Brandied, 79 (FG)
Cream Sauce, Veal Chops
  in, 67 (BE)
Creole Sauce, 50 (CC); 81 (SE)
Creole Sauce, Baked Liver
  in, 113 (BE)
Cucumber Sauce, 31, 127 (SE)
Dessert
  Apricot Sauce, 75 (DE)
  Blackberry Sauce, 104 (FG)
  Blueberry Sauce, 36 (BB);
    66 (DE)
  Bourbon Sauce, 136 (DE);
    44 (PP); 15 (SP)
  Brandy Sauce, 24 (DE)
  Brown Sugar Sauce, 20 (DE)
  Butterscotch Sauce, 85 (GR)
  Butterscotch Sauce, Frances
    Virginia Tea
    Room, 132 (DE)
  Butterscotch Sauce, High
    Hampton, 132 (DE)
  Caramel Sauce, 75, 132 (DE);
    85 (GR)
  Cherry Sauce, 70 (CA);
    21 (DE)
  Chocolate Sauce, 105,
    133 (DE); 82 (FG); 86 (GR)
  Chocolate Sauce,
    Rich, 102 (DE)
  Chocolate Sauce,
    Sherried, 133 (DE)
  Custard Sauce, 70, 76 (DE)
  Custard Sauce over
    Strawberries and
    Raspberries,
    Chilled, 84 (SP)
  Eggnog Sauce,
    Irma's, 136 (DE)
  Fig Sauce, 88 (GR)

  Fruit Sauce,
    Tropical, 135 (DE)
  Fruit Starter,
    Brandied, 135 (DE)
  Fudge Sauce, 105 (DE);
    111 (PO)
  Fudge Sauce, Hot, 133 (DE);
    86 (GR)
  Grape Wine Sauce, 13 (DE)
  Hard Sauce, 116 (CE);
    135 (DE); 49 (FG)
  Hard Sauce,
    Brandied, 37 (CA)
  Hard Sauce,
    Sherried, 12 (CC); 40 (FG)
  Lemon Cream Sauce, Mary
    Randolph's, 86 (GR)
  Lemon Hard Sauce, 36 (DE)
  Lemon Sauce, 13, 18,
    41 (DE); 54 (SS)
  Lemon Sauce,
    Creamy, 136 (DE)
  Lemon Sauce, Old-Fashioned
    Golden, 137 (DE)
  Lemon Sauce, Tangy, 65 (CA)
  Lemon Sauce, Tart, 137 (DE)
  Orange-Pineapple
    Sauce, 134 (DE)
  Orange Sauce, 137 (DE);
    88 (GR)
  Peach Sauce, 133 (DE)
  Peanut Butter Sauce, 82 (FG)
  Plum Pudding Sauce, 26 (DE)
  Raisin-Chocolate
    Sauce, 86 (GR)
  Raspberry Sauce, 111 (DE)
  Rum Butter Sauce, 88 (GR)
  Rum Sauce, 25 (DE); 94 (PO)
  Sabayon Sauce, 40 (SS)
  Sherry Sauce, 88 (GR)
  Sherry Sauce, Hot, 137 (DE)
  Strawberry Sauce,
    Brandied, 134 (DE)
  Strawberry Sauce,
    Fresh, 134 (DE)
  Strawberry Sauce over Vanilla
    Ice Cream, 56 (SP)
  Tutti-Frutti, 84 (GR)
  Vanilla Sauce,
    Creamy, 22 (DE)
  Vanilla Sauce,
    Greenbrier, 136 (DE)
  Whipped Cream-Chocolate
    Sauce, 16 (DE)
  Whiskey Sauce, 12 (DE)
  Wine Custard Sauce, 137 (DE)
  Wine Sauce, 27, 137 (DE)

**BB** *Breakfast & Brunch*   **BE** *Beef, Veal & Lamb*   **BR** *Breads*   **CA** *Cakes*   **CC** *Company's Coming*   **CE** *Celebrations*
**CJ** *Cookie Jar*   **DE** *Just Desserts*   **FG** *Family Gatherings*   **GR** *Gift Receipts*   **PK** *All Pork*   **PO** *Plain & Fancy Poultry*
**PP** *Pies & Pastry*   **SE** *Sea & Stream*   **SO** *Soups & Stews*   **SP** *Sporting Scene*   **SS** *Socials & Soirees*   **VE** *Vegetables*

Sauces, Dessert, *continued*
  Wine Sauce, Oranges
    in, 20 (SP)
Dill and Mustard
  Sauce, 129 (SE)
Dill Marinade, 114 (SP)
Dill Sauce, 29 (SE); 134 (VE)
Drawn Butter, 132 (VE)
Egg-Lemon Sauce, 56 (CE)
Egg Sauce, 129 (SE)
Egg Sauce, Asparagus and Peas
  with, 12 (VE)
Fruit Sauce, Spicy, 129 (BE)
Gargogle Sauce, 131 (CC)
Gravy Sauce, Red, 95 (PO)
Green Sauce, 35 (CC)
Ham Sauce, Sherried, 92 (PK)
Herb Butter, 136 (VE)
Herb Butter, Tarragon, 136 (VE)
Hollandaise Sauce, 122 (BB);
  128 (SE)
Hollandaise Sauce,
  Blender, 133 (VE)
Hollandaise Sauce, Broccoli
  with, 111 (CC)
Hollandaise Sauce,
  Mock, 133 (VE)
Hollandaise Sauce, Steamed
  Asparagus with, 84 (SS)
Hollandaise Sauce
  Supreme, 133 (VE)
Hollandaise Shrimp
  Sauce, 118 (SE)
Horseradish and Sour Cream
  Sauce, 128 (BE)
Horseradish-Mustard
  Sauce, 128 (BE)
Horseradish Sauce, 17, 21,
  128 (BE); 120 (SS); 132 (VE)
Horseradish Sauce,
  Kehoe, 92 (PK)
Hot Pepper Sauce, 135 (VE)
Hot Sauce, 48 (BE)
Jardiniere Sauce, 126 (BE)
Jelly Sauce, 70 (PK)
Jezebel Sauce, 92 (PK)
Lemon-Butter Sauce, 132 (VE)
Lemon Sauce, 128 (SE)
Lemon Sauce, Baked Haddock
  with, 70 (SE)
Lemon Sauce, Broiled
  Sweetbreads with, 115 (BE)
Madeira Sauce, 125 (BE);
  121 (CC)
Marinade Sauce,
  Tangy, 127 (BE)
Maître d'Hôtel Sauce, Brussels
  Sprouts with, 39 (FG)
Mayonnaise, Blender, 134 (VE)
Mayonnaise,
  Homemade, 127 (SE);
  134 (VE)
Mexican Sauce, 38 (BB);
  129 (BE)
Mint-Rum Sauce, Melon Balls
  in, 72 (SS)
Mint Sauce, 129 (BE)
Mint Sauce, Tangy, 130 (BE)
Mushroom Cream
  Sauce, 113 (SE)

Mushroom Sauce, 126 (BE); 59,
  117 (PO); 66, 93 (SE); 48 (SS)
Mushroom Sauce, Tuna Steaks
  with, 100 (SE)
Mushroom-Wine Sauce, Broiled
  Flounder with, 65 (SE)
Mushroom-Wine Sauce, Broiled
  Steak with, 27 (BE)
Mustard Dip Sauce, 134 (VE)
Mustard, Hot Sweet, 92 (PK)
Mustard Sauce, 21, 58 (PK)
Mustard Sauce, Cooked, 87 (PK)
Mustard Sauce, Ham in, 75 (PK)
Mustard Sauce, Tangy, 97 (SE)
Oil and Lemon Sauce, 134 (VE)
Orange Sauce, 132 (CC)
Orange Sauce, Beets in, 25 (VE)
Orange Sauce, Roast Duckling
  with, 43 (PO)
Orange Sauce, Savory, 31 (SP)

Oyster Sauce, 49 (PO); 130 (SE)
Oyster Sauce, Baked Snapper
  with, 90 (SE)
Oyster Sauce, Chicken
  with, 98 (PO)
Pico de Gallo, 37 (BE); 75 (GR)
Piquant, Sauce, 129 (SE)
Plum Sauce, Leg of Lamb
  with, 90 (BE)
Plum Sauce,
  Sweet-and-Sour, 126 (PO)
Raisin Sauce, 47 (CC)
Raisin Sauce, German Tongue
  with, 120 (BE)
Raisin Sauce, Spiced, 92 (PK)
Remoulade Sauce, 127 (SE)
Robert Sauce, 25 (PK)
Rochambeau, Sauce, 106 (PO)

Salsa de Tomates, 82 (VE)
Sausage Sauce
  Piquant, 108 (PK)
Seafood
  Cocktail Sauce, 92 (SP)
  Cocktail Sauce,
    Seafood, 126 (SE)
  Cocktail Sauce, Spicy, 97 (SP)
  Marinade Sauce,
    Seafood, 132 (SE)
  Marinade, Spicy
    Seafood, 132 (SE)
  Red Sauce, Boiled Shrimp
    with, 91 (FG)
  Seafood Sauce, 26 (FG)
  St. Augustine Seafood
    Sauce, 136 (SS)
  Tartar Sauce, 25 (FG);
    126 (SE)
  Tartar Sauce, Sour
    Cream, 126 (SE)
Sherry-Mushroom
  Sauce, 11 (BE)
Sherry Sauce, Brains
  in, 108 (BE)
Sherry Sauce, Lobster
  in, 32 (SE)
Sour Cream and Chive
  Sauce, 127 (BE)
Sour Cream Sauce, 46 (BE)
Sour Cream Sauce, Bratwurst
  in, 113 (PK)
Sour Sauce, Old, 131 (SE)
Spaghetti Caruso, 127 (PO)
Spanish Sauce, 129 (BE);
  130 (SE)
Spanish Sauce, Grouper
  with, 69 (SE)
Spicy Sauce, 108 (SE)
Steak Sauce, Henry
  Bane, 127 (BE)
Sweet-and-Sour Sauce, 131 (SE)
Tomato Sauce, 128 (BE);
  70 (GR); 130 (SE)
Tomato Sauce, Fresh, 135 (VE)
Tomato Sauce,
  Sweet-and-Sour, 129 (BE)
Tomato-Wine Sauce, 73 (SE)
Vegetable Hot Sauce, 134 (VE)

**Sauces,** *continued*
White Sauce, 47 (SP)
White Sauce, Basic, 132 (VE)
White Sauce, Thick, 133 (VE)
Wine Meat Sauce, 124 (CC)
Wine Sauce, Port, 120 (PK)
Wine Sauce, Spiced
    Port, 130 (BE)

**Sauerkraut**
Balls, Kraut, 103 (SS)
Brisket with Sauerkraut,
    Sweet-and-Sour, 17 (BE)
Frankfurter Skillet, Kraut
    and, 112 (PK)
German Sauerkraut, 33 (VE)
Klobase with
    Sauerkraut, 112 (PK)
Pork and Sauerkraut
    Dinner, 31 (PK)
Pork and Sauerkraut, Old
    Dominion, 34 (PK)
Relish, Sauerkraut, 136 (CC);
    76 (GR)
Soup, Sauerkraut, 100 (SO)
Spareribs and
    Sauerkraut, 34 (PK)
Stuffing, Sauerkraut, 49 (PO)
Wine Sauerkraut, 33 (VE)

**Sausage**
Apples, Sausage with, 107 (PK)
Arroz con Pollo, Hearty, 67 (PO)
Balls, Kraut, 103 (SS)
Barbecued Sausage, 40 (CC)
Beef Sausage, Country, 50 (BE)
Belle Meade Specials, 24 (SP)
Bratwurst in Sour Cream
    Sauce, 113 (PK)
Bratwurst,
    Sauer-Beckman, 102 (PK)
Brioche, Sausage in, 48 (BR)
Burritos de Huevos con
    Chorizo, 119 (BB)
Cakes, Sausage, 130 (BB)
Casserole, Jo's Egg, 110 (CE)
Casserole, Sausage, 131 (BB)
Casserole, Sausage and
    Egg, 76 (BB)
Casserole,
    Sausage-Cheese, 105 (PK)
Casserole,
    Turkey-Sausage, 119 (PO)
Castroville Sausage, 97 (PK)
Chorizo, 37 (BB); 100 (PK)
Chorizo and Hominy
    Skillet, 113 (PK)
Cornbread,
    Sausage-Apple, 131 (BB)
Country Sausage, 100 (PK)
Dip, Sausage-Cheese, 107 (PK)
Dressing,
    Sausage-Cornbread, 31 (PO)
German Sausage Dish, 108 (PK)
Grilled Polish Sausage and
    Cabbage, 59 (PK)
Grits and Sausage,
    Country, 131 (BB)

Gumbo, Cajun, 120 (SO)
Gumbo,
    Chicken-Andouille, 113 (PK)
Gumbo, Duck, 59 (SP)
Gumbo,
    Turkey-Sausage, 117 (SO)
How-To, Fresh Pork
    Sausage, 98 (PK)
Jambalaya,
    Chicken-Sausage, 109 (PK)
Jambalaya, Creole, 109 (PK)
Kielbasa, 102 (PK)
Klobase, 102 (PK)
Klobase with
    Sauerkraut, 112 (PK)
Lima Beans with Sausage,
    Dried, 15 (VE)
Loaf, Apple-Sausage, 105 (PK)
Mixed Grill, 58 (PK)
Muffins, Sausage Corn, 18 (BR)
Mushrooms, Broiled
    Stuffed, 62 (VE)
Panned Sausage, 12 (BB)
Pie, Sausage, 105 (PK)
Pie, Tony's Italian
    Pasta-Meat, 43 (BE)
Pork Sausage, Fresh, 98 (PK)
Pork Sausage,
    Kentucky, 100 (PK)
Red Beans and Rice, 110 (PK)
Red Beans and Sausage,
    Lasyone's, 18 (VE)
Rolls, Sausage, 13 (CE);
    107 (PK)
Sauce Piquant,
    Sausage, 108 (PK)
Stew, Owens Sausage, 107 (PK)
Sticks, Sausage
    Cornbread, 134 (SP)
Stuffing, Crown Roast of Pork
    with Sausage, 20 (PK)
Stuffing, Roast Goose with
    Sausage, 41 (PO)
Stuffing, Rock Cornish Hens
    with Sausage, 39 (PO)
Stuffing, Tennessee Country
    Sausage, 36 (PO)
Swirls, Sausage, 84 (CC)
Tamales, Hot, 48 (BE)
Toad-in-the-Hole, 104 (PK)
Veal Birds, 74 (BE)

**Scallops**
au Gratin, Scallops, 44 (SE)
Baked Scallops,
    Virginia, 44 (SE)
Broiled Scallops, 43 (SE)

Casserole, Low Country
    Seafood, 54 (SE)
Cocktail, Scallop, 45 (SE)
Fried Scallops, 43 (SE)
Sautéed Scallops with Garlic
    Butter, 43 (SE)
Seafood au Gratin,
    Baked, 55 (SE)
Seviche, 45 (SE)
Shells, Scallops in, 45 (SE)

**Seafood.** *See also* specific types
    and Fish.
Baked Seafood au
    Gratin, 55 (SE)
Boil, Bluffton Seafood, 55 (SE)
Bouillabaisse, New
    Orleans, 55 (SE)
Brochette of Shrimp and
    Oysters, Hotel Ponce de
    Leon, 56 (SE)
Casserole, Low Country
    Seafood, 54 (SE)
Good to Know, 134-137 (SE)
Gumbo, Cajun, 120 (SO)
Gumbo, Louisiana, 119 (SO)
Gumbo, Seafood, 119 (SO)
Marinade, Spicy
    Seafood, 132 (SE)
Newburg, Seafood, 54 (SE)
Paella, 56 (SE)
Paella Valenciana, 68 (PO)
Salad, Hot Seafood, 136 (BB)
Salad, Old St. Augustine
    Seafood, 136 (SS)
Sauce, Cocktail, 92 (SP)
Sauce, Seafood, 26 (FG)
Sauce, Seafood
    Cocktail, 126 (SE)
Sauce, Seafood
    Marinade, 132 (SE)
Sauce, Spicy Cocktail, 97 (SP)
Sauce, St. Augustine
    Seafood, 135 (SS)
Soup, Seafood-Mushroom,
    64 (SO)
Stock, Seafood, 12 (SO)
Stuffed Red Snapper,
    Baked, 50 (CC); 92 (SE)
Trout Marguéry, 118 (SE)

**Seasonings**
Bouquets Garnis, 66 (GR)
Creole Seasoning, 66 (GR)
Herbes Aromatiques, 66 (GR)
Herb Mix, Dried, 66 (GR)
Salt, Fresh Herb, 64 (GR)
Salt Galore, Seasoned, 65 (GR)
Salt, Seasoned, 64 (GR)
Spice, Kitchen, 65 (GR)
Sugar, Cinnamon, 62 (GR)
Sugar, Lemon-Mint, 62 (GR)
Sugar Mold, Colored, 64 (GR)
Sugar, Orange-Spice, 62 (GR)
Sugar, Vanilla, 62 (GR)

**Seatrout**
Baked Seatrout, Hotel
    Chamberlain, 86 (SE)

**BB** *Breakfast & Brunch*    **BE** *Beef, Veal & Lamb*    **BR** *Breads*    **CA** *Cakes*    **CC** *Company's Coming*    **CE** *Celebrations*
**CJ** *Cookie Jar*    **DE** *Just Desserts*    **FG** *Family Gatherings*    **GR** *Gift Receipts*    **PK** *All Pork*    **PO** *Plain & Fancy Poultry*
**PP** *Pies & Pastry*    **SE** *Sea & Stream*    **SO** *Soups & Stews*    **SP** *Sporting Scene*    **SS** *Socials & Soirees*    **VE** *Vegetables*

80

*The catch was obviously spectacular this day in 1900 at Manteo, North Carolina.*

Seatrout, *continued*
  Florida Seatrout, 87 (SE)
  Meunière, Seatrout, 87 (SE)
  Pan-Fried Seatrout, 87 (SE)
**Shad**
  Bacon, Shad Roe with, 28 (BB)
  Baked Shad, 88 (SE)
  Baked Shad with Roe
    Stuffing, 88 (SE)
  Broiled Shad Roe, 89 (SE)
  Fried Shad Roe, 89 (SE)
  Planked Shad, 89 (SE)
**Sherbets.** *See* Ice Creams and
  Sherbets.
**Shrimp**
  Aspic, Shrimp, 87 (SS)
  Baked Stuffed Redfish,
    Mississippi Sound, 81 (SE)
  Barbecued Shrimp, 104 (SS)
  Batter-Fried Shrimp, 47 (SE)
  Bisque, Shrimp, 56 (SO)
  Boiled Shrimp, 46 (SE)
  Boiled Shrimp with Cocktail
    Sauce, 129 (SP)
  Boiled Shrimp with Red
    Sauce, 91 (FG)
  Boil, Gulf Coast
    Shrimp, 47 (SE)
  Breakfast Shrimp, 136 (BB)
  Brochette of Shrimp and
    Oysters, Hotel Ponce de
    Leon, 56 (SE)
  Broiled Marinated
    Shrimp, 46 (SE)
  Cardinal Sauce, Shrimp
    in, 105 (FG)

Chayote Squash, Mississippi
  Style, 112 (VE)
Cocktail, Marinated
  Shrimp, 128 (SS)
Creole, Shrimp, 50 (SE)
Curried Shrimp in Rice
  Mold, 97 (SS)
Curry, Shrimp, 49 (SE)
Dill Shrimp, 114 (SP)
Eggplant with Shrimp,
  Smothered, 52 (VE)
Étouffée, Shrimp, 124 (SO)
Flounder en Papillote, 64 (SE)
Flounder Marguéry, Fillet
  of, 63 (SE)
French Fried Shrimp, 47 (SE)
Fricassee, The Homestead
  Shrimp Creole, 49 (SE)
Fritters, Shrimp, 47 (SE)
Gravy, Shrimp, 48 (SE)
Gumbo, Shrimp, 50 (SE)
Hominy, Shrimp with, 135 (BB)
Ice, Shrimp on, 109 (CC)
Jambalaya, Shrimp and
  Oyster, 124 (SO)
Mold, Shrimp, 135 (CE)
Mousse, Shrimp, 51 (SE)
Mousse, Shrimp and
  Crabmeat, 103 (FG)
Mull, Shrimp, 125 (SO)
Paste, Shrimp, 51 (SE)
Pickled Shrimp, 23 (CE); 51 (SE)
Pickled Shrimp, Chilled, 22 (SP)
Pie, Shrimp, 48 (SE)
Pilau, Pirates' House
  Shrimp, 48 (SE)

Pilau, Plantation
  Shrimp, 21 (CC)
Pompano en Papillote, 77 (SE)
Puffs, Curried Shrimp, 106 (SS)
Puffs, Shrimp, 79 (CE)
Remoulade, Shrimp, 53 (SE)
Rolls, Shrimp, 81 (SP)
Sandwiches, Shrimp
  Paste, 72 (SS)
Sauce, Hollandaise
  Shrimp, 118 (SE)
Soup, Chilled Shrimp,
  57 (SO)
Soup, Cream of Shrimp, 57 (SO)
St. Augustine Shrimp, 53 (SE)
Stuffing, Flounder Fillets with
  Shrimp, 64 (SE)
Stuffing, Mullet Fillets with
  Shrimp, 75 (SE)
Stuffing, Roast Chicken with
  Shrimp, 36 (PO)
Stuffing, Shrimp and
  Crabmeat, 78 (SE)
Triangles, Shrimp and Cream
  Cheese, 81 (SS)
**Snapper**
  Baked Snapper,
    Greek-Style, 90 (SE)
  Baked Snapper with Oyster
    Sauce, 90 (SE)
  Baked Snapper with Oyster
    Stuffing, 92 (SE)
  Baked Stuffed Red
    Snapper, 50 (CC); 92 (SE)
  Chowder, Florida Fish, 87 (SO)
  Fried Red Snapper, 93 (SE)

Snapper, *continued*
  Mediterranean
    Escabeche, 93 (SE)
  Poached Red Snapper in
    Aspic, 94 (SE)
  Pudding, Fish, 24 (SS)
  Red Snapper Floridian, 90 (SE)
  Timbales, Snapper, 93 (SE)
**Soufflés**
  Asparagus Soufflé, 14 (VE)
  Blueberry Soufflé, 66 (DE)
  Bourbon Soufflé, The Greenbrier
    Cold, 80 (DE)
  Broccoli Soufflé, 27 (VE)
  Broccoli, Souffléed, 133 (CC)
  Caramel, Soufflé of, 105 (CC)
  Carrot Soufflé, 118 (SP)
  Cheese Soufflé, 82 (BB)
  Cheese Soufflé, Easy, 126 (BB)
  Chestnut Soufflé, 67 (DE)
  Chocolate Soufflé,
    Dixie, 65 (DE)
  Crabmeat Soufflé, 20 (SE)
  Crêpes Soufflé, 122 (DE)
  Grits Soufflé, 112 (FG)
  Grits Soufflé, Cheese, 72 (BB)
  Ham Soufflé, 83 (PK)
  Lemon Soufflé, Hot, 67 (DE)
  Oyster Soufflé, 40 (SE)
  Spinach Soufflé, 76 (CC)
  Spinach Soufflé with Mushroom
    Sauce, 48 (SS)
  Sweet Potato Soufflé, 54 (CC)

Tomato Vermicelli
    Soufflé, 134 (FG)
  Turkey Soufflé, 120 (PO)
  Veal Soufflé, 81 (BE)
**Soups.** *See also* Chili, Chowders,
    Gumbos, Stews.
  Accompaniments
    Bread and Butter
      Balls, 15 (SO)
    Cereal Bits, 17 (SO)
    Cheesebits, 20 (SO)
    Cheese Fingers, 19 (SO)
    Cheese Rolls,
      Quick-Fried, 19 (SO)
    Cheese Toast, 19 (SO)
    Cornbread, Mexican, 23 (SO)
    Crackers, Soda, 20 (SO)
    Crackers, Souffléed, 20 (SO)
    Crackers, Wheat, 23 (SO)
    Croûtes, 35 (SO)
    Croutons, 130 (BR); 18 (SO)
    Croutons, Baked, 18 (SO)
    Croutons, Cheese, 18 (SO)
    Custard, Royal, 16 (SO)
    Dumplings, Danish, 13 (SO)
    Dumplings, Rolled, 13 (SO)
    Egg Balls, 15 (SO)
    Farina Balls, 101 (BE)
    Garnish for Cream
      Soups, 20 (SO)
    Garnish, Julienne, 17 (SO)
    Matzo Balls, 59 (CE); 16 (SO)
    Noodles, Homemade, 13 (SO)

Nuts, Soup, 18 (SO)
  Parmesan
    Breadsticks, 23 (SO)
  Parmesan Rosettes, 23 (SO)
  Peanuts, French-Fried,
    17 (SO)
  Quenelles, 15 (SO)
  Rice Balls, 15 (SO)
  Sesame Crisps, 20 (SO)
  Sippets, 130 (BR); 18 (SO)
  Sippets, Cornmeal, 18 (SO)
  Soup Nuts, 18 (SO)
  Spaetzle, 16 (SO)
Artichoke Soup, Cream
  of, 60 (SO)
Asparagus Soup, Cream
  of, 60 (SO)
Bean Soup, 93 (SO)
Bean Soup, Black, 35 (CC);
  94 (SO)
Bean Soup from Avery Island,
  Red, 96 (SO)
Bean Soup, Pinto, 93 (SO)
Bean Soup, Senate
  Navy, 94 (SO)
Bean Soup, Spanish, 97 (SO)
Beef-Noodle Soup,
  German, 79 (SO)
Beef-Vermicelli Soup,
  79 (SO)
Beer Cheese Soup, 47 (SO)
Borscht, 99 (SO)
Borscht, Traditional, 99 (SO)

*Eating soup properly is practiced by this domestic science class, c.1900.*

Soups, *continued*

Bouillons and Consommés
Avgolemono Soup, 33 (SO)
Barley Broth, 32 (SO)
Beef Bouillon, 26 (SO)
Beef Consommé, 28 (SO)
Beef Soup with Liver
Dumplings, 32 (SO)
Clam Madrilene, 30 (SO)
Clams in Bouillon, 38 (SS)
Court Bouillon, 132 (SE)
Court Bouillon of
Redfish, 83 (SE)
Egg Soup, 33 (SO)
Flounder Court
Bouillon, 66 (SE)
French Broth, 31 (SO)
Iced Bouillon, 26 (SO)
Indian River Soup, 36 (SO)
Jellied Consommé, 29 (SO)
Lettuce Soup, 35 (SO)
Madrilene, 30 (SO)
Madrilene à la Russe, 30 (SO)
Mushroom Broth, 35 (SO)
Onion Soup, French, 35 (SO)
Onion Soup,
Huguenot, 35 (SO)
Sherried Consommé, 73 (FG)
Tomato Bouillon, 27 (SO)
Tomato Consommé,
Herbed, 31 (SP)
Tomato Soup,
Home-Style, 37 (SO)
Tomato Soup, Quick, 37 (SO)
Vegetable Bouillon, Old
South, 27 (SO)
Vegetable Consommé, 29 (SO)
Wine Consommé, 29 (SO)
Broccoli Soup, 18 (SP)
Broccoli Soup, Cream
of, 60 (SO); 56 (SS)
Cabbage Soup,
Sweet-and-Sour, 100 (SO)
Carrot Soup, Cream of, 62 (SO)
Cauliflower Soup, 62 (SO)
Celery Soup, Cream of, 129 (CE)
Cheese Soup, Driskill
Hotel, 46 (SO)
Cheese Soup,
Emergency, 47 (SO)
Cheese Soup, Jalapeño, 47 (SO)
Chestnut Soup, Cream
of, 49 (SO)
Chicken and Corn Soup, 82 (SO)
Chicken Mulligatawny, 82 (SO)
Chicken Noodle Soup, 22 (PO);
83 (SO)
Chicken Soup and Filled
Dumplings, 84 (SO)
Chicken Soup, Cream
of, 59 (SO)
Chicken Soup, Golden, 81 (SO)
Chicken Soup, Hearty, 22 (PO)
Chicken Soup, Rich, 59 (SO)
Chicken Soup with Matzo
Balls, 59 (CE)

Chicken Vegetable
Soup, 81 (SO)
Chicken Velvet Soup, 104 (CC)
Clam Bisque, 52 (SO)
Collard Green Soup, 101 (SO)
Corn Soup, Cream of, 62 (SO)
Crab Bisque, 52 (SO)
Crab Soup, Beaufort Cream
of, 54 (SO)
Crayfish Bisque, 26 (SE)

Cream Soup, 48 (SO)
Cucumber Soup, Cold, 21 (CC);
114 (SP)
Cucumber Soup, Cream
of, 63 (SO)
Dessert
Apple Soup, Cold, 38 (SO)
Cantaloupe Soup,
Cold, 38 (SO)
Champagne-Lemon
Soup, 38 (SO)
Cherry Soup, Cold, 40 (SO)
Fruit Soup, Dried, 43 (SO)
Fruit Soup,
Scandinavian, 43 (SO)
Papaya Soup, Cold, 40 (SO)
Peach-Orange Soup,
Cold, 41 (SO)
Peach Soup, Cold, 41 (SO)
Raspberry Soup,
Chilled, 42 (SO)
Strawberry Soup, 42 (SO)
Strawberry Soup,
Marilyn's, 42 (SO)
Easter Soup with Egg-Lemon
Sauce, 56 (CE)
Eggplant Soup, Cream
of, 63 (SO)
Frijole-Cheese Soup, 93 (SO)
Gazpacho, 102 (SO)
Gazpacho, Lola's, 102 (SO)
Gazpacho, Spanish, 129 (CC)
Ham Bone Soup, 81 (SO)
How-To, Basic Cream
Soup, 48 (SO)
Lamb and Vegetable
Soup, 80 (SO)
Lentil Soup, 98 (SO)
Lobster Soup, Cream of, 54 (SO)

Macaroni-Beef Soup, 80 (SO)
Meatball Soup, Mexican, 77 (SO)
Minestrone, 106 (SO)
Mushroom Soup, Cream
of, 64 (SO)
Noodle Soup, Filled, 79 (SO)
Okra Soup, Savannah, 101 (SO)
One-Dish Supper
Soup, 106 (SO)
Onion Soup, Green, 66 (SO)
Oyster Bisque, 54 (SO)
Oyster Soup à la New
Orleans, 93 (PO)
Oyster Soup, Baked, 55 (SO)
Oyster Soup,
Charleston, 60 (CC)
Oyster Soup, Jefferson
Davis', 55 (SO)
Peanut Soup, Cream of, 49 (SO)
Pea Soup, Cream of, 129 (CE)
Pea Soup, Green, 65 (SO)
Pea Soup, Split, 65 (SO)
Pepper Pot, 76 (SO)
Potato Soup, 67 (SO)
Potato Soup, Creamy
Herb, 67 (SO)
Pot-au-Feu, 76 (SO)
Pumpkin Soup,
Baked-in-a-, 68 (SO)
Rice Soup, Cream of, 50 (SO)
Salsify Bisque, 69 (SO);
100 (VE)
Sauerkraut Soup, 100 (SO)
Seafood-Mushroom
Soup, 64 (SO)
She-Crab Soup, 23 (SE)
Shrimp Bisque, 56 (SO)
Shrimp Soup, Chilled, 57 (SO)
Shrimp Soup, Cream of, 57 (SO)
Southern Jugged
Soup, 106 (SO)
Spinach and Crabmeat
Soup, 52 (SO)
Spinach Soup, 69 (SO)
Spinach Soup, Cream
of, 51 (SS)
Squash Soup, Cold
Curried, 69 (SO)
Stocks
Beef Stock, 10 (SO)
Brown Roux, 10 (SO)
Brown Stock, 11 (SO)
Brown Stock, Basic, 125 (BE)
Chicken Stock, 11 (SO)
Fish Stock, 12 (SO)
Fish Stock, Basic, 132 (SE)
Seafood Stock, 12 (SO)
Seasoned Soup Stock, 11 (SO)
To Clarify Stocks or
Soups, 10 (SO)
Vegetable Soup Mix, 12 (SO)
White Stock, 11 (SO)
Sweet Soup, 18 (FG)
Tomato Bisque, 70 (SO)
Tomato Refresher, 107 (CC)
Tomato Soup, 94 (FG); 110 (PO)

---

**BB** *Breakfast & Brunch*  **BE** *Beef, Veal & Lamb*  **BR** *Breads*  **CA** *Cakes*  **CC** *Company's Coming*  **CE** *Celebrations*
**CJ** *Cookie Jar*  **DE** *Just Desserts*  **FG** *Family Gatherings*  **GR** *Gift Receipts*  **PK** *All Pork*  **PO** *Plain & Fancy Poultry*
**PP** *Pies & Pastry*  **SE** *Sea & Stream*  **SO** *Soups & Stews*  **SP** *Sporting Scene*  **SS** *Socials & Soirees*  **VE** *Vegetables*

83

**Soups,** *continued*
Tomato Soup, Cream of, 70 (SO)
Tomato Soup, Essence
of, 42 (SS)
Tomato Soup, Quick, 37 (SO)
Tomato Soup,
Savoury, 116 (CC)
Tomato-Vermicelli
Soup, 83 (SO)
Tortilla Soup, 131 (FG); 84 (SO)
Tortilla Soup, Rio
Grande, 86 (SO)
Turkey Bone Soup, 129 (PO)
Turkey-Noodle Soup, 86 (SO)
Turkey Soup, Creamy, 86 (SO)
Turnip Soup, 71 (SO)
Turtle Soup, Charles Bronger's
Louisville, 92 (SO)
Vegetable-Beef Soup,
Homemade, 105 (SO)
Vegetable Hambone
Soup, 124 (PK)
Vegetable Soup, 105 (SO);
31 (SS)
Vegetable Soup, Cold, 10 (CC)
Vegetable Soup, Cream
of, 72 (SO)
Vegetable Soup, Oxtail, 105 (SO)
Vegetable Soup Puree, 72 (SO)
Vegetable Soup,
Spring, 104 (SO)
Vegetable Soup,
Summer, 104 (SO)
Vichyssoise, 67 (SO)
Watercress Soup, 71 (SO)
White Bisque,
Charleston, 58 (SO)
Wild Rice Soup, Cream
of, 50 (SO)
Zucchini Soup, Cream
of, 72 (SO)
**Spaghetti**
Caruso, Spaghetti, 127 (PO)
Chicken Spaghetti,
Alabama, 71 (PO)
Chicken Spaghetti,
Mother's, 71 (PO)
Chicken Spaghetti,
Panhandle, 72 (PO)
Chicken Spaghetti,
Party, 72 (PO)
Chicken Tetrazzini, 73 (PO)
Crab Sauce Lorenzo, 22 (SE)
Tetrazzini, Ham, 81 (PK)
**Spinach**
au Gratin, Spinach, 103 (VE)
Balls, Spinach, 23 (SP)
Basil, Spinach with, 15 (CC)
Boiled Spinach, 103 (VE)
Casserole, Spinach, 55 (CE)
Dip, Sour Cream
Spinach, 115 (FG)
Eggs Florentine, 63 (BB)
Eggs Sardou, 122 (BB)
Eggs, Spinach with
Stuffed, 105 (VE)

How To Prepare Fresh
Spinach, 102 (VE)
Loaf, Menger Hotel
Spinach, 105 (VE)
Mold, Spinach, 114 (SP)
Pie, Spinach, 62 (FG)
Puffs, Spinach, 124 (SS)
Quiche, Spinach, 125 (BB)
Ramekins,
Spinach-Egg, 103 (VE)
Sautéed Spinach
Special, 103 (VE)
Soufflé, Spinach, 76 (CC)
Soufflé with Mushroom Sauce,
Spinach, 48 (SS)
Soup, Cream of
Spinach, 51 (SS)
Soup, Spinach, 69 (SO)
Soup, Spinach and
Crabmeat, 52 (SO)

Stew, Caesar, 131 (SO)
Timbales, Spinach, 105 (VE)
Tomatoes, Spinach
Stuffed, 129 (SS)
Tomatoes Stuffed with Spinach
Rockefeller, 73 (FG)
**Spreads**
Bacon and Egg Sandwich
Spread, 120 (PK)
Ham Sandwich Spread, 89 (PK)
Herb Spread, 136 (VE)
Mint Spread, Cream, 136 (VE)
Mustard Spread, 74 (GR);
104 (SS)
Olive Spread, Toasted Biscuits
with, 64 (CE)
Salmon Spread,
Smoky, 129 (SP)
Shrimp Paste, 51 (SE)
Spinach Mold, 114 (SP)
**Squab**
Compote of Pigeons, 106 (PO)
Fried Squab, Crispy, 80 (PO)
Good to Know, 130-137 (PO)
Pie, Pigeon, 57 (PO)
Roast Squab Pilau, 46 (PO)

Roast Squab with Rice Pilau,
Low Country, 46 (PO)
Toast, Squab on, 46 (PO)
**Squash**
Acorn
Baked Acorn
Squash, 114 (VE)
Brussels Sprouts and Onions
in Acorn Squash,
Creamed, 118 (CC)
Cranberries, Acorn Squash
with, 29 (PO)
Orange-Glazed Acorn
Squash, 114 (VE)
Pudding, Winter
Squash, 114 (VE)
Butternut
Glazed Butternut Squash,
Smith House, 114 (VE)
Pie, Butternut
Squash, 63 (PP)
Chayote Squash, Creole
Stuffed, 111 (VE)
Chayote Squash, Mississippi
Style, 112 (VE)
Chayote Squash, Special
Stuffed, 111 (VE)
Cushaw Pudding, 116 (VE)
Cushaw Pudding,
Spiced, 116 (VE)
How To Prepare Fresh Summer
Squash, 106 (VE)
How To Prepare Winter
Squash, 112 (VE)
Pattypan Squash
Casserole, 109 (VE)
Yellow
Baked Stuffed
Squash, 52 (CC)
Cakes, Squash, 107 (VE)
Casserole, Crunchy
Squash, 107 (VE)
Casserole, Smith House
Squash, 107 (VE)
Casserole, Squash, 16, 76 (FG)
Drumsticks, Squash, 109 (VE)
Muffins, Squash, 116 (BR)
Onions, Summer Squash
and, 13 (PO)
Pickles, Squash, 45 (GR)
Pie, Yellow Squash, 63 (PP)
Relish, Squash, 52 (GR)
Salad, Ports of Call, 130 (CC)
Savory Southern
Squash, 107 (VE)
Soup, Cold Curried
Squash, 69 (SO)
Stuffed Crookneck
Squash, 109 (VE)
Stuffed Squash,
Savory, 116 (SP)
Stuffed Yellow
Squash, 120 (SS)
Zucchini
Baked Zucchini and
Tomatoes, 110 (VE)

*An illustration in the 1893 Peter Henderson & Co. seed catalog.*

**Squash, Zucchini,** *continued*
Bread, Zucchini, 120 (SP)
Buttered Zucchini, 110 (VE)
Lamb with Zucchini,
    Greek, 98 (BE)
Pickles, Zucchini, 45 (GR)
Soup, Cream of
    Zucchini, 72 (SO)
Stuffed Zucchini, 110 (VE)
Tomatoes, Zucchini Stuffed
    with, 110 (VE)

**Squirrel**
Stew, Squirrel, 51 (SP)

**Stews**
Beef Ragout, 54 (BE)
Beef Stew, 32 (CC)
Beef Stew, Baked, 126 (SO)
Beef Stew, Big-Batch, 78 (SP)
Beef Stew, Creole, 126 (SO)
Beef Stew, Irish, 44 (CE)
Beef Stew,
    Old-Fashioned, 54 (BE)
Beef Stew, Old-Time, 126 (SO)
Beef Stew, Texas, 128 (SO)
Beef Stew with Dumplings,
    Wine, 128 (SO)
Bouchées à la Reine,
    133 (SO)
Bouillabaisse, 136 (SO)
Brisket Stew, 54 (BE)
Brunswick Stew, 65 (PO);
    135 (SO)
Brunswick Stew,
    Carolina, 47 (PK)
Burgoo, 135 (SO)
Burgoo, Kentucky, 87 (CE);
    61 (PO)
Burgoo, Old-Fashioned
    Kentucky, 15 (SP)
Caesar Stew, 131 (SO)
Campers' Stew, 76 (SP)
Camp Stew, 134 (SO)
Carbonades à la
    Flamande, 129 (SO)
Carne Guisada on
    Rice, 131 (FG)

Catfish Stew, 112 (SE)
Catfish Stew, Georgia, 97 (CE)
Chicken Stew, 132 (SO)
Chicken Stew, Farmer's, 66 (PO)
Conch Stew, 13 (SE)
Corn Stew, Pioneer, 130 (SO)
Crayfish Stew, 136 (SO)
Fish Stew, 102 (SP)
Ham Stew, 83 (PK)
Hopkins County Stew, 61 (PO)
Hungarian Goulash, 130 (SO)
Indian Stew, 100 (BE)
Irish Stew, 131 (SO)
Lamb, Ragout of, 101 (BE)
Lamb Stew, 99 (BE)
Lamb Stew, Creole, 99 (BE)
Lamb Stew, Ireland, 46 (CE)
Meatball Stew, 129 (SO)
Mullet Stew, Florida's, 76 (SE)
Mulligan Stew,
    Kentucky, 135 (SO)
Navajo Stew, 100 (BE)
Old South Stew, 133 (SO)
Oyster Stew, 53 (FG); 42 (SE)
Pine Bark Stew, 136 (SO)
Pine Bark Stew,
    Otranto, 108 (SE)
Redfish, Court Bouillon
    of, 83 (SE)
Roast, Stew from
    Sunday's, 55 (BE)
Salt Pork and Potato
    Stew, 123 (PK)
Sausage Stew, Owens, 107 (PK)
Scottish Brew, 132 (SO)
Son-of-a-Gun Stew, 120 (BE)
Southern Stew, Easy, 39 (PK)
Squirrel Stew, 51 (SP)
Veal and Noodle Stew, 78 (BE)
Veal Stew, 79 (BE); 130 (SO)
Vegetable and Chicken Stew,
    Fresh, 66 (PO)
Vegetable Stew, Fresh, 129 (VE)
Venison, Ragout of, 40 (SP)

**Strawberries**
à la Mode, Strawberries, 34 (DE)

Bavarian Cream,
    Strawberry, 71 (DE)
Blancmange with
    Strawberries, 76 (DE)
Charlotte, Strawberry, 84 (DE)
Chocolate Dipped
    Strawberries, 129 (SS)
Cobbler, Rhubarb-
    Strawberry, 43 (PP)
Conserve, Strawberry-
    Pineapple, 30 (GR)
Cream, Strawberries with
    Rich, 23 (SP)
Crème Fraîche, Strawberries
    with, 37 (CE)
Crêpes Fitzgerald, 121 (DE)
Custard Sauce over Strawberries
    and Raspberries,
    Chilled, 84 (SP)
Delight, Strawberry, 81 (DE);
    107 (FG)
Flambé, Strawberry, 136 (SS)
Frosted Strawberries, 34 (DE)
Ice Cream, Strawberry, 101 (DE)
Ice, Strawberry, 27 (SS)
Jam, Strawberry, 24 (GR)
Jam, Strawberry-
    Orange, 24 (GR)
Jelly, Strawberry, 13 (GR)
Meringues, Strawberry, 79 (CC)
Mousse, Strawberry, 109 (DE)
Muffins, Strawberry, 26 (SP)
Parfait, Strawberry
    Rum, 133 (CC)
Paste, Strawberry
    Turkish, 104 (GR)
Pie, Plant City
    Strawberry, 49 (PP)
Preserves, Strawberry, 16 (CC);
    19 (GR)
Preserves, Strawberry-Lemon,
    19 (GR)
Rose Hill Strawberries, 33 (DE)
Roulage, Strawberry, 87 (DE)
Sauce, Brandied
    Strawberry, 134 (DE)
Sauce, Fresh
    Strawberry, 134 (DE)

Sauce over Vanilla Ice Cream,
    Strawberry, 56 (SP)
Shortcake, Old-Fashioned
    Strawberry, 52 (CA)
Shortcake, Strawberry, 52 (CA);
    55 (CE); 13 (PO); 28 (SP)

Strawberries, *continued*
  Soup, Marilyn's
    Strawberry, 42 (SO)
  Soup, Strawberry, 42 (SO)
  Surprise, Strawberry, 47 (SS)
  Tarts, Glazed
    Strawberry, 67 (CE); 117 (PP)
  Torte, Schaum, 118 (DE)
  Torte, Strawberry
    Meringue, 118 (DE)
  Trifle, Classic English, 62 (DE)
  Watermelon Bowl, 32 (DE)
  Wine, Strawberries in, 34 (DE)
**Striped Bass**
  Baked Striped Bass, 95 (SE)
  Bake, Striped Bass, 96 (SE)
  Grilled Striped Bass, 96 (SE)
**Stuffings and Dressings**
  Apple Stuffing, Roast Duckling
    with, 41 (PO)
  Avocado Dressing with Creamed
    Chicken, 63 (CE)
  Breadcrumb Dressing, 97 (CC)
  Bread Dressing, 48 (PO)
  Celery Stuffing, Colonial Roast
    Chicken with, 35 (PO)
  Chestnut Stuffing, 29 (PO)
  Cornbread Dressing, Wild Turkey
    with, 132 (CE)
  Cornbread Stuffing, Roast
    Ducklings with, 42 (PO)
  Duck Dressing, Wild, 42 (SP)
  Fruit Dressing, 85 (BE)
  Lemon Stuffing, Baked Grouper
    with, 67 (SE)
  Mushroom Cornbread
    Dressing, 64 (SP)
  Onion-Bread Dressing, 13 (PK)
  Onion Dressing Patties, 48 (PO)
  Orange-Rice Stuffing, Ham Steak
    with, 78 (PK)
  Oyster Cornbread Stuffing, Rock
    Cornish Hens with, 39 (PO)
  Oyster Dressing, 117 (CC)
  Oyster Stuffing, Baked Snapper
    with, 92 (SE)
  Oyster Stuffing, Roast Capon
    with Virginia, 37 (PO)
  Oyster Stuffing, Roast Turkey
    with, 38 (FG)
  Peanut Dressing, 48 (PO)
  Potato and Peanut Stuffing,
    Roast Goose with, 41 (PO)
  Potato Stuffing, 48 (PO)
  Raisin Dressing, Pork Steaks
    with, 23 (PK)
  Raisin Pecan Stuffing,
    Spit-Roasted Cornish Hens
    with, 38 (PO)
  Raisin Stuffing, 32 (PO)
  Rice-Pecan Stuffing, Roast
    Turkey with, 54 (FG)
  Rice Stuffing, 62 (BE)
  Roe Stuffing, Baked Shad
    with, 88 (SE)
  Sage Dressing, 134 (CC)

  Sage Dressing with Giblet
    Gravy, 114 (CE)
  Sage Stuffing, Roast Cornish
    Hens with, 38 (PO)
  Sauerkraut Stuffing, 49 (PO)
  Sausage-Cornbread
    Dressing, 31 (PO)
  Sausage Stuffing, Crown Roast
    of Pork with, 20 (PK)
  Sausage Stuffing, Roast Goose
    with, 41 (PO)
  Sausage Stuffing, Rock Cornish
    Hens with, 39 (PO)
  Sausage Stuffing, Tennessee
    Country, 36 (PO)
  Shrimp and Crabmeat
    Stuffing, 78 (SE)
  Shrimp Stuffing, Flounder Fillets
    with, 64 (SE)
  Shrimp Stuffing, Mullet Fillets
    with, 75 (SE)
  Shrimp Stuffing, Roast Chicken
    with, 36 (PO)
  Wild Rice Dressing, 49 (PO)
**Sweet-and-Sour**
  Beans, Sweet-and-Sour, 22 (VE)
  Beets, Sweet-and-Sour, 24 (VE)
  Brisket with Sauerkraut,
    Sweet-and-Sour, 17 (BE)

  Carrots, Sweet-and-Sour,
    64 (SP); 36 (VE)
  Dressing, Sweet-and-Sour,
    135 (VE)
  Pickles, Sweet-and-Sour, 48 (SS)
  Pork, Sweet-and-Sour, 37 (PK)
  Sauce, Sweet-and-Sour,
    131 (SE)
  Sauce, Sweet-and-Sour
    Plum, 126 (PO)
  Sauce, Sweet-and-Sour
    Tomato, 129 (BE)
  Slaw, Sweet-and-Sour, 119 (CE)
  Soup, Sweet-and-Sour
    Cabbage, 100 (SO)
  Spareribs, Grilled
    Sweet-and-Sour, 56 (PK)
  Spareribs, Sweet-and-Sour,
    32 (PK)
  Tongue, Sweet-and-Sour,
    119 (BE)
**Sweetbreads.** *See* Veal.
**Swiss Chard**
  Creamed Swiss Chard, 58 (VE)
  Sautéed Swiss Chard, 58 (VE)
  Steamed Swiss Chard, 58 (VE)
**Swordfish**
  Baked Swordfish
    Steaks, 98 (SE)

Brown Brothers

**BB** *Breakfast & Brunch*  **BE** *Beef, Veal & Lamb*  **BR** *Breads*  **CA** *Cakes*  **CC** *Company's Coming*  **CE** *Celebrations*
**CJ** *Cookie Jar*  **DE** *Just Desserts*  **FG** *Family Gatherings*  **GR** *Gift Receipts*  **PK** *All Pork*  **PO** *Plain & Fancy Poultry*
**PP** *Pies & Pastry*  **SE** *Sea & Stream*  **SO** *Soups & Stews*  **SP** *Sporting Scene*  **SS** *Socials & Soirees*  **VE** *Vegetables*

The stuffed bird is getting
a final basting before going
back in the oven, c.1911.

Swordfish, *continued*
Grilled Swordfish, 98 (SE)
Marinated Swordfish
Steaks, 98 (SE)
Peppered Swordfish
Steaks, 97 (SE)
Supreme, Swordfish, 98 (SE)

**Syrups**
Banana Syrup, 92 (CC)
Grape Syrup, 92 (CC)
Orange Syrup, 86 (CA)
Plain Syrup, 92 (CC)
Simple Syrup, 109 (CA);
28 (CC); 92 (FG)

# T

**Tacos**
Tacos, 48 (BE)
**Tamales**
Hot Tamales, 48 (BE)
Pie, Hot Tamale, 46 (BE)
Tamales, 36 (CC)
**Tea**
Five o'Clock Tea, 71 (SS)
Good Tea, 90 (BB)
Irish Tea Brack, 43 (CE)
Mint Tea, Iced, 33 (SS)
Muffins, Tea, 112 (FG)
Punch, Iced Tea, 36 (SS)
Punch, Mint Tea, 126 (SS)
Punch, Tea, 66 (SS)
Rum Tea, Hot, 18 (CE)
Spiced Hot Tea, 29 (FG)
Spiced Tea, 90 (BB); 108 (CE)
Springtime Punch, 71 (CE)
**Timbales**
Dessert Timbales, 120 (DE)
Ham Timbales with Béchamel
Sauce, 80 (PK)
Snapper Timbales, 93 (SE)
Spinach Timbales, 105 (VE)
**Tomatoes**
Aspics, Individual
Tomato, 107 (FG)
Aspic, Spicy Tomato, 49 (SS)
Aspic, Tomato, 44 (CC)
Baked Stuffed
Tomatoes, 58 (BB)
Baked Tomatoes, 110 (CC)
Baked Tomatoes,
Seasoned, 119 (VE)
Baked Tomato Halves, 25 (BB);
35 (FG)
Bisque, Tomato, 70 (SO)
Bouillon, Old-South
Vegetable, 27 (SO)
Bouillon, Tomato, 27 (SO)
Broccoli in Tomato Cups,
Braised, 11 (CC)
Broiled Tomatoes, 78 (BB);
93 (PO); 98 (SS)
Brown, Tomatoes, 120 (VE)
Casserole, Baked Creole
Egg, 123 (BB)
Catsup, Tomato, 70 (GR)
Chicago Hot, 76 (GR)
Chutney, Tomato, 48 (SP)
Consommé, Herbed
Tomato, 31 (SP)
Cucumbers with Tomatoes,
Dressed, 116 (SS)
Cups, Green Peas in
Tomato, 25 (SS)
Eggs, Tomato, 123 (BB)
Fried Red Tomatoes, 120 (VE)
Fried Tomatoes with
Gravy, 121 (VE)
Gazpacho, Spanish, 129 (CC)
Gravy, Tomato, 103 (BE)
Green
Casserole, Green
Tomato, 121 (VE)

Chow Chow, Green
Tomato, 52 (GR)
Fried Green
Tomatoes, 16 (BB); 16 (CC)
Marmalade, Green
Tomato, 22 (GR)
Mincemeat, Green
Tomato, 52 (GR)
Pan-Fried Green
Tomatoes, 121 (VE)
Piccalilli, 53 (GR)
Pickles, Green
Tomato, 45 (GR)
Pie, Green Tomato, 63 (PP);
68 (SP)
Sauce, Green, 35 (CC)
How To Prepare Fresh
Tomatoes, 117 (VE)
Juice, Hot Spiced
Tomato, 92 (BB)
Juice, Spiced Tomato, 14 (CC)
Leeks with Tomatoes, 60 (VE)
Mushrooms, Tomatoes Stuffed
with, 111 (SP)
Okra and Tomatoes, 66 (VE)
Parmesan Scalloped
Tomatoes, 51 (SP)
Piccalilli, 53 (GR)

Pico de Gallo, 37 (BE); 75 (GR)
Pie, Tomato, 68 (BB)
Preserves, Favorite
Tomato, 20 (GR)
Refresher, Tomato, 107 (CC)
Relish, Tomato, 52 (GR)
Rice and Tomatoes,
Sautéed, 119 (VE)
Salad, Cold Tomato, 13 (PO)
Salad, Congealed
Tomato-Tuna, 32 (SS)
Salad, Fire and Ice, 65 (SP)
Salad, Marinated
Tomato, 81 (SP)
Salad, Poinsettia, 130 (CE)
Salad, Summer, 52 (CC)
Salad, Tomato Caviar, 131 (CC)
Salad, Tomato Juice, 82 (BB)
Salsa, Chile, 75 (GR)
Salsa de Tomates, 82 (VE)
Sandwiches,
Tomato-Egg, 11 (SS)
Sauce, Fresh Tomato, 135 (VE)
Sauce, Sweet-and-Sour
Tomato, 129 (BE)

*This 1897 Currier & Ives print is appropriately titled* Home from the Brook/ The Lucky Fisherman.

Tomatoes, *continued*
Sauce, Tomato, 128 (BE);
   70 (GR); 130 (SE)
Sauce, Tomato-Wine, 73 (SE)
Scalloped Tomatoes, 121 (FG)
Soufflé, Tomato
   Vermicelli, 134 (FG)
Soup, Cream of Tomato, 70 (SO)
Soup, Essence of
   Tomato, 42 (SS)
Soup, Home-Style
   Tomato, 37 (SO)
Soup, Indian River, 36 (SO)
Soup, Lentil, 98 (SO)
Soup, Quick Tomato, 37 (SO)
Soup, Savoury
   Tomato, 116 (CC)
Soup, Tomato, 94 (FG);
   110 (PO)
Soup, Tomato-Vermicelli,
   83 (SO)
Spinach Rockefeller, Tomatoes
   Stuffed with, 73 (FG)
Spinach Stuffed
   Tomatoes, 129 (SS)
Stacks, Tomato, 119 (VE)
Stewed Tomatoes,
   Summertime, 120 (VE)
Stew, Old South, 133 (SO)
Stew, Pine Bark, 136 (SO)
Zucchini and Tomatoes,
   Baked, 110 (VE)
Zucchini Stuffed with
   Tomatoes, 110 (VE)

**Tortillas.** *See also* Enchiladas.
Burritos de Huevos con
   Chorizo, 119 (BB)
Chips, Fried Tortilla, 34 (CC);
   126 (CE)
Corn Tortillas, 129 (BR)
Flour Tortillas, 129 (BR);
   64 (CC); 132 (FG)
Huevos Rancheros, 38 (BB)
Soup, Mexican Meatball, 77 (SO)
Soup, Rio Grande
   Tortilla, 86 (SO)
Soup, Tortilla, 131 (FG); 84 (SO)
**Tripe**
Breaded Tripe, 120 (BE)
Pepper Pot, 76 (SO)
**Trout**
Almond-Lemon Sauce, Trout
   with, 121 (SE)
Amandine, Trout, 120 (SE)
Baked Trout, 118 (SE)
Balls, Fried Fish, 122 (SE)
Broiled Trout, 135 (BB)
Broiled Trout Fillets, 120 (SE)
Cedarvale Gardens Trout
   Ida, 123 (SE)
Chowder, Trout, 88 (SO)
Fried Trout, 25 (FG)
Grilled Trout, 123 (SE)
Hollandaise Shrimp Sauce, Trout
   with, 118 (SE)
Marguéry, Trout, 118 (SE)
Marinated Grilled
   Trout, 122 (SE)

Meunière, Trout, 121 (SE)
Nuggets, Fried Trout, 121 (SE)
Sautéed Trout, 120 (SE)
Skillet Dinner, Trout, 122 (SE)
**Tuna**
Casserole, Tuna, 101 (SE)
Creamed Tuna, 100 (SE)
Grilled Tuna Steaks, 100 (SE)
Pie, Tuna Pot, 101 (SE)
Salad, Congealed
   Tomato-Tuna, 32 (SS)
Salad, Tuna, 101 (SE)
Salad, Tuna-Rice, 12 (SP)
Steaks with Mushroom Sauce,
   Tuna, 100 (SE)
**Turkey**
au Gratin, Turkey, 119 (PO)
au Rochambeau,
   Turkey, 106 (PO)
Barbecued Turkey,
   Lemon-, 88 (PO)
Barbecued Turkey,
   Oven-, 34 (PO)
Breast of Turkey Supreme, Chef
   Crawford's, 100 (PO)
Casserole,
   Turkey-Sausage, 119 (PO)
Chowder, Turkey, 66 (PO)

Turkey, *continued*
  Creamed Turkey in
    Shells, 125 (PO)
  Galantine of Turkey, 135 (SS)
  Good to Know, 130-137 (PO)
  Gumbo, Turkey-Sausage,
    117 (SO)
  Hash, Tennessee
    Turkey, 111 (FG)
  Hash, Turkey, 16 (BB);
    116 (PO)
  Hash with Cornmeal Waffles,
    Turkey, 77 (CE)
  Mole, Turkey, 126 (CE)
  Roasted Wild Turkey Breast with
    Cream Gravy, 62 (SP)
  Roast Turkey, 113 (CE)
  Roast Turkey, Basic, 31 (PO)
  Roast Turkey in Wine and
    Brandy, 32 (PO)
  Roast Turkey,
    Old-Fashioned, 117 (CC)
  Roast Turkey, Texas, 118 (CE)
  Roast Turkey with Chestnut
    Stuffing, 29 (PO)
  Roast Turkey with Oyster
    Stuffing, 38 (FG)
  Roast Turkey with Raisin
    Stuffing, 32 (PO)
  Roast Turkey with Rice-Pecan
    Stuffing, 54 (FG)
  Roast Turkey with
    Sausage-Cornbread
    Dressing, 31 (PO)
  Rolls, Smoked Turkey, 83 (CC)
  Salad, Normandy
    Luncheon, 56 (SS)
  Salad, Turkey, 49 (SS)
  Sandwich, Meal-in-a-, 74 (SP)
  Sandwich, The Duke of
    Windsor, 115 (PO)
  Smoked Turkey, 34 (PO)
  Smoked Turkey Breast, 99 (SS)
  Smoked Turkey,
    Overnight, 23 (CE)
  Smoked Wild Turkey, 62 (SP)
  Soufflé, Turkey, 120 (PO)
  Soup, Creamy Turkey, 86 (SO)
  Soup, Turkey Bone, 129 (PO)
  Soup, Turkey-Noodle, 86 (SO)
  Spoonbread, Turkey, 120 (PO)
  Wild Turkey with Cornbread
    Dressing, 132 (CE)
**Turnips**
  Browned Turnips, 123 (VE)
  Casserole, Baked
    Turnip, 123 (VE)
  Creamed Turnips, 69 (SP);
    123 (VE)
  Diced Turnips, 118 (CE)
  How To Prepare Fresh
    Turnips, 122 (VE)
  Mustard Greens and
    Turnips, 54 (VE)
  Pork and Turnips over
    Rice, 35 (PK)

Soup, Turnip, 71 (SO)
**Turtle**
  Soup, Charles Bronger's
    Louisville Turtle, 92 (SO)

**Vanilla**
  Cookies, Shaker Vanilla, 66 (CJ)
  Cookies, Vanilla Nut
    Icebox, 66 (CJ)
  Crescents, Vanilla, 96 (FG)
  Custard, Vanilla, 50, 120 (DE)
  Frosting, Vanilla, 86 (CA)
  Ice Cream, Easy Vanilla, 96 (DE)
  Ice Cream, Homemade
    Vanilla, 78 (PO)
  Ice Cream, No-Cook
    Vanilla, 96 (DE)

  Ice Cream, Vanilla, 123 (CC);
    90 (CE); 95 (DE); 81 (FG)
  Muffins, The Peabody's Famous
    Vanilla, 109 (BR)
  Piecrust, Vanilla Wafer, 22 (PP)
  Pie, Vanilla Chiffon, 104 (PP)
  Pie, Vanilla Cream, 88 (PP)
  Pudding, Vanilla, 31 (SS)
  Sauce, Creamy Vanilla, 22 (DE)
  Sauce, Greenbrier
    Vanilla, 136 (DE)
  Sugar, Vanilla, 62 (GR)
  Wafers, Charleston
    Vanilla, 32 (CJ)
  Wafers, Vanilla, 113 (SS)
**Veal**
  Baked Veal with
    Noodles, 77 (BE)
  Birds with Sour Cream,
    Veal, 75 (BE)

  Brains in Sherry
    Sauce, 108 (BE)
  Broth, French, 31 (SO)
  Burgoo, 135 (SO)
  Chops
    Asparagus, Veal Loin Chops
      with, 67 (BE)
    Baked Veal Chops, 66 (BE)
    Breaded Veal Chops, 66 (BE)
    Casserole, Veal Chops
      in, 67 (BE)
    Cream Sauce, Veal Chops
      in, 67 (BE)
    Lorraine, Veal, 68 (BE)
    Mushrooms, Veal Chops
      with, 69 (BE)
  Croquettes, Veal, 80 (BE)
  Curry, Veal, 77 (BE)
  Cutlets
    Baked Sesame Veal
      Cutlets, 74 (BE)
    Birds, Veal, 74 (BE)
    Birds with Sour Cream,
      Veal, 75 (BE)
    Collops with Oyster Forcemeat,
      Hannah Glasse's
      Veal, 76 (BE)
    Grillades Louisiane, 69 (BE)
    Grillades Panée, 69 (BE)
    Hungarian Goulash, 130 (SO)
    Marsala, Veal, 70 (BE)
    Paprika Veal, 70 (BE)
    Parmigiana, Veal, 70 (BE)
    Pedernales with Glazed Apples,
      Veal, 104 (CC)
    Picatta, Hotel Roanoke
      Veal, 71 (BE)
    Provençal, Veal
      Cutlets, 73 (BE)
    Scallopini Maryland,
      Veal, 73 (BE)
    Scallopini, Veal, 73 (BE);
      133 (FG)
    Wiener Schnitzel, 74 (BE)
  Cuts of Veal, 134 (BE)
  Fricassee, Veal, 78 (BE)
  Good to Know, 133-137 (BE)
  Gumbo, Monticello, 121 (CC)
  Loaf, Congealed Veal, 95 (FG)
  Loaf, Veal, 79 (BE)
  Louisiane, Veal, 129 (BB)
  Meatballs, Veal, 80 (BE)
  Omelet, Open-Face Veal, 58 (BB)
  Oysters, Veal, 78 (BE)
  Paprika Cream, Veal in, 78 (BE)
  Ring, Savory Ham-Veal, 87 (PK)
  Roasts
    Daube Glacé, 65 (BE)
    Marinated Veal Roast, 60 (BE)
    Oven-Roasted Veal with New
      Potatoes, 60 (BE)
    Pot Roast, Veal, 65 (BE)
    Pot Roast with Dumplings,
      Veal, 65 (BE)
    Rice Stuffing, Veal Roast
      with, 62 (BE)

---

**BB** *Breakfast & Brunch*   **BE** *Beef, Veal & Lamb*   **BR** *Breads*   **CA** *Cakes*   **CC** *Company's Coming*   **CE** *Celebrations*
**CJ** *Cookie Jar*   **DE** *Just Desserts*   **FG** *Family Gatherings*   **GR** *Gift Receipts*   **PK** *All Pork*   **PO** *Plain & Fancy Poultry*
**PP** *Pies & Pastry*   **SE** *Sea & Stream*   **SO** *Soups & Stews*   **SP** *Sporting Scene*   **SS** *Socials & Soirees*   **VE** *Vegetables*

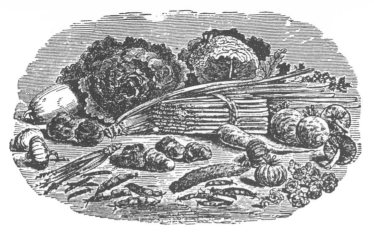

Veal, Roasts, *continued*
Rolled Roast of Veal,
Savory, 60 (BE)
Rolled Veal Roast,
Louisiana, 62 (BE)
Stuffed Veal Roast, 63 (BE)
Stuffed Veal Roast with
Dauphine Potatoes, 64 (BE)
Soufflé, Veal, 81 (BE)
Stew, Camp, 134 (SO)
Stew, Kentucky
Mulligan, 135 (SO)
Stew, Son-of-a-Gun, 120 (BE)
Stew, Veal, 79 (BE); 130 (SO)
Stew, Veal and Noodle, 78 (BE)
Sweetbreads
Bacon, Sweetbreads Wrapped
in, 115 (BE)
Breaded Sweetbreads,
116 (BE)
Broiled Sweetbreads with
Lemon Sauce, 115 (BE)
Deluxe, Sweetbreads,
116 (BE)
Deviled Sweetbreads, 80 (CE)
Green Peas, Sweetbreads
with, 60 (BB)
Pie, A Savory Lamb, 103 (BE)
Pie, Sweetbread and
Oyster, 118 (BE)
Sautéed Sweetbreads with
Gravy, 116 (BE)
Sherried Sweetbreads in Pastry
Shells, 118 (BE)
Stew, Son-of-a-Gun, 120 (BE)
Sweetbreads over Luncheon
Biscuits, Creamed, 39 (SS)
Woodstock, 81 (BE)
**Vegetables.** *See also* specific types.
Blue Cheese Whip, Vegetables
with, 88 (SS)
Bowl, Fresh Vegetable, 95 (FG)
Casserole, Fresh Corn, 45 (VE)
Casserole, Summer
Vegetable, 124 (VE)
Casserole, Vegetable, 93 (SP)
Chartreuse of Vegetables,
Thomas Jefferson's, 129 (VE)

Chops with Vegetables,
Baked, 30 (PK)
Colache, 125 (VE)
Combo, Cucumber, 125 (VE)
Creole Black-Eyed Peas, 80 (VE)
Garden Vegetables,
Mixed, 124 (VE)
Glossary of Cooking
Methods, 138 (VE)
Green Peppers Stuffed with
Fresh Vegetables, 82 (VE)
Gumbo, Vegetable, 126 (VE)
Gumbo z'Herbes, 114 (SO);
126 (VE)
Hash, Vegetable, 127 (VE)
Herb Dip with
Vegetables, 22 (SP)
Jambalaya, Vegetable, 125 (VE)
Maque Chou, 44 (VE)
Medley, Fresh
Vegetable, 124 (VE)
Pickles, Mixed
Vegetable, 46 (GR)
Potato Medley, 127 (VE)
Pot Roast and Vegetables,
German, 21 (BE)
Ratatouille, Italian-Style,
129 (VE)
Relish Bowl, 14 (CC)
Relish, Summer
Vegetable, 54 (GR)
Ring Tum Diddy, 127 (VE)
Roast Loin of Pork with
Vegetables, 18 (PK)
Salads
Fresh Vegetable Salad, 73 (SP)
Marinated Vegetable Salad,
78 (CE); 89 (FG); 20 (SP)
Mold, Vegetable
Salad, 111 (SP)
Riverboat Salad, 72 (BB)
Seven-Layer Congealed
Vegetable Salad, 98 (FG)
Summer Salad, 52 (CC)
Vinaigrette, Vegetables,
125 (SP)
Sandwiches, Vegetable, 21 (SS)
Sauce, Vegetable Hot, 134 (VE)

Soups
Beef Soup, Homemade
Vegetable-, 105 (SO)
Borscht, Traditional, 99 (SO)
Bouillon, Old South
Vegetable, 27 (SO)
Chicken Vegetable
Soup, 81 (SO)
Cold Vegetable Soup, 10 (CC)
Consommé, Vegetable, 29 (SO)
Cream of Vegetable
Soup, 72 (SO)
Hambone Soup,
Vegetable, 124 (PK)
Lamb and Vegetable
Soup, 80 (SO)
Minestrone, 106 (SO)
Mix, Vegetable Soup, 12 (SO)
One-Dish Supper
Soup, 106 (SO)
Oxtail Vegetable
Soup, 105 (SO)
Puree, Vegetable
Soup, 72 (SO)
Soup Mix, Vegetable, 12 (SO)
Southern Jugged
Soup, 106 (SO)
Spring Vegetable
Soup, 104 (SO)
Summer Vegetable
Soup, 104 (SO)
Vegetable Soup, 105 (SO);
31 (SS)
Steamed Winter
Vegetables, 14 (PK)
Stew, Fresh Vegetable, 129 (VE)
Stew, Fresh Vegetable and
Chicken, 66 (PO)
Succotash, 127 (VE)
**Venison**
Barbecued Venison
Steaks, 52 (SP)
Chili, Venison, 113 (SO)
Ragout of Venison, 40 (SP)
Roast, Venison, 134 (CC)
**Vermicelli**
Cavatoni, Chicken Eggplant
Francesca, 95 (PO)
Soufflé, Tomato
Vermicelli, 134 (FG)
Soup, Beef-Vermicelli, 79 (SO)
Soup, Tomato-
Vermicelli, 83 (SO)
**Vinegars**
Basil Vinegar, 67 (GR); 136 (VE)
Chile Pepper Vinegar, 69 (GR)
Chive Blossom
Vinegar, 135 (VE)
Chive Vinegar, 136 (VE)
Datil Pepper Vinegar, 69 (GR)
Garlic-Chive Vinegar, 67 (GR)
Herb Vinegar, Mixed, 67 (GR)
Mint Vinegar, 69 (GR)
Red Wine Vinegar, 69 (GR)
Tarragon Wine Vinegar, 67 (GR)
Violet Vinegar, 69 (GR)

---

**BB** *Breakfast & Brunch*   **BE** *Beef, Veal & Lamb*   **BR** *Breads*   **CA** *Cakes*   **CC** *Company's Coming*   **CE** *Celebrations*
**CJ** *Cookie Jar*   **DE** *Just Desserts*   **FG** *Family Gatherings*   **GR** *Gift Receipts*   **PK** *All Pork*   **PO** *Plain & Fancy Poultry*
**PP** *Pies & Pastry*   **SE** *Sea & Stream*   **SO** *Soups & Stews*   **SP** *Sporting Scene*   **SS** *Socials & Soirees*   **VE** *Vegetables*

# W

## Waffles
Basic Waffles, 114 (BB)
Cheese Waffles, 114 (BB)
Cornmeal Waffles, 77 (CE)
Corn Waffles, 115 (BB)
Crispy Waffles, 114 (BB)
Gingerbread Waffles, 115 (BB)
Ham Waffles, 114 (BB)
Orange Pecan Waffles with
    Orange Butter, 20 (BB)
Raisin Waffles, 61 (BB)
Sweet Potato Waffles, 116 (BB)
Whole Wheat Waffles, 115 (BB)

*A variety of foods is
depicted by a class of
costumed children in 1923
at the Lucia Avenue School
in Louisville, Kentucky.*

## Walnuts
Brittle, Black Walnut, 111 (GR)
Cake, Black Walnut
    Spice, 50 (CA)
Cake, Orange-Walnut, 50 (CA)
Cinnamon Walnuts, 96 (GR)
Coffee Walnuts, 96 (GR)
Cookies, Chocolate-Walnut
    Christmas, 115 (CJ)
Cookies, Chocolate-Walnut
    Refrigerator, 68 (CJ)
Cookies, Christmas
    Fruit, 117 (CJ)
Cookies, Crunchy
    Oatmeal, 44 (CJ)
Cookies, Maryland Black
    Pepper, 37 (CJ)
Figs, Holiday Stuffed, 81 (GR)
Holiday Nuts, 96 (GR)
Karethopeta (Walnut
    Cake), 58 (CE)
Logs, Holiday Delight, 119 (GR)
Meat Loaf with Walnuts and
    Oranges, Rolled, 38 (BE)
Pie, Black Walnut, 55 (PP)
Pralines, Maple, 130 (GR)
Rocks, Maryland, 69 (BB);
    34 (CJ)
Sautéed Walnuts, 24 (CE)
Sugared Walnuts, 95 (GR)
Wafers, Walnut, 55 (CJ)

# Z

**Zucchini.** *See* Squash.

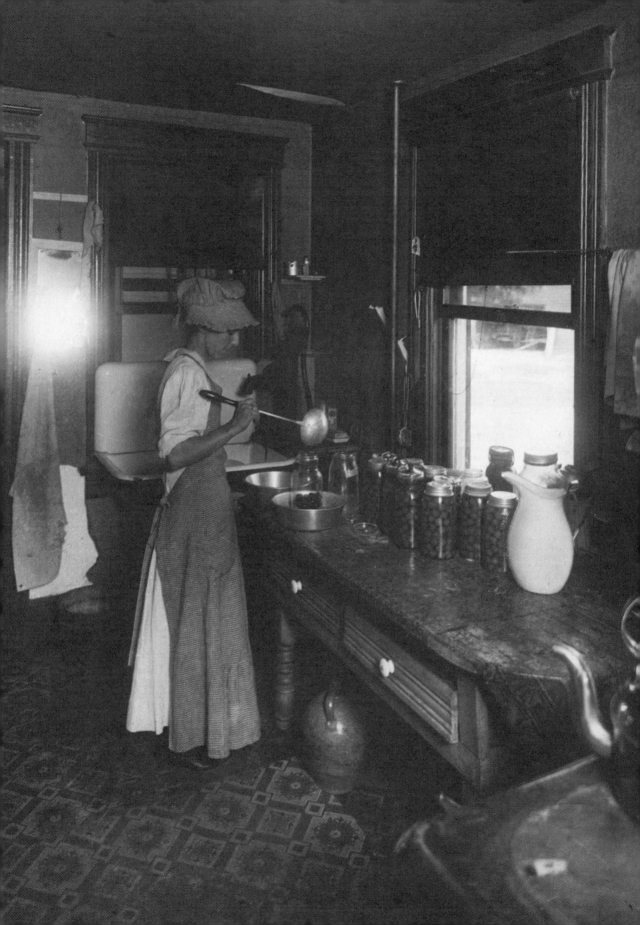

# SOUTHERN HERITAGE SUBJECTS

hroughout the eighteen volumes of cookery books that comprise *The Southern Heritage Cookbook Library*, tantalizing references have been made to important people in Southern history. Such vignettes or "cameo appearances" may have piqued the reader's curiosity to know more about, say, Dolley Madison than the fact that she was a sensational hostess for her husband, our fourth president. Certainly that is our hope. The lives of the persons whom we have glimpsed so randomly were as full of pleasure and pain as were the lives of those whose names escaped the history books; all are deserving of further study.

Beginning with Martha Dandridge Custis Washington (1732-1802) and ending with Mary Virginia Hawes Terhune (1831-1922), who wrote under the name of Marion Harland and whose recipes we've borrowed so shamelessly, only think! We are looking at nearly two centuries of the South's culinary and social history. We move with Martha, gentle mistress of Mount Vernon, to her invention of herself as first lady without precedent and reach beyond America's "flapper age"; Marion Harland died in 1922, the year after F. Scott Fitzgerald's *The Beautiful and Damned* was published. A novelist herself, she would have known of his earlier works.

In the nineteenth century, the primitive facilities that birthed the mystique of Southern cooking evolved into the beginnings of real labor-savers, such as iron ranges in the 1870s, first, with wood as fuel and then, as the century turned, coal. Next, in time for Marion Harland to see it, came the gas stove, soon to be followed by the electric range. Mechanical refrigeration took more time; the first patent had been granted in 1834, but it was to be nearly a century before it became standard household equipment.

The political ferment of these years from which we've extracted only the food-related moments is another book and can only be touched upon here.

We envision the Washingtons, married in 1759, holding forth graciously at Mount Vernon with throngs of guests, especially during fox hunting season. Martha loved the hunt

*The "putting up" of the fruit harvest was a sizable task for the farm woman of 1905.*

too, but often found herself overseeing dinner for the others. It was during this time that Washington referred to their home as "a well-resorted tavern." But not everyone came to hunt; Patrick Henry came and George Mason, author of the Bill of Rights. The Revolution was brewing; Valley Forge was coming. Eventually, Martha was to move to New York as the president's wife. Unaccustomed to the sophistication of the capital, she confided to a friend that she felt like a state prisoner and always referred to her time there as her "lost days."

The six American presidents preceding Andrew Jackson had conducted affairs of state with ceremony, more or less along the lines of the English court. Four were Virginians (Washington, Jefferson, Madison, and Monroe), and two (the Adamses) were from Massachusetts—all East Coast Brahmins. Jackson belonged to another breed of American politicians, those molded by the frontier, risen from the ranks, elected by the citizens. But two women suffered as Jackson gained political prominence: his wife Rachel and Mary Randolph, author of the first truly Southern cookbook.

Rachel Jackson, born in Virginia in 1767, had, at age thirteen, come with her father, Captain Donelson, in the first wave of settlers to Nashville. When Jackson came to Nashville in 1788 as public prosecutor, she was already separated from her husband, Lewis Robards. In 1791, on hearing that Robards had procured a divorce, Jackson and Rachel were married. Two years into the marriage, it was discovered that Robards had not divorced her; the couple went through the ceremony again, and that was that—until Jackson started to rise politically. His fight for the presidency was marred by unparalleled mudslinging, with Rachel's honor being called into question. Rachel had seen enough of high life anyway; she had accompanied Andrew to Philadelphia when he was senator. The Jacksons' frontier manners didn't fit in, and her pipe smoking had been criticized as Dolley Madison's snuff taking never had been. Rachel died, perhaps mercifully, just weeks before his inauguration.

Mary Randolph's family connections and political leanings eventually inspired a wrath in her for Andrew Jackson and all he stood for. She had not affixed her name to that famous cookbook, *The Virginia Housewife*, when the first edition came out in 1824. Modesty, perhaps, interfered or some embarrassment at offering it for sale. She and her cousin/husband, David Meade Randolph, were in financial straits. And their families, intricately intermarried with the Jeffersons, were torn by the bitterest of personal strife, matters of public knowledge, which, in our day, would have the makings of a lurid best-seller. But their animosity toward Jackson came from his tie-in with Jefferson's politics.

The early 1800s was a time of political polarization. Mary and David were part of the conservative, pro-British Federalist party, which favored a strong central government partial to the upper class. Among their leaders were John Marshall, Alexander Hamilton, and John Adams. In the

vanguard of the liberal Republican party were Jefferson and Madison. David, at this juncture, had put his money on the wrong horse when he came out against Jefferson and his party, of which Jackson was a member. David was summarily fired from the political job he had gained through Jefferson's influence. The families carried their hatred to the grave—in Mary's case, only months before "Old Hickory" was elected president in 1828.

Dorothea Payne Todd Madison was eighty-one when she died in 1849, the year of the California gold rush. She had known eleven presidents, and her life spanned America's evolution from the colonial period into the industrial age. When the British burned the executive mansion during the War of 1812, Dolley risked her life to save all the president's papers. The restoration of the building, which included a new white facade, was completed in time for the Monroes to take up residency. Dolley was welcome at the "White House" all her life and made her last public appearance at the Polks' farewell reception. President Zachary Taylor, who succeeded Polk, headed her funeral cortege, the largest, to that time, ever in Washington.

I f society changed quickly for Dolley Madison, it moved even faster for Mary Virginia Hawes Terhune, whose pen name Marion Harland became a household word. Born in rural Virginia under Jackson's presidency, she lived to see Warren Harding take office. Nothing stood still in this frenetic time frame. An unmechanized America turned into a nation powered by steam, gasoline, and electricity. The privations of the Civil War over, an expanded network of railroads fed industry. Most significant to Mary Terhune was the birth of the publishing industry that, by 1870, supported a record audience (chiefly female), which was receptive to her *Common Sense in the Household*, 1871. The constricted women of the 1870s and 1880s, bound by rules of propriety and relegated to indoor labor, welcomed Marion Harland's voice of sympathy when she spoke to their discontent, advising them to accept their "profession" cheerfully.

These are but a sampling of the many Southern women and their men who populate the pages of *The Southern Heritage Cookbook Library* and who have in common their frequent use, in letters and speeches, of such words as duty, honor, and pride. They have much to teach us; we have only to read. Read of them, as chronicled by their contemporaries. Or read their inmost thoughts; many of those men and women were tireless letter-writers and diarists, who had good reason to explain and position themselves historically as they went along.

The following subject index will serve to locate references to the many persons mentioned throughout the series. Use the index also as a guide to many of the South's historic landmarks, such as the Hermann-Grima House in New Orleans and the Snowden House in Alexandria, Virginia.

To use index: Each entry is followed by the page number and, in parenthesis, the code for the book where the entry can be found. The book codes are identified in the key below.

## A

Absinthe, 28 (CC); 34 (CE)
Acadians, 108 (PK)
Adams, John, 82 (CE); 14 (SS)
Agar, 105 (GR)
Aiken's Row, 113 (CJ)
Alabama, 14, 18 (BR); 11, 73 (CA); 43 (CC); 124 (FG); 49 (SP); 72, 105, 108 (SS)
Allison's Little Tea House, 87 (PP)
All Saints' Day, 100 (CE)
Almonds, 9, 13 (CJ)
Ambrosia, 11 (CA); 31, 49 (DE)
Americana, 18 (BR)
"American General Gazette," 1777, 7 (DE)
Ames Plantation, 60 (SP)
Anniversaries, 7, 65, 83 (FG)
Antipasto, 133 (FG)
Apples, 40 (PO)
  apple bee, 37 (CA)

bobbing, 103 (CE)
cake, 35 (CA)
drying, 37, 40 (CA)
history, 27 (PP)
pectin, 9, 13 (GR)
"smoked," 37 (CA)
stack cake, 40 (CA)
Winesap, 35 (CA)
Appleseed, Johnny, 27 (PP)
Aquatic Club of Georgia, 88 (SP)
Arkansas, 9 (BR); 30 (FG); 45 (PO); 109 (SO); 39, 57, 62 (SP)
Arm & Hammer Baking Soda, 9 (CA)
Arnaud's, 64 (DE)
Artichokes, 12 (PO)
*Art of Cookery Made Plain and Easy, The* (Hannah Glasse, 1747), 73, 76 (BE); 111 (CA); 29, 49, 89 (DE); 9 (GR)
Asheville, 13 (BE); 110 (BR)
Ashton Villa, 62 (BB); 67, 80 (CC); 20 (SS)
Asparagus, 14 (VE)
Athenæus, 79 (PP)
"At home," 83 (CC); 62 (SS)
Atlanta, 65 (BB); 83 (CC); 134 (DE); 47 (SP); 7, 10, 16, 19, 96 (SS)
Audubon, John James, 87 (CE); 106 (PO); 67, 71 (SP)
Audubon Society of America, 71 (SP)

Avegolemono, 33 (SO)
Avery Island, 96 (SO); 82 (VE)
Azalea Trail, 51 (SS)

## B

Bachelor Buttons, 33 (CJ)
Bacon, 9, 115, 119, 126 (PK)
Baked Alaska, 89 (DE)
Baking powder, 8, 11, 75 (BR); 9 (CA); 19 (PO)
Ballooning, 67, 80 (SP)
Banbury Tarts, 115 (PP)
Barbecue, 9 (BE); 9, 38, 67 (CC); 87 (CE); 15 (FG); 43, 44, 48, 53, 54, 57 (PK); 8, 75, 87 (PO); 134 (SO); 33, 67, 71 (SP)
Bar cookies, 89 (CJ)
Bar Mitzvah, 7, 97 (FG)
Barnum Hotel, 7 (SO)
Bartram, John, 31 (DE)
Bartram, William, 107 (SE)
Bas Mitzvah, 97 (FG)
Bass, 95, 105 (SE); 102 (SP)
Bavarian, 109 (DE)
Bay leaves, 79 (GR)
Baylor University, 27 (FG)
Beach Hotel, 59 (BB)
Beans, 20, 23, 131 (VE)

Fall Games—the Apple Bee, *a wood engraving by Winslow Homer, 1859.*

Beef, 7, 10 (BE); 38 (CC); 43 (PK); 80 (SO)

Beetroot wine, 25 (VE)

Beets, 95 (GR); 99 (SO); 58 (VE)

Beignets, 32 (BB); 9, 121 (BR); 68 (CC)

Belle Meade Mansion, 10, 33 (FG); 24 (SP)

Belvidere, 82 (CJ)

Benedict, Jennie, 11 (CA)

Benne Seed Cakes, 31 (CJ)

Berkeley Hundred, 112 (CE)

Bermuda, 12 (CC)

Biltmore House, 13 (BE)

Bird-watching, 67 (SP)

Birthdays, 7, 65, 66, 68, 69, 71, 74, 76 (FG); 130, 131 (SS)

Biscuits, 7 (BB); 9, 75, 77, 80, 83, 88, 93 (BR); 26 (GR); 84 (PO)

Bizcochos, 111 (CJ)

Blackbird Pie, 57 (PO)

Black-eyed peas, 80 (VE)

Black, Justice Hugo, 79 (DE)

Blancmange, 70 (DE)

Bloomer, Amelia, 74 (VE)

Blueberries, 42 (DE)

Bluefish, 61 (SE)

Boats, 87, 88 (SP)

"Bœuf Gras," 45 (BE)

Boiling process, 20 (PO)

Boiling-water bath, 35, 58 (GR)

*Boke of St. Albans* (1496), 121 (SE)

Bonfire, 100, 101 (CE)

Bon Ton Restaurant, 12 (DE)

Boone, Daniel, 72 (PP)

Borden, Gail, 51 (DE); 112 (PP)

Borscht, 99 (SO)

Boston Tea Party, 93 (BR); 14 (SS)

Bouillon cube, 25 (SO)

*Bowl of Red, A* (Francis X. Tolbert, 1966), 53 (BE)

Brady, Diamond Jim, 96 (DE)

Braising, 23 (PO)

Brandy, 83 (GR)

Breads
  fry bread, 32 (CC)
  German pancake, 49 (CC)
  history, 7, 8 (BR)
  kogle, 63 (BR)
  muffins, 102 (BB)
  pita bread, 49 (CC)
  "platter bread," 32 (CC)
  quick breads, 99 (BR)
  rusk/sippets, 131 (BR)
  soda bread, 42 (CE)
  spoonbread, 30, 33 (BR)
  starters, 39 (BR)
  wheat bread, 53 (BR)

Breakers, The, 115, 128 (CC)

Breakfast/Brunch, 7, 9, 10, 12, 15, 19, 22, 24, 27, 28, 30, 32, 34, 37, 40, 41, 43, 44, 49, 52, 56, 59, 62, 65, 66, 70, 75, 78, 81, 84, 89, 95, 102, 125 (BB); 78, 94, 111 (FG); 64 (PK); 9 (SE); 24, 39, 117 (SP); 24 (SS)

*Breakfast, Luncheon and Tea* (Marion Harland, 1877), 116, 120, 123 (BE); 105 (FG); 103 (PP); 64 (SS)

Bream, 115 (SE)

Brewing/breweries, 59 (CA)

Bridal shower, 83 (SS)

Bridge, 80 (CC)

Briquette, 89 (PO)

Brisket, 9 (BE)

Brownies, 89 (CJ)

Browning, Robert, 97 (GR)

Brunn, Gustaw C., 98 (CE)

Brunswick Stew, 44 (PK); 65 (PO); 109, 134 (SO)

Buffalo, 52 (SP)

Buffet, 99, 105 (SS)

Burgoo, 61 (PO); 109, 134 (SO); 14, 16 (SP)

Buster Holmes Restaurant, 109, 132 (SP)

Buttermilk, 75 (BR); 57, 66 (PP)

Butters, 9, 26 (GR); 10 (SS)

Butterscotch, 89 (CJ); 132 (DE); 116 (GR)

# C

Cabbage, 125 (PK); 33, 112 (VE)

Cabrito, 43 (PK)

Cades Cove, 74 (SP)

Cafeterias, 128 (DE)

Cajun cooking, 24 (CC); 12 (DE); 87 (PO); 9 (SE); 109 (SO)

Cake decorating, 129 (CA)

Cakes
  Angel food, 7, 111 (CA)
  Apple stack, 40 (CA)
  Ash, 11 (BR)
  Baltimore Cakes, Lord and Lady, 9, 11, 13 (CA)
  Beer Cakes, 59 (CA)
  Blackberry Jam Cake, 46 (CA)
  Brown's Church Jam Cake, 46 (CA)
  Chiffon, 111, 114 (CA)
  Dolly Varden, 9, 11, 20 (CA)
  Fruitcake, 89 (CA); 79 (GR)
  German Chocolate, 27 (CA)
  John Garner Cake, 73 (CA)
  Johnny Cakes, 11 (BR)
  King Cake, 89 (CA); 38 (CE)
  Lane Cake, 9, 11, 14 (CA)
  La Reine, 9 (CA)
  Minnehaha, 11 (CA)
  Mississippi Mud, 73 (CA)
  Pineapple Upside-Down Cake, 71 (CA)
  Pork Cake, 62 (CA)
  Pound, 111 (CA)
  Red Watermelon Cake, 73, 79 (CA)
  Scripture, 61 (CA)
  Shortcake, 52 (CA)
  Shrewsbury Cakes, 57 (CJ)
  Stellar's Funeral Cakes, 59 (CA)
  Tutti-Frutti, 11 (CA)
  Wedding, 89 (CA); 86 (SS)
  Whiskey Cake, 59 (CA)
  White Mountain, 9 (CA)
  "Yankee cakes," 45 (BB)

Calf fries/mountain oysters, 113 (BE)

Camping, 76 (SP)

Camp meeting, 52 (PO)

Candies, 99, 100, 113, 124, 126 (GR)

Cane River, 9, 24 (CC)

Canning, 9 (GR)

Cantaloupe, 96 (DE)

Cape Cod, 12 (SE)

Capon, 94 (CC)

Caramels, 116 (GR)

Card-playing, 81 (BB)

Carolina Cup, The, 10 (SP)

*Carolina Houswife, The,* 67, 80 (BE)

Carrots, 35, 52 (VE)

Carter's Grove, 9 (CC); 60 (SS)

Carver, George Washington, 81 (CJ)

Cassleman Inn, 99 (BR)

Catalpa, 89 (BB)

Catholics, 34, 94 (FG)

Catsup, 61 (GR)

Cauliflower, 39 (VE)

**BB** *Breakfast & Brunch*  **BE** *Beef, Veal & Lamb*  **BR** *Breads*  **CA** *Cakes*  **CC** *Company's Coming*  **CE** *Celebrations*
**CJ** *Cookie Jar*  **DE** *Just Desserts*  **FG** *Family Gatherings*  **GR** *Gift Receipts*  **PK** *All Pork*  **PO** *Plain & Fancy Poultry*
**PP** *Pies & Pastry*  **SE** *Sea & Stream*  **SO** *Soups & Stews*  **SP** *Sporting Scene*  **SS** *Socials & Soirees*  **VE** *Vegetables*

97

Celebrations, 7, 8, 22, 36, 42, 44, 46, 48, 49, 68, 69, 72, 82, 89, 92, 100, 112, 113, 117, 121, 123 (CE); 7, 65, 76, 78, 83, 93 (FG); 80 (SP); 87, 130, 131 (SS)
Celery, 40, 42 (VE)
Cereal, 23 (PP)
Chafing dish, 37 (SS)

Chandler, Asa G., 16, 19 (SS)
Charivari, 106 (CA)
Charleston, 9, 63 (BR); 9, 21, 60, 83 (CC); 127 (CE); 113 (CJ); 40 (DE); 53 (FG); 51 (PP); 9 (SE)
Cheesecakes, 101 (FG); 74, 79, 84 (PP)
Cherry Winks, 116 (CJ)
Chesapeake Bay, 28 (BB); 98 (CE); 12, 59 (SE); 91 (SP)
Chess pies, 74 (PP)
Chicken, 44 (CC); 119 (FG); 7, 9, 51, 62, 71, 75, 79, 83, 84, 91, 96, 101, 109, 113, 117, 127 (PO)
    history, 27 (PO)
Chicory, 68 (CC)
Chiffon pies, 103, 105 (PP)
Chile peppers, 82 (VE)
Chili, 53 (BE); 64 (CC); 109 (SO)
Chili powder, 51 (BE); 111 (SO)
China/Chinese, 136 (BR); 8 (CE); 105 (GR); 37 (PK); 114 (SO)
Chocolate, 28 (CA); 57, 89, 103 (CJ)
    history, 82 (CA)
Chocolate chip cookies, 31, 38 (CJ)
Chop suey, 37 (PK)
Chowder, 12 (SE); 75, 91 (SO)
Christening, 93, 94 (FG)
Christmas, 89 (CA); 7, 12 (CC); 22, 23, 50, 53, 113, 121, 123, 125, 127, 129, 132, 135 (CE); 111, 130, 135 (CJ); 33, 44, 47, 50, 53 (FG); 7, 35, 61, 79, 84, 99 (GR)
Church and Co., 9 (CA)

Churchill Downs, 74 (CE)
Church supper, 9 (FG)
Cider, 57 (CC)
Citrus, 52, 53 (BB); 36 (SO)
Civil War, 49, 89 (BB); 21 (BR); 65, 117 (CA); 14, 43, 71 (CC); 36, 112 (CE); 82 (CJ); 132 (DE); 119 (FG); 84 (GR); 8 (PP); 9 (SE); 30, 46, 47 (SP); 7 (SS)
Clambake, 11 (SE); 87 (SP)
Clams, 11, 12 (SE)
Cloister Hotel, 75 (CJ)
Coca Cola®, 9, 16, 19 (SS)
Cocktail party, 80 (BE); 10 (SP); 99, 102, 105 (SS)
Coconut, 93 (CJ); 124 (GR)
Coffee
    a coffee, 9, 10, 13 (SS)
    café au lait, 32, 37 (BB); 68 (CC)
    café con leche, 37 (BB)
    café noir, 68 (CC)
    history, 93 (BR); 14 (SS); 97 (VE)
Cognac, 83 (GR)
Collation, 86 (SS)
Columbus, Christopher, 27 (PO)
*Common Sense in the Household* (Marion Harland, 1873), 21 (BR); 8, 9 (CA); 45 (VE)
Condiments, 7 (GR)
Confections, 99, 105 (GR)
Confederacy, The, 46 (SP); 105, 108 (SS)
Connemara, 57 (DE)
Conner's Toll House, 58 (CJ)
Conserves, 9, 28 (GR)
*Consolidated Library of Modern Cooking, The* (1905), 7 (SO)
Consommé, 25 (SO)
Continental Congress, 82 (CE)
Cookies. *See also* specific types. 7, 31, 57, 58, 70, 73, 89, 111, 116, 125, 135 (CJ)
Cooking equipment (cookware)
    biscuit brake, 77, 78 (BR)
    braizer, 23 (PO)
    broche, 47 (PK)
    candy-making, 99 (GR)
    cheese press, 78 (PP)
    clay pot, 11 (PO)
    Dover rotary (egg) beater, 8 (CA)
    gaufrette iron, 73 (CJ)
    iron kettle, 7, 20 (PO)
    krumkake iron, 73 (CJ)
    "muffin" irons, 18 (BR)
    "oven-pot," 44 (CE)

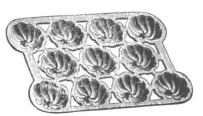

pickling equipment, 35, 58 (GR)
rosette iron, 73 (CJ)
sausage stuffer, 12 (BB)
"spider," 11, 34 (BR)
stew-hole, 94 (PO)
stove, 117 (CA); 120 (FG)
"tin kitchen," 32 (PO)
wafer iron, 73 (CJ)
waffle iron, 73 (CJ)
Corbitt, Helen, 104 (CC); 109 (PO)
Corn, 7 (BB); 7 (PK); 7, 11, 17, 24, 45, 129 (VE)
Cornbread, 7, 8, 9, 11, 24, 27 (BR); 17 (PK)
Corn dogs, 110 (PK)
Cornmeal, 7, 17 (BR); 10 (DE); 123 (PP)
Cortez, 82 (CA); 64 (CC)
*Cottage Kitchen, The* (1883), 119 (PK)
County fair, 93 (CE)
Court bouillon, 81 (SE)
Cownes Plantation, 43 (CC)
Crabs, 7, 9, 14, 17, 21 (SE); 87, 91 (SP)
Cracker Jack, 114 (GR)

Cracker Jack
AMERICA'S FAMOUS CONFECTION

"THE MORE YOU EAT—
THE MORE YOU WANT"
REG. U. S. PAT. OFF.

Borden, Inc.

Crackling, 11 (BR)
Crappies (sunfish), 115 (SE)
Crawford, Chef Fred, 12 (BB); 100 (PO)
Crayfish, 9 (SE)
Cream, 90 (BR)
Cream cheese, 79 (PP)
Cream pies, 9, 87 (PP)
Cream soups/purees/bisques, 45, 58, 72 (SO)

---

**BB** *Breakfast & Brunch*   **BE** *Beef, Veal & Lamb*   **BR** *Breads*   **CA** *Cakes*   **CC** *Company's Coming*   **CE** *Celebrations*
**CJ** *Cookie Jar*   **DE** *Just Desserts*   **FG** *Family Gatherings*   **GR** *Gift Receipts*   **PK** *All Pork*   **PO** *Plain & Fancy Poultry*
**PP** *Pies & Pastry*   **SE** *Sea & Stream*   **SO** *Soups & Stews*   **SP** *Sporting Scene*   **SS** *Socials & Soirees*   **VE** *Vegetables*

Creole, 33 (BE); 7, 9, 24, 28, 43, 67, 90 (CC); 108, 109 (PK); 69, 91 (PO); 9 (SE); 121 (SO); 112 (SS); 23 (VE)
Crêpes, 121 (DE)
Croquet, 109, 110 (SP)
Cross Creek (Marjorie Kinnan Rawlings, 1942), 83 (BR)
Cross Creek Cookery (Marjorie Kinnan Rawlings, 1942), 28 (BR); 73 (CA)
Crudité tray, 42, 131 (VE)
Crusts, 57 (PO); 7, 8, 17, 21, 23, 27, 65, 87, 115 (PP)
"Cubbing," 109 (CE)
Cucumber, 49 (VE)
Curing meats, 7 (BB); 8, 63, 83, 115, 121 (PK)
Curry, 102, 103 (PO)
Custard, 49, 70 (DE)
Custard, chess, and cheese pies, 65, 74 (PP)
Custis, Mary, 19 (CA)
Customs and traditions, 27 (BB); 45 (BE); 106 (CA); 7, 67, 71, 83, 115 (CC); 13, 19, 22, 38, 48, 72, 100, 113, 121, 123, 132 (CE); 59, 65, 93, (FG); 90 (GR); 52 (PO); 29, 57 (PP); 25, 94 (SO); 91 (SP); 19, 59, 62, 79, 127 (SS); 31, 49, 80, (VE)
Cycling, 67, 74 (SP)

Dale, Governor Thomas, 8 (PK)
Dallas, 76 (CC); 128 (DE); 110 (PO)
Davis, Jefferson, 87, 89 (PP); 55 (SO); 105, 108 (SS)
De Bonnes Choses à Manger, 33 (BE)
Delaware, 18, 91 (SP)
Delightes for Ladies (Sir Hugh Plat, 1600), 7, 13 (CJ)
Delineator, The, 37 (FG)
Dennis Cookbook, Annie (1901), 41, 78, 83 (BE)
Derby Day, 74, 76 (CE)
Desserts, 7, 29, 49, 55, 96, 109, 115, 131 (DE)
party, 92 (SS)
Dewberry, 70 (PP)
Dictionary of American Food and Drink, The (John F. Mariane, 1897), 89 (CJ)
Dixieland, 102 (SS)
Domestic Receipt Book, 85 (CC)
Doughnuts, 45 (BB); 121, 124 (BR)
Driskill Hotel, The, 46 (SO)
Ducks, 109 (BR); 60 (CC); 45 (PO); 57 (SP)

Dumplings, 29 (DE); 19 (PO); 127, 128 (PP); 15 (SO)
Dunleith Mansion, 115, 131, 132 (CC)

# E

Eagle Brand Sweetened Condensed Milk, 51 (DE); 112 (PP)
Easter, 47 (CC); 48, 49, 51, 53, 56, 121 (CE); 125 (CJ); 7, 33, 34 (FG)
East India Company, 93 (BR)
Easy Entertaining, 34 (SS)
Edwards House, 106 (PO)
Eggnog, 19, 21, 135 (CE); 50 (FG)
Eggplant, 52 (VE)
Eggs, 48, 51, 56 (CE); 65 (PP); 33 (SO)
Egyptians, 7, 37 (BR); 8 (CE); 80 (VE)
England/English, 7, 83, 110 (BE); 7, 93, 121 (BR); 10 (CC); 8, 23, 27, 62, 68, 72, 121 (CE); 7, 9, 19, 26, 55, 111 (CJ); 7, 9, 27, 42, 49 (DE); 33, 36 (FG); 79 (GR); 11 (PK); 14, 27, 57 (PO); 7, 8, 9, 11, 27 (PP); 7, 125 (SE); 7 (SO); 7, 110, 126 (SP); 59, 62 (SS); 25, 35, 49, 52 (VE)
English Housekeeper (Elizabeth Raffald, 1769), 89 (DE)
Etiquette, 55 (BR); 67 (CC); 59, 64 (SS)
Étouffée, 125 (SO)
Excelsior House, 99 (BR)

# F

Fabergé, 51 (CE)
Fall, 54 (CC)
"Famous Chocolate Wafers," 86 (DE)
Fancy Farm, 43 (PK)
Farmer, Fannie, 7 (CA)
Farrar, Geraldine, 96 (SS)
Father's Day, 80 (FG)
Fedler's Camp Ground, 52 (PO)
Ferguson, "Ma," 100 (PP)
Fifty Years in a Maryland Kitchen (Mrs. Benjamin Chew Howard, 1873), 82 (CJ)
Figs, 81 (GR)
Filé powder, 62 (PO); 9 (SE); 109, 114, 117 (SO)
Fish. See also specific types. 7, 59, 103, 109 (SE); 104 (SP)
fry, 96 (CE); 25 (FG); 7, 103 (SE); 60 (SP)

Maryland State Archives/Merrick Photo Archives

A father-son fishing team, Little Orleans, Maryland, 1896.

Fishing, 40, 41 (BB); 44, 87, 102, 104, 107 (SP)
Flagler, Henry Morrison, 115, 128, 129 (CC); 57 (SE); 111, 134 (SS)
Florida, 27 (BB); 9 (BE); 115, 128, 129 (CC); 56, 96 (CE); 7, 75, 93, 122 (CJ); 31 (DE); 11, 57 (PK); 8, 38 (PP); 9, 12, 31, 53, 57, 61, 77 (SE); 36 (SO); 96, 107 (SP); 111, 134 (SS)
Florida Seminoles, 107 (SE)
Flounder, 59, 62 (SE)
Flour, 7, 8, 53, 59 (BR); 11, 123 (PP)
Flower Cookery, The Art of Cooking with Flowers (Mary MacNicols, 1967), 97 (GR)
"Fool," 29 (DE)
Football, 65, 75 (BB); 109, 124, 126, 128, 130, 132 (SP)
Ford, Henry, 89 (PO)
Forks, 7 (SO)
Fort Worth, 115, 134 (CC); 35 (SP)
Fourth of July, 82, 83, 87 (CE); 15 (FG)
France/French, 7, 120 (CC); 16, 32, 36, 48 (CE); 33, 40, 89 (DE); 130 (GR); 87, 101 (PO); 103 (PP); 9, 75 (SO)
Franklin, Benjamin, 120 (CC); 82 (CE); 28 (PO)

Fredericksburg, Texas, 93, 97 (CC)
Fredericksburg, Virginia, 88 (CC)
French cooking, 34 (BB); 74 (BE); 24 (CC); 73 (CJ); 49 (DE); 91 (PO); 11 (PP); 114 (SO); 23 (VE)
French Market, 9, 121 (BR); 31 (CC); 117, 122 (SO)
French Quarter, 32 (BB); 7 (PO); 132 (SP)
Fricassee, 11, 12 (PO)
Fried pies, 127 (PP)
Frigidaire Corporation, 57 (CJ)
Fritters, 121, 127 (BR)
Frostings/icings, 129, 133, 136 (CA)
Fruit. *See also* specific types. 29, 31, 49 (DE); 84 (GR)
Fruit leathers, 79 (GR)
Fruit peel, 90 (GR)

# G

Galt House, 11 (CA)
Galveston, 59, 62 (BB); 59 (CA); 67, 80 (CC); 95 (PK); 7, 20 (SS)
Games, 35, 109, 134 (SP); 92, 94 (SS)
*Garden Book for Houston, A*, 51 (SS)
Garden Pilgrimages, Natchez, 49 (BB); 63 (CE) Maryland, 65 (CE)
Garner, John Nance, 76 (CA)
Gazpacho, 75, 102 (SO)
Gebhardt, William, 51 (BE); 111 (SO)
Geese, 8, 45, 91 (PO)
Gelatin, 107 (BE); 109 (DE); 103 (PP)
General Mills, 114 (CA)
Gentlemen's Club, 93, 106 (CC)
Georgia, 75 (BB); 14, 28, 63 (BR); 44 (CE); 46, 75, 81 (CJ); 9, 21 (FG); 43 (PK); 65 (PO); 103 (SE); 9, 21, 24, 46, 87, 88, 109, 117 (SP); 16 (SS)
German clubs, 7, 111, 123 (SS)
German's Sweet Chocolate (Baker & Co.), 27 (CA); 89 (CJ)
Germany/Germans, 65 (BR); 18 (CC); 98, 123 (CE); 7, 73, 111, 130 (CJ) 21, 33, 44 (FG); 79, 88, 95, 112 (PK); 23 (PP); 75 (SO); 32 (VE)
Gifts, 106 (CA); 7, 30, 35, 61, 79, 81, 83, 99, 130 (GR)
Ginger, 9 (CJ)
Gingerbread, 59, 66 (CA); 88 (CC); 57, 111 (CJ)

Girl Scouts of America, 46, 47 (CJ); 39 (SP)
Glasse, Hannah, 7, 9, 13, 57 (CJ); 25, 91 (SO)
Golf, 109, 117, 122 (SP)

*Good Housekeeping Cookbook* (1942), 105 (PP)
Gottlieb's Bakery, 94 (CJ)
Graduation, 102 (FG)
Graham crackers, 53 (BR); 21 (PP)
Graham flour, 53 (BR); 21 (PP)
Graham, Sylvester, 53 (BR); 21 (PP)
Grandfather Mountain, 109, 134 (SP)
Grand Prize Race, 67, 82 (SP)
Gravy/sauces, 30, 123, 131 (BE); 131, 132, 134 (DE); 61 (GR); 48, 84 (PO); 79, 131 (VE)
Great Depression, The, 128 (DE)
Greek cooking, 56 (CE); 7, 111 (CJ); 61 (FG); 33 (SO)
Greenbrier Hotel, 99, 116 (BR)
Greens, 54, 57 (VE)
Grits, 7 (BB); 30 (BR); 47 (VE)
Grove Park Inn, 110 (BR)
"Grunt," 29 (DE)
Gulf Islands National Seashore, 99 (SP)
Gulf Shores, Alabama, 134 (SO)
Gum Arabic, 105 (GR)
Gumbo, 28 (CC); 62 (PO); 9 (SE); 109, 117, 121 (SO)

# H

Halloween, 129 (CA); 100, 101, 103 (CE)
Ham, 7, 9, 66 (BB); 7 (BE); 34 (FG); 8, 9, 63, 64, 71, 79, 83, 115 (PK)
Hamantaschen, 123 (CJ)

Hambuck, Carl, 88 (PK)
Hammond-Harwood House, 65 (CE)
Hancock, John, 82 (CE)
Hanukkah/Chanukah, 121 (CE); 111 (CJ)
Harland, Marion, biography, 21 (BR) eggs, 65 (BB) hogs, 75 (PK) mince pie, 120 (CE) sauerkraut, 33 (VE)
Harris County Heritage Society, 62 (SS)
Harrison, President Benjamin, 59 (BB); 21 (CE); 68 (FG)
Harrison, President William H., 115 (CC); 21 (CE)
Harvests, 35 (CA); 54 (CC); 112, 113 (CE); 51 (PP); 109 (SO); 55 (SS); 72 (VE)
Head cheese, 115, 129 (PK)
Hedrick's Restaurant ("Goodie Garden"), 79 (CC)
Heinz, Henry J., 35 (GR)
Henry, Patrick, 7 (PK)
Herbs/spices, 58, 61, 65 (GR)
*Here's How* (W. C. Whitfield), 95 (BB)
Heritage House, The, 76 (SS)
Hermann-Grima House, 48 (BR); 14, 91, 92, 94 (PO)
Hermitage, The, 111 (FG); 58 (PP); 111, 134 (SS)
Hermits, 31 (CJ)
Herrick, Robert, 68 (CE)
High Hampton Inn and Country Club, 132 (DE); 106 (PP)
Highland Park Pharmacy, 110 (PO)
Highland Park Village, 76 (CC)
Hill, Corrie, 99 (BR)
Hines, Duncan, 12 (BB); 29 (PP)
Hogg, Ima, 51 (SS)
Hogmanay, 13 (CE)
Homecoming, 9, 21, 27 (FG)
Homestead in Virginia, The, 96 (PO)
Hominy, 47 (VE)
Honey, 79 (GR)
Hope Farm, 33, 50 (FG)
Horses, 71 (BB); 107 (CE); 7 (PK); 7, 9, 14, 18, 24 (SP)
Horseshoes, 68 (SP)
Hotel Roanoke, The, 71 (BE); 33 (BR)
*House and Home* (1800s), 129 (CE)
*Housekeeping in Old Virginia* (Marion Cabell Tyree), 8, 9 (PP)
*Housekeeping in the Bluegrass*, 85 (CA); 89 (CJ)
Housewarmings, 65, 83, 87 (FG)
Houston, 39 (SP); 41, 51, 62 (SS)
Houston, Sam, 11, 17 (CA); 34 (CC)

*Inspecting the crop for jack o'lantern candidates, c.1927.*

*How We Cook in Tennessee,*
    37 (SS)
Huguenots, 40 (DE)
Humble Oil Company,
    39 (SP)
Humble pie, 110 (BE)
Hunting, 65, 70, 71 (BB);
    106, 107, 109 (CE); 9,
    45 (PO); 7, 9, 24, 39, 40, 44,
    46, 47, 49, 57 (SP)
Hush puppies, 28 (BR)

# I

Ice, 91 (DE)
Ice boxes, 60 (BR); 103 (PP)
Icebox pies, 103,
    105 (PP)
Ice cream, 89 (CE); 89,
    92, 96, 98, 109 (DE);
    80 (FG)
Ice cream cone, 89 (DE)
Ice cream freezer, 89 (DE)
Ices, 89 (DE)

*Idle Hens Don't Lay,* 107 (VE)
India, 57 (GR); 103 (PO)
Indian River, 36 (SO)
Indians, 9 (BE); 7, 11, 24, 45,
    129 (BR); 42 (CA); 9, 32 (CC);
    55, 81 (CJ); 42 (DE); 25 (FG);
    7, 11, 43 (PK); 8 (PO); 8,
    20 (PP); 11 (SE); 47 (VE)
Indian Summer, 57 (CC)
Invitations, 59, 131 (SS)
Ireland/Irish, 41, 42, 44, 46,
    100 (CE); 13 (GR); 131 (SO);
    18 (SP)
Iroquois Hounds of Lexington,
    109 (CE)
Italian cooking, 133 (FG); 114 (SO)

# J

Jack o' Lantern, 100 (CE)
Jackson, Andrew, 9 (BB); 24 (BE);
    31 (CJ); 111 (FG); 58 (PP); 7,
    111, 134 (SS)
Jackson, General Thomas J.
    "Stonewall," 53 (PK)

Jambalaya, 109 (PK); 69 (PO); 7,
    109, 114, 125 (SO)
James River, The, 7 (BE); 99 (BR);
    42 (CA); 9, 10, 85 (CC); 62,
    112 (CE); 7, 8 (PK); 60 (SS);
    112 (VE)
Jams/jellies/preserves, 7 (BB);
    107 (BE); 7, 69 (DE);
    9, 13, 18, 28 (GR); 103 (PP)
Jarvis, Anna M., 78 (FG)
Jaubert, Gus, 61 (PO)
Java, 95 (GR)
Jefferson, Thomas, 89 (BB); 33,
    65, 74, 107, 123 (BE);
    8 (BR); 75, 111 (CA); 115,
    120 (CC); 82, 89 (CE);
    13, 31, 33, 73 (CJ); 115 (DE);
    7, 83 (PK); 11, 71, 101 (PO);
    11 (PP); 88 (SE);
    119 (SS); 26 (VE)
Jekyll Island, 122 (SP)
Jewish Sabbath, 7, 128 (FG)
Jones, Bobby, 117 (SP)
Jousting/ring tournament,
    9, 27 (SP)
Julius Caesar, 35 (GR)
Jumbles, 85 (CA); 9, 22, 24,
    57 (CJ)

# K

Keeneland, 9, 14, 16 (SP)
Kelly, Harold Osman,
104 (PK)
Kennedy, President John F.,
112 (CE)
Kentucky, 24, 83 (BE); 9, 14,
43 (CC); 76, 79, 87, 107,
109 (CE); 97, 101 (FG);
43 (PK); 61, 75 (PO); 29,
65, 87, 99 (PP); 38 (SE);
134 (SO); 9, 14,
16, 21 (SP)
  cream candy, 111 (GR)
King Ranch, 7, 112 (CC)
Kitchens, 57 (CJ); 120 (FG);
14 (PO)
Kossuth, Louis, 125 (DE)

# L

Labor Day, 92, 98 (CE)
Lady managers, 61 (CJ)
Lafayette, General Marquis de,
67, 88 (CC); 89 (CE)
Lamb/mutton, 7, 83, 88, 92, 94,
100 (BE); 10 (CC); 43 (PK);
80, 131 (SO)
Lane, Emma Rylander, 11 (CA)
Lang, Helen, 37 (PK)
Lard, 9 (PK)
LBJ Ranch, 67 (CC)
Lebkuchen, 111 (CJ)
Lee, General Robert E., 121, 127
(BR); 76, 111 (CA); 65 (CE);
53 (PK); 76 (PP)
  cake, 11 (CA)
  marriage, 19 (CA)
  Hotel, 106 (PO)
  King Ranch, 7, 112 (CC)
  Shirley Plantation, 9 (CC)
Lee, "Mother Ann," 105 (CA);
14 (CC)
Lent, 45 (BE); 32 (CE); 117 (SO);
45 (SS)
Lentils, 98 (SO); 80 (VE)
Life with Father, 81 (FG)
Liquid Smoke, 53 (PK)
Liver, 107 (BE)
Lobster, 7, 9, 31 (SE)
Long Run Hounds of Louisville,
109 (CE)
Long, Senator Huey P., 7 (PO)
Lord's Supper, 7 (BR)
Louisiana, 24 (CC); 7 (CJ); 47,
108 (PK); 7, 87 (PO); 9,
24 (SE); 96, 109 (SO);
112 (SS); 82 (VE)

Louisville, 11 (CA); 74, 87 (CE);
38 (SE)
Louisville Jockey Club, 74 (CE)
Louisville Turf, 74 (CE)
Low Country, 9, 21 (CC)
Low, Juliet Gordon, 46, 47 (CJ);
39, 107 (SP)
Luck, 16 (CE)
Luncheons, 74, 75 (CC); 65 (CE);
97, 102, 105, 108 (FG); 113
(PO); 30, 34, 37, 41, 45, 48,
51, 55, 59 (SS)

# M

Macaroons, 7, 9 (CJ)
Mackerel, 59, 72 (SE)
McKinley, Mrs. William, 24, 27 (SS)
Mme. Bégué's Restaurant, 7,
56 (BB)
Madison, Dolley, 91 (CA); 7, 111,
119, 131 (SS)
Magnolia Grove, 72, 75 (SS)
Magnolia Hall, 49 (BB)
Magnolia Hotel, 96, 97 (SP)
Magnolia Springs, 49 (SP)
"Maids of Honor," 115 (PP)
Mangos, 57 (GR); 38 (PP)
Mardi Gras, 45 (BE); 89 (CA); 32,
34, 36 (CC); 83 (PP)
Marion, General Francis, 97 (VE)
Martha White Foods, 123 (PP)
Maryland, 7, 27, 28, 70, 71,
101 (BB); 99 (BR); 11 (CA);
50 (CC); 62, 65, 98, 106,
113 (CE); 24, 31 (CJ); 34 (FG);
96 (PO); 9 (SE); 121 (SO); 9,
21, 27, 91 (SP); 114 (SS)
Marzipan, 13 (CJ)

Mason-Dixon Line, 7 (BB); 29 (DE)
Masters Tournament, The, 109,
117 (SP)
Matador Ranch, 7 (CC); 132 (CE)
May Day, 68, 69, 72 (CE)
Maypole, 68 (CE)
Meat loaf, 79 (BE)
Meat pies, 57 (PO); 7 (PP)
Melrose Plantation, 24, 27 (CC)

Memphis, 9, 99, 109 (BR); 59 (CE)
Menger Hotel, 105 (VE)
Meringue, 49, 53, 115 (DE);
25 (PP)
Merrimac, The, 75 (SS)
Metropolitan Opera, 96 (SS)
Mexican food, 37 (BB); 46,
51 (BE); 129, 136 (BR); 34,
64 (CC); 125 (CE); 73,
111 (CJ); 59, 131 (FG);
126 (GR); 91 (PO); 75, 77,
111 (SO)
Mexico, 82 (CA); 34, 64 (CC); 125
(CE); 73 (CJ); 59, 131 (FG);
62 (SS); 82 (VE)
Middle Plantation, 14 (BB);
124 (CC)
Middleton Place, 33, 53, 55,
76 (FG)
Mint Juleps, 24, 89 (BB); 88,
115, 124 (CC); 79 (CE); 99 (CJ);
21 (SP)

*Julep
strainer.*

*Miss Ann Chase's Book,* 12 (PO)
Mississippi, 28 (BR); 65, 66 (CA);
133 (CC); 62, 83, 93 (CE); 52,
106 (PO); 111 (PP); 134 (SO);
60 (SP); 13, 99 (SS)
Mississippi River, 9, 19 (BB);
66 (CA)
*Miss Leslie's New Cookery Book*
(Eliza Leslie, 1857), 7, 75 (BR);
9 (CJ); 35 (GR); 51 (PO);
7 (PP); 84, 125 (SE)
Mobile, 32, 36 (CE); 49 (SP)
*Modern Priscilla Cookbook, The*
(1924), 83 (BE)
Molasses, 88 (BR); 9 (CJ); 25 (DE)
Monticello, 13 (CJ); 7 (PK); 11 (PP);
88 (SE); 26 (VE)
Mooreland Hunt, The, 70 (BB)
Moravians, 65, 115 (BR); 9, 18
(CC); 49, 121 (CE)
"Morning call," 67, 71 (CC)
Mother's Day, 78, 79 (FG)
Mount Vernon, 67, 88, 116 (CC);
57 (CJ); 11, 68 (VE)
Mousse, 69, 79, 109 (DE)
Muffins, 102 (BB); 99, 110 (BR)
Mullet, 74 (SE)
Muscadines, 36 (PP)
Mustard, 61 (GR)

---

**BB** Breakfast & Brunch    **BE** Beef, Veal & Lamb    **BR** Breads    **CA** Cakes    **CC** Company's Coming    **CE** Celebrations
**CJ** Cookie Jar    **DE** Just Desserts    **FG** Family Gatherings    **GR** Gift Receipts    **PK** All Pork    **PO** Plain & Fancy Poultry
**PP** Pies & Pastry    **SE** Sea & Stream    **SO** Soups & Stews    **SP** Sporting Scene    **SS** Socials & Soirees    **VE** Vegetables

*An engraving of New Orleans harbor by Alfred R. Waud.*

# N

Napoleon, 47 (PK); 101 (PO)
Nashville, 7, 86 (BE); 10, 108 (FG); 65 (PP); 134 (SS)
Nashville Centennial Club, 108 (FG); 9, 24 (SS)
Nasturtium seeds, 54 (GR)
Natchez, 49 (BB); 115, 131 (CC); 62, 63 (CE); 50 (FG)
National Biscuit Company, 86 (DE)
National Field Trial Championship, 7, 39, 60 (SP)
National Register of Historic Places, 110 (BR); 115 (CC); 30 (SP)
National Trail, 99 (BR)
National Wild Turkey Calling Contest, 62 (SP)
*Natural History of Virginia* (William Byrd, 1737), 9 (CJ); 70 (FG); 7 (VE)
Naval Academy, Annapolis, 7, 111, 127 (SS)
Neiman-Marcus, 104 (CC); 109 (PO)
Nestlés, 38 (CJ)
*New Dixie Cookbook, The* (1895), 115 (PK); 99 (SS)
New Ebenezer, 63 (BR)
*New Family Cookbook, The* (Juliet Corson), 51 (PO)
New Orleans, 7, 9, 19, 20, 32, 56 (BB); 45 (BE); 9, 49, 121 (BR); 66, 89 (CA); 7, 28,

New Orleans, *continued* 47, 68, 90 (CC); 19, 28, 32, 34, 38 (CE); 9, 12, 25, 64 (DE); 130 (GR); 7, 14, 69, 91, 92, 94, 96 (PO); 9, 125 (SE); 109, 132 (SP); 111, 112 (SS)
New Smyrna, 122 (CJ)
New Year's, 84 (BB); 67, 85 (CC); 8, 10, 13, 16, 18, 19 (CE); 111 (CJ); 7, 33, 59, 61 (FG); 41 (SS); 80 (VE)
New York, 67 (CC); 19 (CJ); 8 (PO); 79 (PP); 61 (SE); 45 (SO)
Nomini Hall, 87 (FG)
Norfolk and Western Railroad, 33 (BR)
North Carolina, 9, 10 (BB); 13 (BE); 51, 110 (BR); 9, 18, 52 (CC); 49 (CE); 19, 26, 81 (CJ); 57, 132 (DE); 12, 17, 44, 71 (PK); 72 (PP); 9, 77, 103 (SE); 9, 21, 109, 110, 134 (SP); 7, 131 (VE)
Nuts, 35 (CA); 93 (GR)

# O

Oakland Race Track, 74 (CE)
Oaklawn Park, 16 (SP)
Oatmeal, 31, 45 (CJ); 57 (PP)

Oklahoma, 7, 32, 93 (CC); 24, 33, 47 (FG); 93 (GR); 43 (PK); 44, 52, 128 (SP); 76 (SS)
Okra, 62 (PO); 9 (SE); 109, 114, 117 (SO)
Old Bay Seasoning, 98 (CE)
Old Glory, 83 (CE)

Old Salem, 115 (BR); 18 (CC); 49 (CE)
Old Salem Tavern, 115 (BR)
Old Talbott Inn, 87, 99 (PP)
Olla Podrida, 120 (BE)
Onions, 131 (VE)
  Vidalia, 70 (VE)
Open house, 67, 85 (CC); 27, 83, 90 (FG)
Oranges, 31 (DE)
*Original Picayune's Creole Cookbook, The* (1901), 58 (SO)
*Out of Kentucky Kitchens* (Marion Flexner, 1949), 111, 112 (CJ); 69, 80, 125 (PP)
Oven-testing, 73 (CA)

Overton, John, 24 (BE)
Oysters, 60 (CC); 24, 25 (FG); 7, 9, 38, 125 (SE); 134 (SO); 7, 87, 96, 97 (SP)

# P

Paine, Thomas, 31 (CJ)
Palm Beach, 115, 128, 129 (CC)
Pancakes/waffles, 27, 34, 89 (BB)
"Pandowdy," 29, 45 (DE)
Paraffin, 9 (GR)
Parkhurst, 114 (SS)
Parsnips, 73 (VE)
Passover, 100 (CA); 48, 59 (CE)
"Pasties," 57 (PO)
Pastries, 44, 117 (BB); 11, 115, 124, 127 (PP)
Pâte Sucrée, 124 (PP)
Peabody Hotel, The, 9, 99, 109 (BR)
Peanuts, 81 (CJ); 8 (PK); 8 (PP)
Pearlash, 7 (BR)
Pears, 18, 49 (GR)
Peas, 78, 79 (VE)
Pecans, 17, 93 (GR); 8, 20 (PP)
   pie, 53, 57 (PP)
Pectin, 9, 13, 18 (GR)
Pemberton, John S., 16 (SS)
Pennsylvania Dutch, 9 (CC)
Pensacola, 87, 99, 100, 104 (SP)
Penuche, 126 (GR)
Peppers, 61 (GR); 84 (VE)
Pepys, Samuel, 27 (CE); 7 (CJ)
Philadelphia, 82 (CE); 7 (PP)
Phillips, Frank, 52, 54 (SP)

Pickles/relishes/chutneys, 35, 46, 53, 54, 57, 58 (GR)
Pickling, 35, 46 (GR)
Picnic, 75 (BB); 69, 83, 87 (CE); 10, 30 (FG); 75, 76, 77 (PO); 11 (SE); 18, 74, 82, 87, 99, 124, 134 (SP)
Pie-throwing, 97 (PP)
Pigs/hogs, 7 (BE); 7, 8, 11, 12, 24, 44, 47, 54, 57, 95 (PK)
Pilgrims, 112 (CE)
Pillsbury® Bake-Off, 116 (CJ); 23 (SO)
Pinckney, Eliza Lucas, 11 (PO)
Pineapple
   history, 71 (CA); 12 (CC)
Pine Bark Stew, 107 (SE); 109 (SO)
Pink House Tearoom, 79 (CC)
Pinwheels, 70 (CJ)
Pirogi, 136 (BR)
Pitchfork Ranch, 93 (CC)
Plantations, 15 (BB)
Plow, 26 (VE)
Plums, 27 (DE)
Point-to-Point, 7, 18 (SP)
Pokeweed/sallet, 57 (VE)
Polk, President James K., 76, 91 (CA); 48 (SS)
Polo, 7, 9, 30 (SP)
Pompano, 77 (SE)
Ponce de Leon Hotel, 128 (CC); 57 (SE); 111, 134 (SS)
Pone, 8, 24 (BR)
Pooka, 13 (GR)
Pooshee Plantation, 40 (SP)
Popcorn, 114 (GR)
Pork, 7, 27 (BB); 7, 9, 11, 17, 24, 27, 31, 43, 49, 54, 59, 95, 115, 116, 121, 123 (PK); 7 (SE)
Porridge, 9, 10 (DE)

Porter's New Southern Cookery Book, Mrs. (1871), 29, 45, 49, 70 (DE); 74 (PP); 54 (SO)
Potash, 7 (BR)
Potatoes, 89, 112 (VE)
Pot likker, 126 (PK); 54, 57 (VE)
Pottage, 75 (SO)
Powdered sugar, 75 (CA)
Practical Cooking and Dinner Giving (Mary F. Henderson, 1877), 43, 84 (BB); 10, 65, 92 (BE); 75 (CC); 24 (PK); 8, 65 (PP)
Praline, 130 (GR)
Preachers, 100 (CC)
Preserving, 7, 18 (GR)
Prosciutto, 79 (PK)
Pudding, 9, 10, 12, 53, 55 (DE); 36 (FG); 8, 127 (PP)
   Hasty, 10 (DE)
   Indian, 10 (DE)
   Plum, 10 (CC); 9, 27 (DE)
   Tapioca, 9, 17 (DE)
   Yorkshire, 49 (CC)
Pueblos, 9 (CC)
Puff paste, 11 (PP)
Pullman Palace Car Company, 111 (SS)
Pumpkin, 57 (PP); 55 (SS); 107 (VE)
Purefoy Hotel, 124 (FG)
Puritans, 8, 53, 68, 72, 121 (CE); 33 (FG); 87 (SP)
"Pyes," 7, 9, 11 (PP)

# Q

Queen Elizabeth, 7 (DE); 100 (PO)
Queen Victoria, 9 (PK)
Quenelles, 15 (SO)
Quilting bee, 7, 30 (SS)

# R

Railroads, 9, 22 (BB); 46 (SP)
Ramos Gin Fizz, 28 (CC)
Randolph, Mary, 65, 107 (BE); 64 (CA); 13 (CJ); 70 (DE); 83 (PK); 11 (PP)
Recipes, 95 (BB); 7, 11, 28, 118 (CA); 22, 61, 116 (CJ); 13 (SS)
Redfish, 59, 81 (SE)
Red River Valley, 44 (SP)
Red snapper, 50 (CC)
Refrigeration, 91 (DE); 105 (PP)
Regattas, 87, 88 (SP)
Retreat Plantation, 79 (SS)
Reunions, 7, 9, 15 (FG)
Revolutionary War, 67, 88 (CC); 31 (DE); 15 (PK); 59 (SE); 9, 114 (SS); 97 (VE)
Rhubarb, 42 (PP)

*Picnics in romantic places like a riverbank were possible with the advent of the Model T.*

Brown Brothers

Rice, 9, 21 (CC); 55 (FG); 50, 109, 114 (SO)
  cakes, 68 (CC)
  festival, 57 (SP)
  muffins, 9 (BR)
  Dirty Rice, 9 (PO)
  growth, 108 (PK)
  Hotel, 41 (SS)
  pilaf (pilau), 69 (PO)
Ring dance, 127 (SS)
Ritz Carlton, 45 (SO)
River Oaks Club, 51 (SS)
"Roaring Twenties," 83 (SS)
Roasting, 32 (PO)
Robert Morris Inn, The, 101 (BB)
Rodeo, 9, 33, 35 (SP)
Rogers, Will, 112 (CC)
Romans, The, 7 (BR); 8, 22, 27, 48, 68, 100, 121 (CE); 7, 9 (CJ); 81 (GR); 27, 45 (PO); 11, 79 (PP)
Rose Hill Plantation, 9, 30 (SP)
Roux, 92 (PO); 109, 117 (SO)
Royal Poinciana, 128, 129 (CC)
Rum, 99 (CJ); 79, 84 (GR)
Rumford Cookbook (1907), 37 (SS)
Run for the Roses, 74 (CE)
Russell, Lillian, 96 (DE)

**S**

S & S Tearoom, 76 (CC)
Saga of Texas Cookery, 79 (VE)
Sailing, 87, 88, 91 (SP)
St. Augustine, 128 (CC); 122, 125 (CJ); 61 (GR); 53 (SE); 96 (SP); 111, 134 (SS)
St. Augustine "Tatler," 96, 97 (SP)
St. Basil, 61 (FG)
St. John's Hunting Club, 40 (SP)
St. Nicholas Day, 121 (CJ)
St. Patrick's Day, 129 (CA); 41, 42, 44, 46 (CE)
St. Simon's Island, 79 (SS)
St. Thomas Manor, 34 (FG)
St. Valentine's Day, 129 (CA); 27, 28, 30 (CE); 111 (CJ)
Saleratus, 7 (BR)
Sally Lunn, 10, 124 (CC)
Salmon, 84, 125 (SE)
Salt, 18 (CC); 35, 58, 61 (GR); 8, 63, 121 (PK); 96 (SO); 16 (VE)
Salt Grass Trail Ride, 67, 78 (SP)
Salzburgers, 63 (BR); 9, 21 (FG)
Sandburg, Carl August, 57 (DE)
Sanders, Colonel Harland, 75 (PO)
Santa Rosa Island, 99 (SP)
Sauer-Beckmann Living History Farm, 44 (FG); 103 (PK)
Sauerkraut, 59, 112 (PK); 33 (VE)
Sausage, 9, 59, 95, 102, 103, 107, 112 (PK)

Savannah, 63 (BR); 9, 79 (CC); 42 (CE); 46, 94 (CJ); 17 (PP); 9 (SE); 67, 82, 84, 107 (SP); 7, 32, 79, 91, 123 (SS)
Scallops, 43 (SE)
Scandinavia, 25 (SO)
Scottish games, 109, 134 (SP)
Scott, Sir Walter, 121 (CE)
Scurvy, 35 (GR)
Sea Island, 75 (CJ)
Seatrout/sea trout, 59, 86 (SE)
Secret Diary of William Byrd of Westover, 1709-1712, The, 17 (BE)
"Secrets," 30 (CE)
Shad, 27, 28 (BB); 59, 88 (SE)

Shakers, 105 (CA); 9, 14, 43 (CC)
Shamrock, 41, 46 (CE)
Shark, 98 (SE)
Shary, John H. 52, 53 (BB)
Sharyland Estate, 52, 53 (BB)
She-crab soup, 9 (SE)
Shellfish. See also specific types. 7, 9, 125 (SE)
Sherbets, 89 (DE)
Sherwood Forest, 86, 124 (CC)
Shirley Plantation, 84 (BE); 99 (BR); 9, 11, 12, 85 (CC); 112 (VE)
Shortbread, 9, 16 (CJ)
Shortening, 76 (BR)
Shrimp, 9, 21 (CC); 9, 51 (SE); 134 (SO)
Shrove Tuesday, 27, 34 (BB); 32 (CE)
"Sirops," 67, 90 (CC); 112 (SS)
Skirvin Plaza Hotel, 93, 109 (CC)
Slang Jang, 44 (SP)
"Slump," 29 (DE)
Smith and Welton's Tea Room, 87, 90 (PP)
Smith, Captain John, 42 (CA); 112 (CE); 7, 8 (PK); 28 (PO); 7, 95, 109 (SE); 111 (SS)
Smithfield Hams, 8, 9, 63, 71, 79 (PK)
Smoked meats, 63, 115 (PK)
Smoky Mountains, 67, 74 (SP)
Smorgasbord, 18 (FG)
Smothering, 23 (PO)
Snow, 92 (DE)
Snowden House, 79 (DE)
Soirees, 67, 90 (CC); 111, 112, 114 (SS)
Sole, 62 (SE)
Son-of-a-Gun Stew, 107 (BE)
Sotterly, 24 (CJ)
Soufflés, 49, 69 (DE)
Soup stock/broth, 7, 9, 15, 25, 27, 31, 66 (SO)

South Carolina, 21, 60 (CC); 127, 129 (CE); 75 (CJ); 53 (FG); 44, 108 (PK); 11 (PO); 51 (PP); 107 (SE); 9, 10, 30, 40 (SP)
Southern Cooking (Henrietta Stanley Dull, 1928), 8 (CA); 105 (PP)
Southern Cotton Oil Company, 17 (PP)
Southern Gardener and Receipt Book, The (1845), 123 (VE)
Southern Gardener, The (1840), 78 (VE)
Spanish, 82 (CA); 9 (CC); 7 (CJ); 31, 49 (DE); 135 (FG); 95 (GR); 87 (PO); 102 (SO); 52 (VE)
Spanish-American War, 75 (SS)
Speculaas, 121 (CJ)
Spit-roasting, 19 (BE); 48 (PK)
Sports, 7, 9, 30, 39, 57, 67, 91, 109, 113 (SP)
Spring, 28 (BB); 43, 44 (CC); 48 (CE); 18, 21 (SP)
Springerle, 111, 130 (CJ)
Squash, 57 (PP); 107 (VE)
Stagecoach Inn, 28, 29 (BR)
Steak, 7, 9, 30, 33, 41 (BE)
Steamboats, 9, 19, 20 (BB)
Steeplechase, 7, 9, 10, 21 (SP)
Stewing process, 20 (PO)
Stews, 61 (PO); 109, 131, 134 (SO)
Stirrup Cup, The, 107 (CE)
Storing meat, 22 (BE)
Strawberries, 27, 28 (BB); 33 (DE)
Stuffings/dressings, 48 (PO)
Sugar, 9 (CJ); 25, 55 (DE); 9, 49, 58, 61, 63, 79, 95 (GR)
Sugar Bowl, The, 109, 132 (SP)
Sugarcane, 95 (GR)
Sundae, 89 (DE)
Sunday dinner, 120, 124 (FG)
Sunday House, 93, 97 (CC)
Sunfish, 115 (SE)
Sweetbreads, 116 (BE)
Sweet potatoes, 57, 111 (PP); 93 (VE)
Sweets, 7 (DE)
Swimming, 87, 94, 95 (SP)
Swiss chard, 58 (VE)
Swordfish, 98 (SE); 104 (SP)
Syllabub, 21, 135 (CE)
Syrup, sorghum, 88 (BR)

**T**

Tabasco sauce, 96 (SO)
Table setting, 124, 125 (BB)
Taffy, 106 (GR)
Taft, President William Howard, 39 (SP)
Tanglewood, 52 (CC); 21 (SP)

---

**BB** Breakfast & Brunch  **BE** Beef, Veal & Lamb  **BR** Breads  **CA** Cakes  **CC** Company's Coming  **CE** Celebrations
**CJ** Cookie Jar  **DE** Just Desserts  **FG** Family Gatherings  **GR** Gift Receipts  **PK** All Pork  **PO** Plain & Fancy Poultry
**PP** Pies & Pastry  **SE** Sea & Stream  **SO** Soups & Stews  **SP** Sporting Scene  **SS** Socials & Soirees  **VE** Vegetables

Tarts/tartlets, 7, 8, 115, 116, 121, 124 (PP)
Tassies, 9, 121 (PP)
Taverns, 9, 10 (BB)
Taylor, Zachary, 31 (CJ); 108 (SS)
Tea/teas, 93 (BR); 7 (CC); 127 (CE); 26 (CJ); 41 (FG); 122 (SP); 14, 59, 64, 67, 72, 76 (SS); 97 (VE)
Tea cakes, 7, 9, 89 (CJ)
Tearoom, 99 (BR); 7, 76, 78 (CC)
Telfair Mansion, 28 (CJ)
Tennessee, 24 (BB); 24 (BE); 46 (CA); 93 (CC); 107 (CE); 81 (CJ); 10, 15 (FG); 43 (PK); 7, 39, 60 (SP); 48, 72, 134 (SS)
Tennis, 109, 113 (SP)
Texas, 52 (BB); 9, 51, 53 (BE); 7, 28, 52, 80, 99 (BR); 17, 59, 73, 76 (CA); 7, 9, 34, 38, 42, 50, 64, 93, 115, 127, 134 (CC); 46, 117, 123 (CE); 111 (CJ); 129 (DE); 7, 9, 18, 27, 33, 44, 74, 131 (FG); 93 (GR); 43, 95, 96, 103, 104, 110, 116 (PK); 61, 87 (PO); 100 (PP); 17, 59 (SE); 46, 109, 111, 134 (SO); 33, 35, 44, 67, 78, 128 (SP); 32 (SS); 80, 82 (VE)
Thanksgiving, 65, 66 (BB); 67 (CC); 112, 113, 117 (CE); 7, 33, 37, 41 (FG); 27, 28 (PO)
Thistle Hill, 115, 134, 137 (CC)
Thomasville, Georgia, 46, 47 (SP)
Toffee, 116 (GR)
Tolbert, Francis X., *A Bowl of Red*, 53 (BE)
Toll House Inn, 38 (CJ)
Tomatoes, 53 (GR); 120 (VE)
Tortillas, 129 (BR); 77 (SO)
Travellers' Rest, 24 (BE)
*Travels* (William Bartram, 1791), 59 (VE)
Trifle, 36 (FG)
Tryon, Governor William, 19 (CJ)
Tryon Palace, 19 (CJ); 12, 15 (PK)
Tuesday Club, 106 (CC)
Tuna, 100 (SE)
Turkey, 8, 27, 28, 45, 109, 117 (PO); 62 (SP)
"Turkey trots," 57 (CJ)
Turnips, 112, 123 (VE)
Turnovers, 136 (BR); 115, 127 (PP)
Twelfth Night, 22, 23, 26, 32, 38 (CE)
Tyler, Julia Gardiner, 115, 127 (CC)
Tyler, President John, 115, 124, 127 (CC); 79 (CE)

## U

University of the South, 72 (SS)

## V

Van Buren, Martin, 31 (CJ)
Vanderbilt Cup, 67, 82, 84 (SP)
Vanderbilt, George Washington, 13 (BE)
Variety meats, 107 (BE); 115 (PK)
Vasilopeta, 61 (FG)
Veal, 7, 59, 66, 68, 73, 74, 78 (BE)
Veal parmigiana, 70 (BE)
Vegetable pies/nut pies, 8, 9, 51, 57 (PP)
Vegetables. *See also* specific types. 35 (CA); 47 (CC); 57 (PP); 66, 72 (SO); 7, 11, 16, 23, 59, 112, 131 (VE)
Verandas, 34 (SS)
Vichyssoise, 45 (SO)
Vicksburg, 16 (SS)
Victorian, 67 (SS)
Vidalia, Georgia, 70 (VE)
Vinegar, 35, 49, 58, 61 (GR); 57 (PP)
Virginia, 9, 27 (BB); 7, 71 (BE); 21, 33 (BR); 59, 76, 91 (CA); 12, 43, 115, 120 (CC); 22, 56, 65, 69, 79, 112 (CE); 9, 28 (CJ); 33, 79 (DE); 71, 87 (FG); 7, 11, 43, 63, 71, 88 (PK); 45, 65, 96, 100, 117 (PO); 8, 51, 53, 87, 90 (PP); 7, 9, 12, 95, 109 (SE); 27 (SO); 9, 21, 91, 110 (SP); 9, 60, 110, 130 (SS); 7, 112 (VE)
*Virginia Housewife or Methodical Cook, The* (Mary Randolph, 1824), 34, 89 (BB); 83, 131 (BE); 124, 127, 131 (BR); 85, 111, 118 (CA); 7, 57 (CJ); 9, 89 (DE); 9 (GR); 51 (PO); 8 (PP); 125 (SE); 54 (SO); 123 (VE)
Visiting Day, 19 (CE)
Vitamins, 35 (GR); 35 (VE)

## W

Wakefield, Ruth, 38 (CJ)
Walden's Ridge, 58 (CJ)
Walnuts, 55 (CJ)
Washington, George, 7, 10 (BB); 57 (BR); 67, 85, 88, 115, 116 (CC); 8, 89, 106 (CE); 57 (CJ); 7, 69 (DE); 9, 11, 43 (PK); 34, 76 (PP); 75 (SO); 7, 111, 130, 131 (SS); 68 (VE)
Washington, Martha, 7 (BB); 57 (CJ); 7 (PP); 75 (SO)

Washington, Martha, *continued*
cake, 89 (CA)
great-grandchildren, 19 (CA)
vegetables, 11 (VE)
Wayside Inn, 8, 51, 53 (PP)
Weddings, 65, 78 (BB); 106 (CA); 7, 93, 108, 110, 111, 114 (FG); 86 (SS)
Weems, Parson Mason Locke, 34 (PP)
Wesson, Dr. David, 17 (PP)
West Virginia, 9 (BB); 99, 116 (BR); 103 (SE)
Whipped cream, 131 (DE)
Whiskey, 59 (CA); 99 (CJ)
Whitehall, 115, 128 (CC)
White Sulphur Springs, 116 (BR)
Wiener roasts, 94, 95 (SP)
Wild game, 39, 46, 47, 49, 57 (SP)
Williamsburg Inn, 12 (BB); 100 (PO)
Williamsburg, Virginia, 9, 10, 14 (BB); 7 (BE); 11 (CA); 9, 124 (CC); 62 (CE); 27 (PP); 60 (SS)
Wine, 7 (BR); 12 (CC); 83 (GR); 64 (SS)

Winston-Salem, 65, 115 (BR); 18, 52, 74 (CC); 49 (CE)
Winterthur Gardens, 18 (SP)
Women's clubs, 7, 32, 41 (SS)
Woodboo Plantation, 40 (SP)
Wood, Grant, 34 (PP)
Woolaroc Lodge, 52, 54 (SP)
World's Fair, 1893, 61 (CJ)
Wyatt's Cafeteria, 128 (DE)

## Y

Yadkin River, 52 (CC)
Yams, 93 (VE)
Yeast, 7, 8, 9, 37, 39, 59, 75 (BR)

## Z

Zwieback, 23 (PP)

---

**BB** *Breakfast & Brunch*   **BE** *Beef, Veal & Lamb*   **BR** *Breads*   **CA** *Cakes*   **CC** *Company's Coming*   **CE** *Celebrations*
**CJ** *Cookie Jar*   **DE** *Just Desserts*   **FG** *Family Gatherings*   **GR** *Gift Receipts*   **PK** *All Pork*   **PO** *Plain & Fancy Poultry*
**PP** *Pies & Pastry*   **SE** *Sea & Stream*   **SO** *Soups & Stews*   **SP** *Sporting Scene*   **SS** *Socials & Soirees*   **VE** *Vegetables*

*Southern biscuits hot from the oven, c.1926.*

**FAVORITE
RECIPES**

FAVORITE
RECIPES